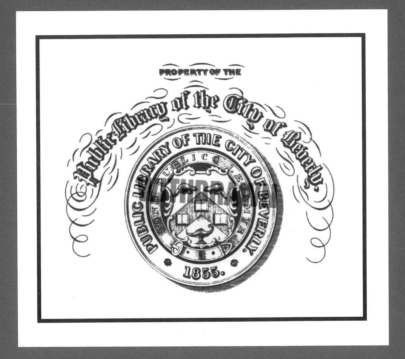

WEIRD
MASSACHUSETTS

Weird

Massachusetts

Your Travel Guide to Massachusetts's
Local Legends and Best Kept Secrets
by Jeff Belanger

Mark Moran and Mark Sceurman,
Executive Editors

WEIRD MASSACHUSETTS

STERLING and the distinctive Sterling logo are registered trademarks of Sterling Publishing Co., Inc.

Library of Congress Cataloging-in-Publication Data Available

10 9 8 7 6 5 4

Published by Sterling Publishing Co., Inc.
387 Park Avenue South, New York, NY 10016

© 2008 by Mark Sceurman and Mark Moran

Distributed in Canada by Sterling Publishing
c/o Canadian Manda Group, 165 Dufferin Street
Toronto, Ontario, Canada M6K 3H6

Distributed in the United Kingdom by GMC Distribution Services
Castle Place, 166 High Street, Lewes, East Sussex, England BN7 1XU

Distributed in Australia by Capricorn Link (Australia) Pty. Ltd.
P. O. Box 704, Windsor, NSW 2756, Australia

Printed in China.
All rights reserved.

Sterling ISBN 978-1-4027-54371

For information about custom editions, special sales, premium and corporate purchases, please contact Sterling Special Sales Department at 800-805-5489 or specialsales@sterlingpublishing.com.

CONTENTS

DEDICATION

For my daughter, Sophie, who was born in the weird state of Massachusetts on March 8, 2007.

Our weird journey began a long, long time ago in a far-off land called New Jersey. Once a year or so, we'd compile a homespun newsletter called *Weird N.J.*, then pass it on to our friends. The pamphlet was a collection of odd news clippings, bizarre facts, little-known historical anecdotes, and anomalous encounters from our home state. The newsletter also included the kinds of localized legends that were often whispered around a particular town but seldom heard outside the boundaries of the community where they originated.

We had started *Weird N.J.* on the simple theory that every town in the state had at least one good tale to tell. The publication soon became a full-fledged magazine, and we made the decision to actually do our own investigating to see if we could track down where all of these seemingly unbelievable stories were coming from. Was there, we wondered, any factual basis for the fantastic local legends people were telling us about? Armed with not much more than a camera and a notepad, we set off on a mystical journey of discovery. Much to our surprise and amazement, a lot of what we had initially presumed

to be nothing more than urban legends turned out to be real—or at least to contain a grain of truth, which had sparked the lore to begin with.

After a dozen years of documenting the bizarre, we were asked to write a book about our adventures, and so *Weird N.J.: Your Travel Guide to New Jersey's Local*

Legends and Best Kept Secrets was published in 2003. Soon people from all over the country began writing to us, telling us strange tales from their home state. As it turned out, what we had perceived to be something of very local interest was actually just a small part of a larger and more universal phenomenon.

After *Weird N.J.*, we wrote *Weird U.S.*, in which we documented the local legends and strangest stories from all over the country. We set out in search of weirdness wherever it might be found in the fifty states. And indeed, we found plenty of it!

After *Weird U.S.* was published, we came to the conclusion that this country had more great tales than could be contained in just one book. Everywhere we looked, we found unwritten folklore, creepy cemeteries, cursed locations, and outlandish roadside oddities. We wanted to document it all in a series of books, each focusing on the peculiarities of a particular state.

One of the first states to spring to our minds when we thought of a good place to find a high concentration of weirdness was Massachusetts. C'mon, any state that can boast literally dozens of places named for the devil himself has got to be kind of weird, right? Just about everybody knows of the state's more famous historically bizarre tales, like those of the Salem Witch Trials and Lizzy Borden's axe murders. But we'd also learned of several of the Bay State's lesser known strange stories through our *Weird U.S.* research, like the legends of the Dover Demon, Danvers Asylum, and phantom kidnapping clowns. Before long, we began to realize that there seemed to be a ghost in just about every old house in the state, and its centuries-old graveyards were just brimming with weird tales waiting to be told. And we knew just the guy to tell them!

We became acquainted with Jeff Belanger while we were writing our *Weird U.S.* book, when we collaborated with a number of great authors around the country who were experts on the oddities of their own particular state. And if anybody can be called an expert on the weird goings-on of Massachusetts, it's Jeff! In the past few years, he's written more than a half-dozen books on ghosts and haunted places, and his Ghostvillage.com Web site has grown into a community of over 30,000 strong! Jeff made some great contributions to our book, but more importantly, turned out to be a real pleasure to work with. We could tell from the beginning of our relationship that he was a true kindred spirit in weirdness, with a real talent and enthusiasm for telling tales of the macabre, offbeat, or just plain odd.

We knew without question that Jeff possessed what we refer to as the Weird Eye. The Weird Eye is what is needed to search out the sort of stories we were looking for. It requires one to see the world in a different way, with a renewed sense of wonder. And once you have it, there is no going back—you'll never see things the same way again. All of a sudden you begin to reexamine your own environs, noticing your everyday surroundings as if for the first time. And you begin to ask yourself questions like, "What the heck is that thing all about, anyway?" and "Doesn't anybody else think *that's* kind of *weird?*"

So come with us now and let Jeff take you on a tour of *his* Bay State, with all its ghostly places, ancient and unexplainable mysteries, and quirky New England charm. It's a place we like to call *Weird Massachusetts.*

—Mark Moran and Mark Sceurman

Introduction

Life in Massachusetts was absolutely normal right up until about 10,000 years ago when the first people arrived in the region—and then things started to get strange.

Maybe it's something in the water (like the Shaker Fountain of Youth in Harvard, the clear-blue H_2O of the Quabbin, or that dirty water of the Charles), or maybe it's our cold winters—forcing people to hibernate and share stories of local monsters, demons, ghosts, giants, or other magical creatures by the fire while they wait for spring's thaw. Maybe it's so many decades of not winning a World Series that made us a bit nuts, but no matter the cause, the end result is that Massachusetts is indeed a very weird place—a fact that takes even some locals by surprise.

When one thinks of gaudy or boisterous people and places, Massachusetts doesn't usually come to the general American mind, but scratch the surface just a little bit, and we see that there are some very odd skeletons in our closet.

In researching *Weird Massachusetts*, I had the opportunity to speak with many people around the state about local points of interest, legends, or history that didn't quite make it to the mainstream, but occurred nonetheless. Some historians and experts that I consulted were a bit put off by the "weird" title. I was shocked! For me, the unusual, the bizarre, and the unique are something to be celebrated. Massachusetts isn't like any other state in the country (we don't even talk like anyone else), and my job was to uncover as much of our strange past and odd present as possible . . . kind of a weird roving reporter. And it wasn't always easy. Fortunately, I got some advice from Mark Sceurman on how to make the approach for gathering up the stories.

"Sometimes you need to make the *d* silent when you make that initial call," Mark said. As in, "Hi, I'm writing a book called *Weir Massachusetts.*"

"Did you say, *Weird Massachusetts?*" the caller/potential interview subject may ask.

"No, no. . . . *We're Massachusetts . . .*"

Thanks, Mark.

The name Massachusetts goes back to the people who first settled here millennia before the English colonists, and the word roughly translates to "at the range of hills" (meaning the Blue Hills located in Milton, just southwest of Boston). Massachusetts is a commonwealth—one of only four states that refer to themselves as such—and in this big melting pot there is a mix of influences from Native American to English, from heavy New England sensibility to a touch of New York brash. It's reflected in our attitude, the way we dress (like our standard-issue YANKEES SUCK T-shirts), the way we drive (who has time for turn signals?), and the way we hold on to ancient sites even if we haven't quite figured them out.

History is sacred 'round these parts. And it should be, considering we're one of the oldest parts of the country. We tend to cling to things from antiques to old buildings, but especially our stories and legends. The Wampanoags' pukwudgees, or little magical people, may still be wreaking havoc on Cape Cod; the Dover Demon, though spotted over only a two-day period back in 1977, may just be poised for a comeback; Bigfoot's been on October Mountain, in western Massachusetts; and Massachusetts is home to America's first UFO sighting back in the late 1630s, when one evening James

Everell and two companions witnessed a huge, bright light hovering in the sky; it turned into the shape of a pig and darted between Boston and Charlton for a few hours before disappearing.

The seeds of the American Revolution were planted in the streets of Boston and sown in Concord when the first shots were fired. I'm sure those brave men who fought at Old North Bridge had no idea that they were laying down their lives so one day Massachusetts could be home to prestigious institutions like the Museum of Bad Art, the Burnt Food Museum, and the birthplace of Toll House cookies.

Then there are our ghosts—literal (if we're to believe the legends and witnesses) reminders of our past. We have haunted inns and hotels, ghost ships that once hailed from Gloucester, and there's the ghost of little Lucy Keyes still lost in the woods and looking for her family. We have founding fathers buried in our soil, plus literary giants. Though long dead, they still seem to exert some influence on who we are.

Weird Massachusetts is a journey through time and space (at least the space between Connecticut, New York, Vermont, New Hampshire, Rhode Island, and the Atlantic Ocean). It's an exploration of our ancient artifacts that must have had some reason for being, a journey through some old abandoned villages, buildings, and places, and a look at the events, people, and curses that have come to help define who we are.

Massachusetts is home to more than 6.4 million people who not only have learned to tolerate our weirdness but maybe have even come to love it.

—*Jeff Belanger*

Local Legends

in *northern climes like ours,* folks tend to hibernate a bit in the winter; they often sit around fires and share stories with each other, which probably explains why some tales are passed down from one generation to the next. Myths and legends are as much a part of our identity as is the actual history of good old weird Massachusetts. We take our past seriously here. You might even say it's sacred.

The Bay State is full of very old legends, from ghostly ships to child-abducting clowns to hidden treasures and even a peanut butter jar endowed with special powers of luck. Most of the stories have some grain of truth to them, although it may be so layered over by time that it's hard to find. Some are mysteries that may never be solved. But all make for very good reading!

The Mary Celeste—Marion's Ghost Ship

Though the great age of sail ended in the early part of the nineteenth century, there were still sailing vessels crossing the seas to foreign ports for another century. One of these last of the great sailing vessels was a 103-foot, 282-ton brigantine called the *Amazon*. The *Amazon* first launched out of Nova Scotia in 1861, and you might say she was born under a bad sign. Her first captain died just after embarking on her maiden voyage. The vessel changed ownership several times, and in 1862 she was driven ashore during a fierce storm in Glace Bay, Nova Scotia. Later that year she was sold to American owners in Marion, Massachusetts, who changed her name to *Mary Celeste*. Ask any sea dog worth his salt, and he'll tell ya changin' a ship's name be bad luck.

Two-hundred-and-eighty-two-ton sailing boats need a skilled captain and crew to work the sails, navigate away from treacherous waters, and find the wind to tack. If left unmanned for even a short time, a ship can put herself into an endless turn or catch the wind the wrong way and capsize. In November 1872, Captain Benjamin Briggs was tasked with putting together an able-bodied crew to take the *Mary Celeste* across the Atlantic.

Clockwise from left, Captain Benjamin Briggs, **Mary Celeste**, *Sarah Briggs, and Sophia Matilda Briggs. Opposite page, Albert Richardson, first mate.*

Captain Briggs and his crew were assigned to pick up a cargo of industrial alcohol from the Meissner Ackermann & Coin Company in Staten Island, New York, and take it to Genoa, Italy. Briggs was a seasoned seaman who knew his way around a ship and around the ocean. He must not have feared the journey ahead, because in addition to his crew of seven sailors, he also brought his wife, Sarah, and daughter, Sophia Matilda. Ten souls left Staten Island aboard the *Mary Celeste* on November 7, 1872. They sailed east into the Atlantic Ocean and into the annals of maritime folklore and mythology.

The next time the *Mary Celeste* was seen was on December 4, 1872—about four hundred miles east of the Azores, near Portugal. Captain David Reed Morehouse was commanding the *Dei Gratia* when one of his crew spotted the *Mary Celeste*. The *Dei Gratia* had left New York harbor one week after the *Mary Celeste*, and captain and crew were a bit surprised to have caught up. Morehouse knew Briggs, and knew what kind of experienced captain he was, and so he suspected something was wrong. Even though there was no distress flag raised and the *Mary Celeste*'s sails were set properly to ride a starboard tack eastward, he decided to take a closer look.

When the *Dei Gratia* drew near, they could see that no one was on deck on the other ship. Oliver Deveau, the chief mate of the *Gratia*, dropped his yawl—or small rowboat—into the Atlantic and led a party over to the seemingly abandoned ship. Once on board, they found the brigantine was sound. The masts and sails were in their place, and the hull was solid. Heading below, they discovered a fair amount of water between the decks and a few feet of water in the hold, but the cargo, over 1,700 barrels of alcohol, was all securely fastened in place, and there was no sign of struggle or any other problems. But Deveau did notice a few things missing from the ship. For one, the lifeboat was gone, as were the sextant and chronometer, which led the search party to assume that the crew deliberately left the *Mary Celeste*. Most of the ship's manifests and papers were gone, but Captain Briggs's log remained.

The last log entry was dated November 24 and placed the *Mary Celeste* one hundred miles west of the Azores, hundreds of miles from where she was now. The ship's slate told Deveau that she was scheduled to reach the island of Santa Maria on November 25, but nothing after that. Sailing ships in 1872 weren't very likely to sail themselves for hundreds of miles on course. Aboard the *Dei Gratia* whispers of a ghost crew and haunted ship began to circulate. The *Dei Gratia's* crew split up to sail both ships into port in Gibraltar, report the find to local authorities, and collect the salvage reward per the law of the sea.

At first, the *Dei Gratia* crew were praised for their bravery, but the praise quickly turned to suspicion about how they had come upon the vessel. In the end, the crew of the *Dei Gratia* were cleared, but the rumors and speculation of the *Mary Celeste* mystery were just beginning. One fact remained: No one from the *Mary Celeste* was ever seen or heard from again.

The world had many questions as the details of the mystery spread: If the *Mary Celeste* had been raided by pirates, wouldn't they have taken the cargo or the ship? If there was a mutiny, wouldn't there be blood or some sign of struggle? And wouldn't the mutineers have taken the ship and its cargo? If the seasoned captain and crew abandoned ship (which is what it looked like) because they felt the ship was in peril, perhaps because of the potentially explosive cargo, wouldn't they remain within sight of the *Mary Celeste* to see if she foundered or not? Setting a small boat full of people and few supplies into the open Atlantic is a death sentence unless another ship is nearby.

These unanswerable questions have led to wild speculation. There was talk of sea monsters abducting the crew; others suggested nature's wrath swept away everyone onboard but left the vessel intact, and even alien abduction was tossed around in the legends. Why did the crew and passengers simply vanish into thin air?

The *Mary Celeste* sailed for twelve more years after the *Dei Gratia* found her floating adrift. She continued to change hands until January of 1885 when Captain Gilman C. Parker sailed her from Boston to Haiti. On January 28, he wrecked her on a reef on Rochelais Bank.

The *Mary Celeste* has since sailed on into popular legend, thanks to everyone from Arthur Conan Doyle's 1884 story titled "J. Habakuk Jephson's Statement" to the *Star Trek* segment where the *Enterprise* comes across a ship with no crew. Next to the infamous *Flying Dutchman*, the *Mary Celeste* is arguably the world's most famous ghost ship, and she hailed from Marion in our own state.

Conducting Visitors through the Cave

Hiram Marble

Dungeon Rock

Yarrgh, ye scalawags, the Caribbean's not the only place where pirates plundered, pillaged, and hid their booty. It was the summer of 1658 when a black ship sailed into Lynn Harbor with nary a flag of identifying country to be seen above her decks. A rowin' boat was lowered to the water, a chest placed inside, and two oarsmen and two young ladies took it to shore.

The buccaneers rowed their boat up the Saugus River and stopped just short of the Saugus Iron Works. They left a note on the door, saying the men wanted to purchase hatchets, shovels, and shackles. The note asked for the goods to be delivered to a specified location, and in exchange, Saugus Iron Works would be rewarded in silver. The tools were delivered and paid for as promised.

Considering the ominous black ship in the harbor and odd request for tools, whispers spread of a pirate encampment in Lynn in a place we know today as Pirate's Glen, right near the river. When British troops caught wind of the talk, they set out to capture the pirates. The raid was mostly successful. The troops caught Captain Harris and the two women, but a man named Thomas Veal narrowly escaped into the woods with what many believed was the pirates' treasure. As Veal ventured deeper into Lynn Woods, he discovered a natural cave in the rocks.

Veal moved into the cave and managed to integrate himself into the Lynn community. He did odd jobs around town for his spending money—he was known to fix shoes for various townspeople—but he mostly kept to himself and quietly lived in his cave . . . until disaster struck.

An earthquake rocked Veal's cave, collapsing a section of the structure, which either sealed the cave shut like a natural dungeon or possibly crushed him. No matter what happened, Veal was never seen alive again.

Two centuries later, in the 1830s, folks once again began to talk about the day the pirates came to Lynn. Many knew Veal had lived in the cave, now known as Dungeon Rock, and they assumed his remains and treasure must still be buried inside. Kegs of black powder were brought into the cave, and were soon only a matchstick away from blowing the lid off the mystery, as well as the cave. But after the dust settled and the smoke cleared, nothing was found.

Two decades later, in 1852, a spiritualist named Hiram Marble came to Lynn because of a message he received from the other side. Spiritualism was a new movement at the time, but the belief system was spreading rapidly. Many were intrigued with the idea of two-way communication with those who had passed on. Marble believed he was communicating with the spirit of Thomas Veal, who had told him to head to Lynn where he would find buried treasure.

Marble was from Charlton, but he moved his family to Lynn and immediately purchased several acres of land, which included Dungeon Rock. If he could find buried treasure, he would prove spiritualism to the world and get rich in the process.

Marble built his family a two-story house near the cave's entrance and set to work digging. Soon his son, Edwin, joined in the excruciatingly slow work. The Marbles would drill holes in the rock, pack the holes with black powder, and then duck! The rock broke away a few inches at a time, and the two would carry off the mess. The tunnels inside the cave often took unexpected turns as Hiram and his son changed their minds or direction in an effort to get to the treasure. They bored through 145 feet of rock, but found nothing but more stone. Other spiritualists came to town, and the site became a center for the movement. Months and years went by, but the riches remained elusive.

Hiram Marble died in 1868, likely with one very sore back but no pirates' gold to show for it. In 1880, his son, Edwin, passed away, never fulfilling his and his father's dream of finding Thomas Veal's treasure and validating spiritualism. Edwin asked to be buried at Dungeon Rock, and today a pink stone marks his grave.

An August 10, 1878, article from *Frank Leslie's Illustrated Newspaper* says of Dungeon Rock: "Every tourist entering the ancient precincts of Lynn, Mass., should pass a few Moments, at least, at Dungeon Rock. If he is a believer in the tenets of modern Spiritualism his stay will be prolonged, for this spot owes its chief interest to the laborious work of a family who have for many years professed to be guided by the directions and encouragement of the spirits." The article concludes that "the treasure was as far from human sight as ever, and to this day it remains an unknown quantity."

Send in the Clowns

Oh no . . . they're already here! Let's face it: Besides bugs, snakes, and monsters, there are few things quite as scary as a clown. The distorted makeup, the overly bright colors, and the fact that the person behind the disguise is relatively anonymous, all of it drums up fears in children and adults alike.

There's a delicious dichotomy to clowns—the happy jester façade with a mysterious lonely man behind the makeup—that has inspired some fantastic tales of horror like Stephen King's *IT* and the *Poltergeist* film. Back in 1981, Boston had its own run-in with terror—terror that allegedly wore a rainbow wig.

In the spring of '81, reports sprang up around town of children being abducted by a clown, and sometimes by a group of clowns. Though the police and even the press could find no victim or even alleged victim of clown harassment, mad clown fever continued to grow.

In May of 1981, Daniel O'Connell, an investigative counselor for the Boston Public School Board, sent a memo to district school administrators stating: ". . . it has been brought to the attention of the police department and the district office that adults dressed as clowns have been bothering children to and from school. Please advise all students that they must stay away from strangers, especially ones dressed as clowns." Sound advice anytime, really.

O'Connell's memo only added fuel to the growing clown fire. Another report came in a few days later around Franklin Park in Roxbury that a man dressed as a clown from the waist up (and naked from the waist down) was trying to lure children with candy to get into his old black van. Clearly the man was an amateur. Had he been a pro, there would have been more clowns, and they would have all fit into a tiny car.

Throughout May and into June, police were receiving reports from all over the greater Boston area of people spotting clowns. The police would send out a patrol car but would find nothing. Even the witnesses who first called the police would second-guess themselves. Maybe they were just seeing things.

Legitimate entertainers who worked children's parties dressed as clowns were not only out of work, but they didn't dare don their garb and walk outside. "Clownism" was the order of the day in the spring of '81, and police were completely at a loss as to what to do. There were no adult eyewitnesses, and no abductions of children could be tied to any clown. Yet the reports continued to come in . . . and they were spreading.

As Loren Coleman points out in his book *Mysterious America*, the legend and fear that began in Boston soon spilled into other states like an overflowing banana cream pie. In May of '81 in Providence, Rhode Island, children were reporting to social workers that they were being stalked by men dressed as clowns.

Then it all went away, almost as suddenly as it had begun. By early summer, the clown reports were just a memory recorded into the annals of a Massachusetts urban legend.

Ain't No Clowning Around

I wanted to tell you about my Clown in a Van story. When I was 12 years old and my brother 8, my parents would bring us to their friend's house who also had two kids, ages 11 and 8. So all the kids would play together and we would gather up other neighborhood kids and play huge games of capture the flag, etc. One night around 10 the four of us were going to meet a huge group of people at this park. On our way there we were closely followed by a big black van with tinted windows and what looked like a dude dressed up like a clown. We started getting a little freaked out, so we cut through some yards to get across the block and avoid the van. A little bit later, we saw the van creeping along another street a little bit down the street from where we were and we ran through some more yards and got to the park and met everyone. In the middle of our game we saw the van pull up to the park and sit there for a while.

It eventually left. So, the next day I see on the news that a guy driving a black van dressed like a clown got arrested in a mall parking lot after he tried to get some teenage girls in his van. He also had a record of being a sexual deviant! This had to be back in like 1992 or '93, but I still have that memory.—*Brandon Perras*

The Angel of Hadley

Some legends have been told and retold so many times that it becomes difficult to separate the legend from the actual history. Sometimes it's hard to know if anything historical ever took place at all. The myth becomes bigger than the people involved and even the actual event.

James Freeman is a professor of English at the University of Massachusetts and has been a resident of Hadley since 1969. He's studied the following legend for many years, and when asked how he first heard about it, he said, "It's almost in the air in Hadley."

Hadley's legendary hero is General William Goffe, a fugitive from England in the seventeenth century. Goffe was wanted for regicide—and there was no higher crime in the empire than killing a king. But it's Goffe who is said to have saved Hadley from murderous invaders.

By the late seventeenth century, English settlers were becoming more and more intrusive in the lands and the lives of the Native Americans. In addition, Wampanoag leader Metacom suspected the English of foul play in the death of his brother Wamsutta. This suspicion played a significant role in what would come to be known as King Philip's War, King Philip being the white man's name for Metacom. It was a bloodbath that left one out of every twenty citizens dead or wounded.

As with any war, there were many factors that contributed to the bloodshed. Not only did the Wampanoag believe their land and well-being were in danger from the encroaching English settlers, they also believed their very souls were at stake, as some of the Puritan groups made it clear that one of their objectives was to convert the natives to Christianity.

The altercation began on June 8, 1675, in Plymouth, when three Wampanoags were convicted and hanged for the murder of John Sassamon. On June 20, a band of Pokanokets retaliated for what they felt was an unjust execution by attacking some isolated homesteads in

Swansea. They burned the homes and barns, and killed several settlers. On June 28, English forces responded to the Swansea attack with a raid of their own on a village in Rhode Island. The war was on.

On Sunday, September 1, 1675, King Philip's War came to Hadley. Though other dates of this attack have been put forth, the basics of the story remain the same: The Wampanoag army pulled a bluff on the English forces. The Wampanoag sent scouts to northern Massachusetts to give the impression that a major offensive was heading that way. When the English moved their troops to defend the north, the Wampanoag attacked the central Massachusetts town of Hadley. According to the legend, Sunday, September 1, found most of the residents of Hadley in church when the Wampanoag roared into town.

Taken by surprise and clearly outnumbered, the residents of Hadley thought they were doomed, until a tall, white-bearded Englishman appeared brandishing a military saber. The stranger took command of the situation; his powerful voice brought all to attention, and he organized a militia and a plan in mere minutes. The figure clearly had military knowledge and leadership prowess. The outnumbered English successfully drove the Wampanoag back into the woods, where they scattered. When the residents of Hadley returned to thank their deliverer, he was gone. The man was dubbed the Angel of Hadley, and word of his accomplishment spread almost as fast as conjecture over exactly who the man was. Whispers turned to rumors, and rumors turned to a legend that the angel was none other than General William Goffe, who had come over to Massachusetts to save his skin.

In 1648, Goffe was one of the fifty-nine judges who signed a death warrant for King Charles I of England.

After the king was beheaded, Oliver Cromwell took over England. His reign barely survived his death in 1658, and Parliament eventually restored the monarchy and gave the throne to Charles's son, who would become Charles II. Young Chuck was hell-bent to avenge his father's death. To give an idea of how upset Charles II was, he had Oliver Cromwell's body exhumed from Westminster Abbey and posthumously executed. Cromwell's decaying remains were hung and quartered, and his severed head was displayed on a pole outside Westminster Abbey. Given that, there's no confusion as to why William Goffe wanted to get as far away from England as possible.

Goffe hid out at various safe houses in Connecticut and Massachusetts. Goffe and fellow fugitive Edward Whalley are believed to have been harbored in Hadley for close to ten years, which leads Freeman to believe that the whole town was in on it. The community was only about fifty families large, making it almost impossible for someone to keep any kind of secret that long.

So was there any record of a battle in Hadley on September 1, 1675? "None," Freeman says. "There were battles nearby on the first of September 1675. Our ancestors are British, and they kept very good records." He explained that there was no mention of a battle in journals or letters of the townspeople and nothing in the official documents of the village. The Angel of Hadley legend may have been born in the 1760s when Massachusetts lieutenant governor Thomas Hutchinson came into possession of some of Goffe's letters and his diary. Hutchinson wrote a history of Massachusetts and mentioned Goffe as the great deliverer of Hadley from the Indian attack. Any evidence of the actual letters and diaries was destroyed in 1765 when Hutchinson's home was ransacked because of his political affiliations.

One Lucky Peanut Butter Jar

There's a very significant peanut butter jar floating around the athletic department of Tufts University in Medford. The jar dates back to 1975, and the contents are definitely not peanut butter anymore. Athletes, students, and coaches all claim it's good luck to rub this special jar before a big game.

The story behind the jar's contents begins in 1861 in the jungles of Africa. A baby elephant had been captured and brought to Cairo, Egypt, where he was sold to a representative of the Paris zoo. The young elephant was named Jumbo, possibly a mix-up of the Swahili word *jumbe,* which translates to "chief."

Though Jumbo was relatively small at the time the name was given, the growing creature would turn the term into a household word.

Soon after arriving in Paris, Jumbo was swapped for a rhinoceros from the Royal Zoological Gardens in London. When Jumbo arrived in London, he was a scant four feet tall, dirty, and malnourished. At the London zoo, keeper Matthew Scott cared for the young pachyderm until it grew to heroic proportions. When Jumbo was seven years old, he was consuming a daily diet of two hundred pounds of hay, two bushels of oats, one barrel of potatoes, fifteen loaves of bread, lots and lots of onions, and all the pails of water he could drink. Jumbo was now eleven-and-a-half feet tall and weighed over six-and-a-half tons.

The giant quickly became a favorite of London

children, and during the next two decades, thousands took rides on the great beast's back. Noted Jumbo passengers included Winston Churchill, Theodore Roosevelt, and one Phineas Taylor Barnum.

An entrepreneur and showman, P. T. Barnum took notice of the giant creature's growing popularity. In 1880, he merged his Greatest Show on Earth circus with James Anthony Bailey's London Circus to create the Barnum and Bailey Circus, which survives to this day. The biggest circus in the world needed the biggest draw in the world, so in 1881 Barnum offered the London zoo $10,000 for Jumbo, a lot of money at the time. Barnum didn't expect the zoo to take the offer, nor did it initially, not until Jumbo got cranky one day and threw some temper tantrums that made his keepers fear the elephant was turning on them. The zoo did not want its employees or customers getting hurt should the elephant go on a rampage, and so the London zoo accepted Barnum's offer.

Londoners were outraged, with a little help from Barnum, who began a whisper campaign aimed at convincing locals that they were giving up a national treasure. How could they let such a prize go to the Americans? Had they no pride?

Protest letters poured into the London zoo and to the newspapers, and even Americans took notice. Considering all the fuss, this must have been quite a spectacle coming to the United States.

Counter offers were made, but Barnum refused every one.

The *London Daily Telegraph* editorial summed up the defeat and national sentiment of England: "Our amiable monster must [now] dwell in a tent, take part in the routine of a circus, and, instead of his by-gone friendly trots with British girls and boys, and perpetual luncheons on buns and oranges, must amuse a Yankee mob and put up with peanuts and waffles."

On April 9, 1882, thousands stood on the docks in New York City to see the colossal creature. Jumbo and his huge ornate crate were carted through the streets of New York to the Hippodrome (now called Madison Square Garden), where he joined Barnum's famous circus. Barnum had spent just over $30,000 in purchasing Jumbo and transporting him home. By the end of his first year in America, Jumbo had earned his new owner about $1.5 million.

"JUMBO" — Killed in St. Thomas, September 15, 1885

COMPLIMENTS OF
ANDERSONS LIMITED, ST. THOMAS, C

"The Towering Monarch of His Mighty Race, Whose Like the World Will Never See Again," the bill read. "Jumbo" even became part of the American lexicon, a word reserved for something truly huge.

But all things do come to an end unless you're P. T. Barnum. On September 15, 1885, Barnum's Greatest Show on Earth was playing in St. Thomas, Ontario. It was near the end of the show, and Jumbo was waiting

next to the railroad tracks to close the show. Suddenly the shrill whistle of an unexpected train sounded. Before anyone had time to react, poor old Jumbo's head was crushed by the train.

P. T. Barnum didn't miss a beat. He immediately contacted taxidermist Henry A. Ward and presented him with the biggest taxidermy job ever offered. Ward high-tailed it to St. Thomas, where he and six local butchers worked feverishly to remove Jumbo's bones and hide. Barnum wanted two Jumbos: one a stuffed hide made to look lifelike, the other a reconstructed skeleton. And Barnum wanted them quickly, because not even death would stop Jumbo's money-making prowess.

The stuffed Jumbo toured the world for the next two years; then P. T. Barnum, a Tufts University trustee, donated the taxidermied pachyderm to the university, where the animal was quickly adopted by the school as a lucky charm. For many years, students would place pennies in Jumbo's trunk or tug on his tail for luck before big events like exams. The behemoth was the pride of the school, and the mascot the sports teams rallied behind.

But tragedy struck Jumbo again on April 14, 1975, when a fire broke out and reduced him to a charred tusk, a fragment of burned tail, and a pile of ashes. A quick-thinking administrative assistant named Phyllis Byrne grabbed an empty peanut butter jar and handed it to George Wilson of the school's maintenance staff. She told Wilson to save whatever he could of the school's mascot, and Wilson scooped up some of Jumbo's charred remains.

The athletic director at the time, Rocco J. "Rocky" Carzo, kept the jar in his office and helped birth a strange tradition and unique legend. Students had been rubbing Jumbo for luck for years, and Carzo saw no need to stop. Athletes would come in and hold the jar before a big game, coaches rubbed it for luck, and students and other fans of the school would ask to see the jar.

Rocky Carzo has long since retired, but the jar of Jumbo's remains is still there. It sits on a shelf with a typed label that reads ENCLOSED ASHES ARE REMAINS OF TUFTS' JUMBO LOST IN A FIRE AT BARNUM MUSEUM ON 4-14-75.

Curse of the Bambino

The Boston Red Sox have won more World Series than any other team in professional baseball . . . at least this was true in 1918. That was the year the Sox took their fifth title—and they owed quite a bit of credit to one of their stars: George Herman Ruth Jr., also known as the Sultan of Swat, the Great Bambino, or simply Babe Ruth.

The Babe came to Boston in 1914, but he didn't earn a spot in the Red Sox pitching rotation until the 1915 season. The team won the 1915 World Series, though Ruth didn't play in much of it. He started coming into his own during the 1916 season, helping bring the Sox to their third World Series in five years. In the 1918 World Series, Ruth went 2–0, giving the Sox yet another championship. The Sox weren't in the 1919 series, but that season Ruth hit a record-breaking twenty-nine home runs.

So what do you do with a talent who's arguably just getting started? Sell him to your archrival, the Yankees, of course.

And so the Boston Red Sox traded Babe to the Yankees in 1920 for $100,000. On January 3, 1920, then Red Sox owner Harry Frazee was quoted as saying, "With this money, the Boston club can now go into the market and buy other players and have a stronger and better team in all respects than we would have had if Ruth had remained with us."

But Frazee didn't use the hundred grand to better his team. Instead, he mortgaged Fenway Park for $300,000 and added that to the $100,000 he got for Ruth in order to finance Broadway plays like the unforgettable classic *No, No, Nanette*.

The rest is baseball history. Over the next eighty-four years, the Red Sox made it to only four World Series and lost each one. The Yankees, on the other hand, won their first World Series with Babe Ruth in 1923. They went on to play in thirty-nine more and win twenty-six of them—twice as many championship titles as any other team in Major League Baseball. Some would say the Red Sox were just in a looooong slump, but many more said the team was cursed.

New York Times sports columnist George Vecsey first wrote that the Red Sox must be cursed for selling Babe Ruth all those years ago, but it was *Boston Globe* sports columnist Dan Shaughnessy who made the concept famous with his 1990 book *The Curse of the Bambino*. "It became such a cottage industry and a handy theme for multiple network announcers, columnists, and out-of-town people," Shaughnessy says. "It just grew into a monster because it was such an easy, catchy phrase."

The curse was now firmly in place. But was it truly something supernatural? In subsequent editions of *The Curse of the Bambino*, Shaughnessy covered the phenomenon and the way some fans were coping and even trying to counteract the curse. Witches from Salem have performed rituals outside Fenway Park in an attempt to break the curse. Priests have been asked to perform exorcisms along Yawkey Way. Maybe none of those things worked, maybe collectively they helped a little. We'll never know for sure. But the Red Sox did finally win a World Series.

The 2004 baseball playoffs were one of the

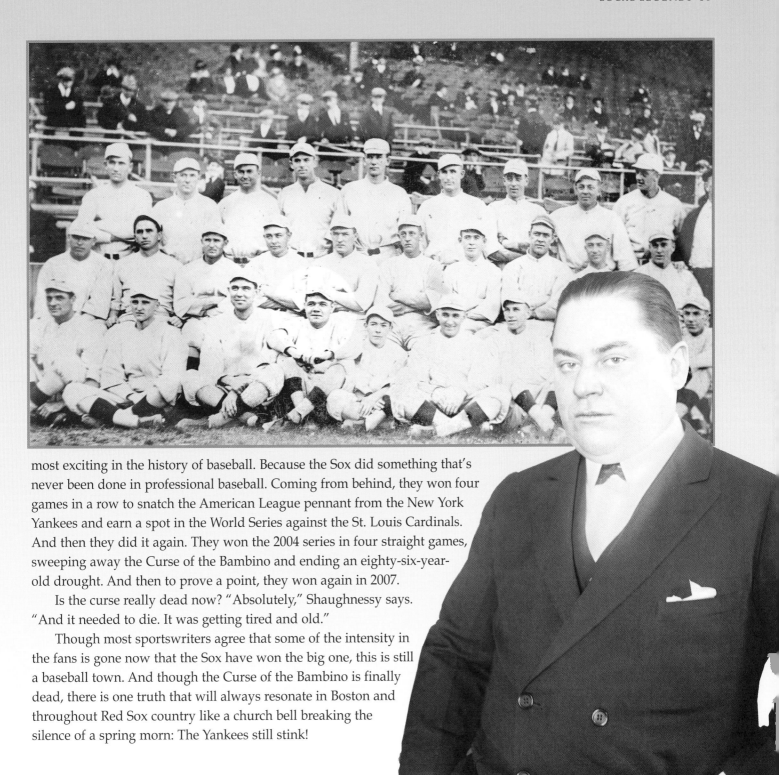

most exciting in the history of baseball. Because the Sox did something that's never been done in professional baseball. Coming from behind, they won four games in a row to snatch the American League pennant from the New York Yankees and earn a spot in the World Series against the St. Louis Cardinals. And then they did it again. They won the 2004 series in four straight games, sweeping away the Curse of the Bambino and ending an eighty-six-year-old drought. And then to prove a point, they won again in 2007.

Is the curse really dead now? "Absolutely," Shaughnessy says. "And it needed to die. It was getting tired and old."

Though most sportswriters agree that some of the intensity in the fans is gone now that the Sox have won the big one, this is still a baseball town. And though the Curse of the Bambino is finally dead, there is one truth that will always resonate in Boston and throughout Red Sox country like a church bell breaking the silence of a spring morn: The Yankees still stink!

Ghosts of the Charles Haskell

Gloucester is a fishing town with more than its share of sea stories: tales of strange monsters lurking in the waters offshore and of cursed ships. The *Charles Haskell* is one such vessel.

Built in 1869, the *Charles Haskell* saw her first bad omen before her sails even caught their first breeze. During a final inspection, one of the workmen slipped on a companionway and broke his neck. Seamen are a superstitious bunch, and that little slip caused the original captain to refuse to sail her. The ship sat idle until Captain Clifford Curtis from Gloucester stepped up and offered to take the helm.

The *Charles Haskell* was rigged for cod fishing, and Georges Bank, east of Cape Cod, was the place to make the big catches. During the winter of 1869–1870, Captain Curtis took the *Haskell* to Georges Bank and anchored her. Across the water, Curtis saw many other fishing vessels also anchored along the shoals with the aim of landing the bounty from below.

There's a saying in New England that if you don't like the weather, don't worry; just wait a minute and it will change. This goes double for weather off the shores of the Cape. Dark clouds rolled up the horizon, and the sea below the *Haskell* began to churn—a violent winter storm had sneaked up on the shoals. Captain Curtis feared for his ship and crew, and he ordered his anchor lines cut so he could maneuver away from the other boats. Though this may have saved the *Charles Haskell*, it proved fatal to the *Andrew Johnson*, a nearby ship that hailed from the port of Salem. The *Haskell* rammed the Johnson, slicing her open. Water flooded the *Andrew Johnson* and the boat, with ten souls on board, sank to a watery grave.

The *Charles Haskell* was seriously wounded from the collision, but she could still float. Captain Curtis brought his ship back to port in Gloucester for repairs. The *Haskell* had just encountered its second death mark, but Curtis wasn't one to give in to flights of fancy. Once it was repaired, he took his ship and crew back to Georges Bank just a few months after the accident.

The crew had a few peaceful days of fishing that spring, and thoughts of the winter horror were slowly drifting away until a certain midnight watch. The Gloucester legend goes that two crew members of the *Charles Haskell* were on the watch that evening when an unexplained chill settled around the boat. At first, the men believed that their eyes were playing tricks on them. They saw dark, shadowy figures rising up out of the sea. There were ten of them in all, and as they reached the *Haskell* the watchmen could see that the figures looked like men. The dark wraiths reached their hands over the rail of the schooner and climbed aboard. Their eyes were black, like hollowed-out holes, and they wore dark and oily sealskins for clothes. The phantoms quickly took up positions around the ship and began to go through the motions of casting lines, rigging sails, and setting the anchor. The watchmen aboard the *Haskell* were in a panic and called for Captain Curtis.

When he arrived on deck, Curtis stood slack-jawed at the sight. The dark figures took no notice of the living crew until Curtis finally approached one of them. When the shadowy fisherman turned to face the captain, the black holes for eyes pierced him and Curtis slunk back to his quarters. When dawn broke, the phantom crew climbed over the rails of the *Charles Haskell*, back into the sea, and back down to the darkness below.

Captain Curtis was spooked and had his crew set the sails for home. The schooner sailed with all her might, but it couldn't cover the miles in the daylight hours. She would need to spend another night at sea. The men on the night watch were all jitters when darkness fell. When midnight rolled around and another chill set around the vessel, the crew was on alert.

Once again, the black shadows rose from below and dark hands and legs hoisted phantom sails aboard the *Haskell*. Again the ghostly crew went to work, fishing on lines that no one could see. The crew of the *Haskell* waited in fear until dawn, when they once again set sail and took their boat into Gloucester's port.

Some say the *Charles Haskell* never sailed again and simply fell into ruin until her hull disintegrated and the harbor took her down to rot into nothingness. Others suggest a Canadian captain came in and bought the vessel. No matter, the *Charles Haskell* and its ghostly crew were out of the life of Captain Curtis and his very shaken-up men.

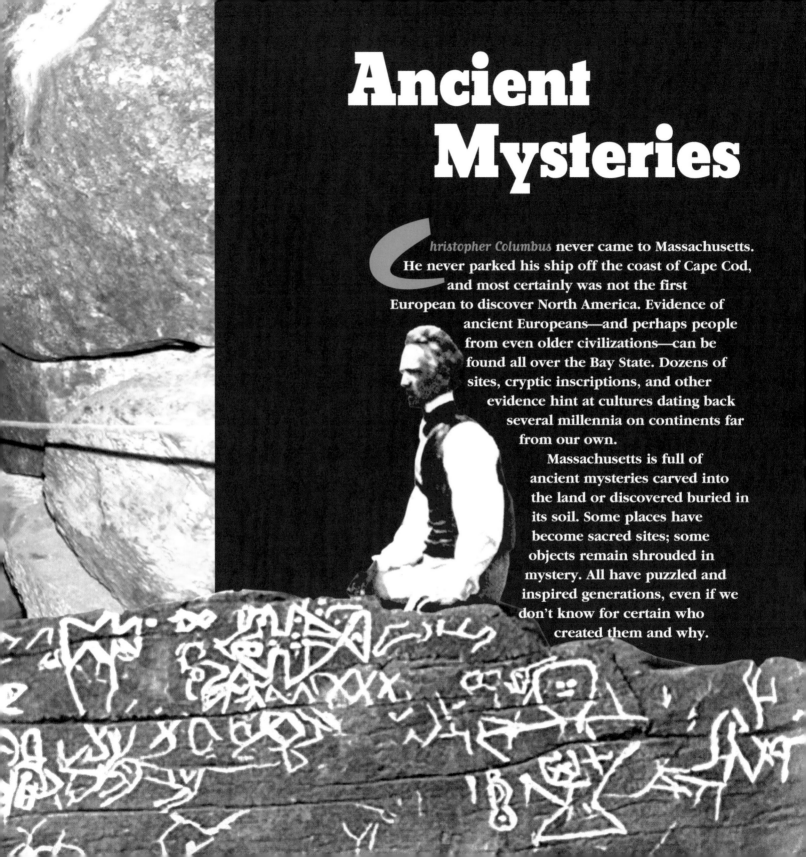

Ancient Mysteries

Christopher Columbus never came to Massachusetts. He never parked his ship off the coast of Cape Cod, and most certainly was not the first European to discover North America. Evidence of ancient Europeans—and perhaps people from even older civilizations—can be found all over the Bay State. Dozens of sites, cryptic inscriptions, and other evidence hint at cultures dating back several millennia on continents far from our own.

Massachusetts is full of ancient mysteries carved into the land or discovered buried in its soil. Some places have become sacred sites; some objects remain shrouded in mystery. All have puzzled and inspired generations, even if we don't know for certain who created them and why.

Standing stones on hill in Heath remain a puzzle

By Trudy Tynan

Associated Press

... — As cold and lonely as
sky, the standing
Burnt Hill have
nation of fiction
tions of blue-

...nd why

'I started out
thinking this
would be a quick
job and got
hooked.'

...es were erected by a
farmer to mark the
his land or some

d it to be very
and very clear,
o historical back-

five years of
rveyor's tran-

"When a traveller in north central Massachusetts takes the wrong fork at the junction of Aylesbury Pike just beyond Dean's Corners, he comes upon a lonely and curious country," wrote H. P. Lovecraft in his 1929 short story "The Dunwich Horror." In that curious country is the town of Heath, where atop an 1,850-foot-tall mountain called Burnt Hill lies a series of standing stones that have intrigued archaeologists and researchers, and fascinated artists and writers.

"The Dunwich Horror" is the tale of a mysterious entity that grows out of control and terrorizes the surrounding village. When you visit the Stone Circle of Burnt Hill, great rings of rough-hewn stone columns on the hilltops, you can see how the area raises more questions than answers, leaving the doorway open to images of mysterious and ancient monsters.

The site is called Burnt Hill because the exposed area of bedrock at the highest point looks as though some supernatural force singed it. Placed on the bedrock are twenty-one megalithic rocks, weighing somewhere between three hundred and five hundred pounds, each standing straight up like a sentinel admiring one of the most spectacular views of the western half of the state.

There are more standing stones and rock clusters as you move southwest of the top, but they get progressively smaller. Because of the expansive view and the obvious trouble someone went through to place the stones, many speculate that this is a calendar site. And then there's the legend that during bad weather, strange flashing blue lights emanate from the stones, creating a very weird vibe.

During the autumn of 2001, Edward Bochnak had a startling experience when he went to the area to take some photographs. He said, "I visited that hill on a rainy autumn day. From the parking lot where I left my car, it took me two hours to hike up with my camera gear. When I got to the top, I started taking pictures of the Standing Stones. To look for a dramatic effect, I used a deep purple filter. I was very surprised later when I discovered on a few pictures a luminous anomaly over the Standing Stones."

The Goshen Mystery

Of the many puzzling structures throughout New England, the Goshen Mystery is absolutely unique. Nothing like it has been discovered before, so it has to serve as its own frame of reference. And we can be sure Mother Nature had very little to do with its construction, though we must credit her with furnishing the building material.

No one among Goshen's 920 residents can tell you what it is. They, and their ancestors, have been scratching their heads since the "Mystery" was first discovered "sodded over" in the late 1800s. There is nothing written about it in the town records. Diaries of founding fathers make no reference to its having been built. And nothing about its origins survives in the oral tradition. The only conclusion is that it predates Goshen town.

As of this writing no one has a clue about its age or why it exists. All theories have been weighed and—for one reason or another—discarded.

Briefly, the Goshen Mystery is a cleverly designed underground stone tunnel, built without mortar. The main shaft is three and a half feet wide, descending straight down for fifteen feet. The knee-jerk assessment is that it is a well, but look again. There's no water. And it is carved out of dense clay hardpan where no water would be expected. To further deep-six the perception of a well, there are horizontal tunnels branching off from the sides. One, at the bottom, leads eastward for about seventy-five feet. It's about three feet in diameter: big enough to crawl into, not big enough to stand in—unless, of course, you're very, very short.

A higher tunnel, branching out about three feet up on the main shaft, has a larger diameter but extends only about fifteen feet. Some examiners have suspected that at one time this shaft may have been longer; it appears to have been truncated by a cave-in. What lies beyond its end is anybody's guess.

But one thing is certain: This unfathomable oddity was constructed in the days of hand tools. Cutting and placing the tons of stones that line its walls and tunnels would have required countless hours of slow, backbreaking labor. The horizontal shafts would have been especially difficult to engineer and build.

How could it have been created without the first settlers realizing it? How did it escape notice for so long? And most important, what was it?

Theories include a den for very short thieves or counterfeiters, an Underground Railroad stop for escaped slaves, a root cellar, a place to store ice, a hideout from the Indians, and an abandoned treasure pit. But most likely it will turn out to be an eternal puzzle.

Whatever it is, or was, the people of Goshen say, "It's always been there."—*Joseph Citro*

Aiming for the Big Dipper

Anyone who has ever stuck a shovel in the Massachusetts soil knows that we've got rocks—and plenty of 'em. This was also true for the Colonists, who in clearing and plowing their farmland would turn up bumper crops of rocks, which they would use to create stone walls that defined their property lines and kept livestock from wandering away. Today, you'll find many of these stone walls as you walk through the state's woods. They are a subtle reminder of the past—gray scars that cut across the land, testifying that someone was here before us.

But settlers are not the only source for these stone formations. Long before the Colonists arrived, many Indian nations lived on the land. And though they didn't typically carve or construct with stones, they did use them. Stone mounds, outcroppings, and possibly some of the many walls lining the landscape may have been created by the hands of the indigenous peoples of North America.

But why?

Ted Ballard is a member of New England Antiquities

Research Association (NEARA) and an officer of the Massachusetts Archaeological Society. He's explored and documented some of our state's ancient features for the last several decades. He is quick to point out that the majority of stone walls in Massachusetts are associated with farming and were created when stones were simply dug up and carted to the edge of a property so the farmer could get on with his plowing.

However, he points out, this kind of construction is on flat ground, primarily farm fields. "But there are other connections of stones with large boulders," he says. "And when these things are on the upper side of hills, my argument is that you better damn well look at the Native American part of that, because the hilltops were ritual sites used for sky observation. When you find stone constructs on hilltops, the first thing you need to do is prove that it's not Native American. Not just arbitrarily say that it's farm field clearance."

Imagine you're a Colonist living in Sharon in the 1600s. You've cleared thousands of heavy rocks from your fields and made fences with them. Do you have the time and energy to cart more heavy rocks to hilltops where you're neither farming nor allowing your animals to graze? It's doubtful.

So when Ted Ballard found some curious U-shaped stone constructs on a hill in the woods in Sharon, he hypothesized that European settlers did not build them. "The stone constructs are on high points of ground and have interesting horizon observation azimuths," he

Dozens of these U-shaped stone constructs exist all over southern New England, and all seem to have some astrological alignment purpose.

says. (An azimuth, for the nonastronomers among us, is a way of measuring direction from a fixed point on the horizon, like true north.)

Dozens of these U-shaped stone constructs exist all over southern New England, and all seem to have some astrological alignment purpose. Some mark the solstice sunrise or sunset, but others seem built for nighttime use. In Massachusetts's early winter, the Big Dipper constellation appears low on the horizon with the handle directly below the cup. When the tail of the Dipper touches the hilltops, it marks the sacred time when the Wampanoag tribe honored one of their gods, Hobomock. Some of these U-shaped rock clusters may mark that specific event.

The U-shaped rocks are by no means the only example of Native Americans' working with stone. On other hilltops there are snakelike walls with large boulders in the middle that don't seem to serve any engineering or farming purpose. Instead, it's possible they had a more sacred use. Other stone constructs may have had more practical uses, like the short stone walls on Martha's Vineyard that have gaping holes in them. Some archaeologists believe these may have been hunting blinds, where Wampanoag hunters could hide yet still see their quarry.

The origin of the stone constructs remains controversial. Years ago the mainstream archaeological community decided that Native Americans in Massachusetts didn't work with stone and that therefore the constructs must be Colonial or evidence of ancient Europeans' visits. Sadly, some sites are being lost to modern-day construction, which is why NEARA and the Massachusetts Archaeological Society are working to document what they can before it's lost forever.

Half Moon Meadow: A Solstice Sunrise Site

One of the most significant early sites in Middlesex County may be Half Moon Meadow Brook, located in Boxborough. Its most outstanding feature is its spectacular winter solstice sunrise alignment. There is also a summer solstice sunrise alignment and a variety of interesting and enigmatic stonework. It is also the location of the last witchcraft accusations in Massachusetts.

The Half Moon Meadow site is within the original sixteen-square-mile boundary of the old Nashoba Praying Indian Village. Nashoba was established in 1651 under the guidance of John Eliot, the "Apostle to the Indians." Interestingly, the Indians were allowed to choose the locations of the Praying Villages—established in an effort to teach Christian ways—and it is believed that they chose their most religiously significant places. Two other important places within Nashoba are the nearby Beaver Brook Esker in Boxborough and the Sarah Doublet Forest in Littleton.

George Krusen, whose land abuts the property, first recognized the Half Moon Meadow Brook site. In 1988, he invited a friend, Byron Dix, to walk the area with him. Byron was immediately intrigued with what he saw. Among other things, he postulated that from a large flat rock in the west corner of the field, the winter solstice sun would rise in a cleft of a large bedrock ridge on the southeast side. He was proved to be absolutely correct.

When the land was put up for sale for house lots in 1998, George was instrumental in arranging for its purchase and preservation by the Sudbury Valley Trustees, a nonprofit conservation trust.

The Half Moon Meadow Brook site is at the junction of roads said to be an old Indian trail. The late Mark Strohmeyer, a writer with more than twenty years' experience in archaeology, believed that the trail was specifically created by the Indians for access to the site. Strohmeyer was well acquainted with Half Moon Meadow Brook and entertained the possibility that there may have been a Native American presence there even in recent times.

The meadow is rectangular, approximately 355 feet long by 245 feet wide, bounded almost entirely by stone rows. The place from which the solstice sunrises are viewed is a low slab set in the stone row at the western corner of the field. This is a massive slab, 14 inches thick and approximately 50 inches in diameter. In fact, all the stonework at this corner is quite large as compared to typical stone rows. It appears that this corner of the field, which is at the edge of a steep drop-off, was built up with stone to give it the needed elevation to view the sunrise points.–*Daniel V. Boudillion*

Dighton Rock

Sitting in Berkeley, just a few feet from its original spot, Dighton Rock holds centuries-old carvings that experts believe date from the area's earliest nonnative visitors. For three centuries, people have been studying this rock in an attempt to decipher whose hand made this ancient graffiti.

This forty-ton sandstone boulder, which was deposited in Massachusetts during the last Ice Age, lies near the shore of the Taunton River, where the brackish water rises and falls with the tide. When the water was at its highest, Dighton Rock was completely submerged. At low tide, a broad section of the rock was exposed for about four hours per day, displaying the many intricate and mysterious carvings on its face.

The land around the rock is now a state park. In 1963, the massive boulder was lifted from the water and placed eleven feet higher in a cofferdam in its same orientation—with the inscriptions facing out toward the water. Over the years, many have come to document and explore the markings, and have come up with four main theories as to their origin.

The Reverend John Danforth offered the first theory in 1680. He sketched the upper half of the inscriptions and believed the markings to be made by the Wampanoag Indians who lived in southeastern Massachusetts. Danforth wrote of the rock:

> [I]t is reported from the tradition of the old Indians, that there came a wooden house (and men of another country in it) swimming up the river Assonet, that fought the Indians and slew their Sachem [chief or king of a tribe]. Some interpret the figures to be hieroglyphical. The first figure representing a ship, without a mast, and meer [mere] wrack cast upon the Shoals. The second representing a head of land, possibly a cape with a peninsula.

The main problem with Danforth's theory is that the Wampanoag typically didn't carve stone sculptures. There are very few examples in New England of Native Americans defacing rocks for the sake of inscriptions.

Other theories hold that the markings are ancient Phoenician symbols or were carved by seafaring Vikings. The most recent theory came in 1918 from Edmund Delabarre, who believed he saw the name of a Portuguese captain, Miguel Corte Real, the year 1511, and several Portuguese coats of arms etched in the stone. This theory ties in with ancient maritime charts in Portugal which state that Miguel Corte Real's brother, Gasper, sailed from Portugal to North America in 1501 but didn't return when he was expected. Miguel Corte Real left Portugal on May 10, 1502, in search of his brother, and he too was never seen again. Could Captain Miguel have wandered the coast of North America for nine years and left his marks on Dighton Rock as some kind of sign should his brother sail by?

Inside the Dighton Rock Museum, visitors can see many photographs that outline the symbols each theorist believed are in the rock. There are many marks, clearly made by human hands, but so worn and faded by time and weather that they could say almost anything.

These days, most scholars subscribe to the Portuguese theory, but the rock continues to be scrutinized. It's clear that this place was important to someone long ago. Whoever it was, they went through great effort to ensure that the markings they left would be seen by as many people as possible. Though some believe they have cracked the Dighton Code, the huge boulder may never give up all its secrets.

DIGHTON ROCK MUSEUM

Nomans Land Rune-Stone

The southernmost tip of Massachusetts is definitely no man's land, figuratively and literally. Nomans Land is a 612-acre island located about three miles southwest of Martha's Vineyard. There's no record of how it got its name. Our best guess is that this tiny island was named for Tequenoman, a Wampanoag chief from the nearby larger island. Tequenoman's Land was shortened to simply Nomans Land.

In the early 1900s, a man named Joshua Crane owned the entire island and made it his home. Late one afternoon in November 1926, Crane was watching the setting sun hit a large black rock on the water's edge. This rock was visible only during the lowest part of low tide, and even then the waves often broke over its face. But that day, Crane noticed strange markings on the rock—clearly man-made, but in an unfamiliar language. The symbols were four inches tall, evenly spaced, and etched in four lines.

The following year, author and researcher Edward F. Gray came to the island to photograph the rock for a book he was writing on Norse voyages to the North American continent. Battling the churning water wasn't easy, but Gray managed to get a clear photo and sent it to professors A. W. Brögger and Magnus Olsen at Oslo University to see if the inscriptions could be interpreted there. The conclusion was pretty dramatic. According to the professors, the first two lines read, "Leif Eriksson, 1001" (or possibly "1016"), and though the lower lines were well worn from ocean waves and New England weather, it was believed that the word "Vinland" was present.

Vinland, or "wine land"—but also interpreted as "pasture land" by some—was the name Leif Eriksson had given to a place he had traveled to sometime around A.D. 1000. For many years, scholars and explorers have tried to figure out where Vinland was, but it wasn't until recent times that many drew the conclusion that it must be somewhere in North America.

In 1960, archaeologists uncovered a Norse settlement in L'Anse aux Meadows on the island of Newfoundland in Canada. The find was conclusive proof that the Vikings were in North America centuries prior to Christopher Columbus. However, it didn't prove that the settlement in L'Anse aux Meadows was indeed the Vinland that Eriksson documented in his travels.

The Nomans Land rune-stone added a new voice to the debate of Vinland's whereabouts. Could this tiny island off the coast of Martha's Vineyard be Eriksson's Vinland?

Researching the enigmatic stone was nearly impossible, and potentially fatal, for more than half the twentieth century. In 1943, the U.S. Navy took ownership of the island and used it for target practice for more than twenty years. Bombers would fly overhead and drop ordnance all over this small dot of land. In 1996, the navy turned the island over to the U.S. Fish and Wildlife Service to be used as a wildlife refuge for migratory birds (clearly some incredibly brave avian breed that didn't mind resting in an area with bombs going off around them).

In August 2003, the New England Antiquities Research Association organized an expedition to the island to look for the rune-stone. The group included geologist and author Scott Wolter, who braved the cold waters of the Atlantic in the name of science. Though the researchers timed their expedition for low tide, the rock was still partially submerged, and they had to swim to it. Wolter was the first to reach it.

"Even though it wasn't a bad day as far as weather

goes," Wolter says, "it was pretty rough surf. I found the stone, and I had a hard time hanging on to it because I was getting knocked around by the waves. But we had some brushes, and we were able to knock off some of the seaweed, and I could actually feel some of the carved characters—it was hard to see the inscription in the direct sunlight—it was far from ideal conditions. But it's still there."

Wolter has been researching and writing about ancient rune-stones like the Nomans Land stone for almost thirty years, and he believes the implications of this rock off the coast of Massachusetts are huge. The initial academic response to the Nomans Land rune-stone was cool because there were both runic symbols as well as Roman numerals in the inscription—a detail some believe would mean this rock couldn't have been carved before the sixteenth century.

Not so, says Scott Wolter. "I don't have a problem with the mixture of Roman numerals and runic symbols at all," he said. "If you look at the Kensington rune-stone [discovered in Minnesota in 1898 and dating back to circa A.D. 1000], we have Latin letters, we have pentadic numerals, and we have runes—it was the practice at that time."

If the Nomans Land rune-stone is the real thing, it implies that Vinland has been found. "I am absolutely convinced that Vinland is the area around Martha's Vineyard and Nomans Land Island," Wolter said.

This stone may well hold secrets to our country's ancient, unknown past. The fact that it's survived not only millennia of weather and waves but also five decades of bombings is a testament to its fortitude. We can only hope that the find will one day be preserved for study so we can finally determine its origin. Who knows, this rock may just be more significant than the one on the side of the bay in Plymouth with "1620" carved into it.

The Westford Knight

When we think of medieval knights, we usually think of European castles and lords and ladies in fancy dress. But the town of Westford offers a centuries-old mysterious carving clad in shining armor that calls into question the geographic boundaries of the medieval era.

On the side of Depot Street near the center of town is a rock—noticeable only because some stone pillars and a headstone-shaped monument mark the spot. Step closer and you still may see only a large, flat rock. This mystery requires that you get closer to the ground. Your knees may get a little dirty, but it's a small price to pay to look back over six centuries. According to the Clan Gunn Society of North America, carved into the rock is the image of one Sir James Gunn, a fallen member of the party of Henry Sinclair, a Scottish earl who may have made a voyage to these parts somewhere around 1398.

But what about Christopher Columbus, whom our textbooks say discovered America—but not until a century later? There is compelling evidence that Columbus was not the first European to set foot on the soil of the New World. Ancient sites, such as America's Stonehenge in nearby North Salem, New Hampshire, indicate that Europeans were coming here millennia before Columbus was born, never mind sailing a ship. The Westford Knight is further evidence of early visits from across the Atlantic.

Henry Sinclair was the Earl of Orkney, a Scottish nobleman, and some say also a Knights Templar. The Knights Templar were religious warriors, formed to protect pilgrims on Crusades to the Holy Land in the twelfth and thirteenth centuries. By Sinclair's time, they had fallen out of favor with various monarchs and popes and were officially disbanded. But some believe they continued on in secret. Sinclair may have enlisted their help in his own crusade of fighting the British. And

when the Knights also became unwelcome in Scotland, one theory holds that Sinclair outfitted a small fleet of ships and headed west to America with his Templar compatriots.

What did this group of men do when they got to America? How can we be sure they were here? Many believe the Westford Knight holds the answer. The carving shows a Scottish knight with a thirty-nine-inch sword and a shield bearing the Gunn clan insignia. The impression is made of punched holes, a series of small impressions that were dug into the rock with a mallet. Or at least that's what the Clan Gunn Society believes.

When the rock carving was first discovered, no one rushed to form a preservation society or to alert the archaeological community. Locals shrugged their shoulders and went about their business, and New England weather continued its erosive work on the exposed slab. Today many of the lines are faded. The T-shaped sword with a break through it (indicating the death of a knight) is still evident, but the rest is left to the imagination.

Not everyone agrees that this work goes back to the late fourteenth or early fifteenth centuries. Some scholars think the carving is graffiti that may be only one hundred and fifty years old at best. But Frank Joseph, who investigated the Westford Knight while researching his book *Discovering the Mysteries of Ancient America,* says, "Some of the assistants to the curators of the British Museum were so excited when they heard about this that they actually traveled out and examined what was known as the Westford Knight by that time. They were able to very easily see that this was a type of sword that's called a hand and a half wheel pummel blade. That's a type of the two-handed sword that was dated to the mid-fourteenth century A.D. They also found that the style of the chain mail and the helmet that this figure wore was definitely part of the uniform that was worn by the Knights Templar in Scotland who belonged to Henry Sinclair."

Westford has a second mystery rock in town, but this one currently resides in the Westford Town Library. The Boat Stone, as locals call it, is an egg-shaped rock measuring about eighteen inches in diameter. Carved onto the rock is an etching of a fourteenth-century ship, the number 184, and an arrow. This rock was discovered in the latter half of the nineteenth century while forest was being cleared for roads. Some speculate that it may be a key to buried Knights Templar treasure. Like the Westford Knight, both rocks are a part of Westford's identity and offer a challenge to those who claim Columbus was the first European to discover America.

Skeleton in Armor

Speak! speak! thou fearful guest!
Who, with thy hollow breast
Still in rude armor drest,
Comest to daunt me!
Wrapt not in Eastern balms,
But with thy fleshless palms
Stretched, as if asking alms,
Why dost thou haunt me?

New England native Henry Wadsworth Longfellow wrote those opening lines of his ballad "The Skeleton in Armor" in 1841. His inspiration was a real-life archaeological find discovered in Fall River in 1832. When workers dug away a portion of a dirt bank just east of the Unitarian meetinghouse (near Hartwell and Fifth Street today), they unearthed a human skull. An account

of the discovery by John Stark appeared in *American Magazine* in Boston in 1837. Stark, who researched Indian mounds and other antiquities from early America, wrote:

> In digging down a hill near the village a large mass of earth slid off leaving in the bank, and partially uncovered, a human skull, which on examination was found to belong to a body buried in a sitting posture; the head being about one foot below what had been for many years the surface of the ground. The surrounding earth was carefully removed, and the body found to be enveloped in a covering of coarse bark of a dark color.
>
> Within this envelope were found the remains of another of coarse cloth made of fine bark, and about the texture of a Manila coffee bag. On the breast was a plate of brass, thirteen inches long, six broad at the upper end and five at the lower. This plate appears to have been cast, and is from one-eighth to three thirty-seconds of an inch in thickness. It is so much corroded that whether or not anything was engraved upon it has not yet been ascertained. It is oval in form, the edges being irregular, apparently made so by corrosion.
>
> Below the breastplate, and entirely encircling the body, was a belt composed of brass tubes, each four and a half inches in length. . . . The tubes are of thin brass, cast upon hollow reeds, and were fastened together by pieces of sinew. This belt was so placed as to protect the lower parts of the body below the breastplate.

Stark went on to point out that the construction of the armor and the brass arrows found with it looked nothing like any known work of Indians. The skeletal body inside the armor measured about five feet five inches tall and was believed to be that of a young man. Much of it was preserved, so it was also believed that an embalming or mummification process was used.

The find sent the archaeological community of the day into an uproar, as many believed the Native Americans didn't work in brass. This person, they conjectured, must be an ancient European or maybe even Phoenician or Egyptian. To add to the mystery, early research into the body's origin brought Dighton Rock into the discussion, as the corpse was discovered just a few miles downriver from that enigmatic boulder.

Stark's article concluded, "That the body was not one of the Indians, we think needs no argument. We have seen some of the drawings taken from the sculptures found at Palenque, and in those the figures are represented with breast-plates, although smaller than the plate found at Fall River. [Palenque is a ruined city in Mexico, dating back hundreds of years B.C.] On the figures at Palenque the bracelets and anklets appear to be of a manufacture precisely similar to the belt of tubes just described. These figures also have helmets precisely answering the description of the helmet of Hector in Homer."

The brass-armor–clad skeleton was moved into the Fall River Athenaeum, a private-subscription library in town, where patrons could study it. Unfortunately, in 1843 a fire destroyed it, so we'll never be able to carbon-date or further analyze the find. We have only descriptions and conjecture to try to determine the skeleton's origin, but it's clear that one can't rule out that the body belonged to a Native American tribe.

Between the years of 1560 and 1590, brass objects did make their way to North America on British trading ships, where they were traded with the Native Americans for furs and other goods. During the first few years of the seventeenth century, traders commented in their journals about Indians in the area around Cape Cod wearing large copper breastplates. So it's possible that Fall River's skeleton in armor was a relic of the early 1600s.

On the other hand, it may come from a much earlier time. A permanent shroud of mystery now veils the body. We'll never know who the brass-clad figure was in life, but we do know he's inspired artists and raised further questions as to what foreign peoples visited Massachusetts and when.

Balance Rock

For many spiritually inclined people, nature's grandeur is proof that God exists. If that's so, then natural oddities like Balance Rock in the northeast corner of Pittsfield State Forest, in the town of Lanesborough, are proof that God also has a sense of humor.

During the last Ice Age, a glacier dropped this 165-ton limestone boulder on a significantly smaller rock. The boulder is poised about three feet off the ground, and it vibrates when touched.

Today, sadly, the rock is covered in graffiti, and more than one visitor has tried his hand at tipping it off of its pedestal. Thankfully, Mother Nature still comes out on top.

Upton Chamber

Upton Chamber is one of the largest and best preserved of about three hundred similar spaces throughout the northeastern United States. Theories vary as to what purpose the strange chambers served. They may have been simply cool storage or root cellars from the Colonial American period or spiritual structures built by Native Americans. The Upton Chamber may have been a ritual site. If you sit there and look straight out of the tunnel, the stone cairns on Pratt Hill appear in your line of vision. On the summer solstice, the sun aligns with the stone piles on Pratt Hill and illuminates the deepest recess of Upton Chamber.

Some believe this chamber and others like it were built by the same Neolithic culture that created stone passageways and tombs in Ireland. It's a controversial theory because the Neolithic period (meaning "new stone age") goes as far back as 8500 B.C. (3000 B.C. in the region that is now Ireland), which raises questions about the structures' age.

In the early to mid-1990s, J. W. Mavor Jr. and B. E. Dix studied the Upton Chamber and concluded that the design was most similar to the chambers that dotted Ireland and the Iberian coast of the Mediterranean. Could similar structures pop up independent of each other thousands of miles apart? Or did ancient peoples get around more than we previously thought?

Mavor and Dix concluded in a 1995 *New England Antiquities Research Association Journal* that "of all the enigmatic structures that we have seen in America, the Upton chamber stands out as one that could have been built under the influence of Irish monks in the 8th century."

Irish in Massachusetts? Can you believe it?

Fabled People and Places

Folks from Massachusetts cherish their history and their legends, but sometimes the two get mixed together a bit. Take the Salem Witch Trials of 1692, for example, a real event that morphs into new meaning for each generation. The facts remain the same, but the story evolves, the legend grows, and from it comes something even bigger. And on the Cape, tales of the sea, of witches, monsters, and devils get passed around over pints of ale. They're as much a part of the local color as the sunrise off the shore of Martha's Vineyard. Inland, through the hills of the Berkshires, Native American legends are no less powerful.

The tales don't get told as often as they once did, and some have already been lost forever. But a few stick around. Maybe Bash Bish is still lurking beneath the waters that bear her name. The mini Pukwudgees could still be luring the unwary to their doom. And there's evidence that modern wizards are still practicing their arts at Wizard's Glen. Don't go there at night.

Bash Bish Falls

Bash Bish State Park lies in the southwestern corner of Massachusetts, right on the border of New York State. The park contains a waterfall—also named Bash Bish—that's almost sixty feet high and the highest in the state. All this bashing and bishing originates in a story from Mohican folklore.

For the Mohicans, adultery was punishable by death. And though the beautiful woman known as Bash Bish maintained her innocence, she was accused of this crime. Her fellow tribe members brought her up the mountain, planning to bind her to a canoe and send her over the waterfall to her death.

But before Bash Bish could be bound, a smoky mist rolled in and dozens of butterflies appeared and circled her head. Those watching drew back in shock. Bash Bish broke free, ran to the edge of the waterfall, and threw herself off. Her body never rose to the surface. The Mohicans felt she had cheated death through the use of sorcery.

Bash Bish's daughter, White Swan, grew to be as beautiful as her mother and eventually married the son of a chief. But she was unable to produce a child, so her husband took a second wife. As time went on, White Swan became depressed and spent much time sitting on the cliff where her mother had taken her dive. Soon White Swan began to dream that her mother would come to her, beckoning her to leave her troubles behind and join her.

White Swan's husband tried to coax her away from the site, but to no avail. One evening she stood on the edge of the

People claim that the cascading water sometimes takes the shape of a woman plunging to her death in the waiting pool.

stone, gazing at the dark pool below, just as her husband emerged from the woods with the finest gift he could find . . . a pure white butterfly. White Swan leaped from the edge just as her husband released the butterfly. Without thinking, he dived after his bride down to his death below.

White Swan's body never surfaced, but her husband's battered and broken remains were quickly recovered. The Mohicans believe that White Swan and Bash Bish were united for all eternity. Today the legend lives on. People claim that the cascading water sometimes takes the shape of a woman plunging to her death in the waiting pool. If you look beneath the surface of the waters pooling below the falls on a moonlit night, you just may see the smiling face of Bash Bish.

The Ecstatic Spirits of Harvard's Holy Hill

To understand something of the Holy Hill of Zion in Harvard, look to the road that leads there. The trailhead is on South Shaker Road. Most people know of the Shakers only by their furniture; what's not so well known is that they also invented modern spiritualism. Their ecstatic meetings on Harvard's Holy Hill were attended by upwards of 40,000 spirits at a whack, including the Angel of Victory, Noah, and the Virgin Mary.

The United Society of Believers in Christ's Second Appearing, as Shakers called themselves, first came to Harvard in 1781; there they established a creative and egalitarian society under the direction of their leader, Mother Ann Lee. Although the spirit world was an integral part of Mother Ann's teachings, the story of spiritualism on Holy Hill begins after her death.

Five decades after she died, in 1784, her remains were moved to a Shaker-owned cemetery in Watervliet, New York, and the reinterment seems to have aroused the Shakers to a new spiritual life. The following decade was known as Mother Ann's Second Appearing, or simply the New Era. At the site of her new resting place, several teenage girls simultaneously began to shake and tremble with extraordinary intensity. They whirled around until they fainted to the floor in a deep trance, and woke with tales of encounters in the spirit land. This phenomenon soon spread to other Shakers and became a codified part of their practice in 1838.

In Harvard, they listened to "testimony from Spirits brought forward through a mortal instrument," typically a young woman between the ages of thirteen and twenty-five. One of the chosen

Fountain Stone footer

instruments was moved to select a high point of land as a feast ground and picked what is now Holy Hill. Over the course of two years, the Shaker Brethren transformed a spot at the top of the hill into a half-acre-square plateau and enclosed a space about eleven feet long and five feet wide with a fence. This was known as the Fountain, an area of energetically upwelling spiritual blessings. At the northern end of the Fountain area a marble slab was erected, variously known in the different Shaker communities as a Fountain Stone, God Stone, or Lord's Stone. It was engraved with this message:

> For the healing of the nations, who shall here seek my favor. And I will pronounce all people who shall come to this fountain, not to step within this enclosure, nor place their hands upon this stone while they are polluted with sin. I am God the Almighty in whose hands are judgment and mercy. And I will cause my judgments to fall upon the willful violator of my commands in my own time according to wisdom and truth, whether in this world, or eternity. For I have created all souls, and unto me they are accountable. Fear ye the Lord.

On meeting occasions, the Holy Hill was approached in procession along an avenue of maple trees and up the north end of the hill in two columns, one of Brothers and one of Sisters. An eyewitness account from nearby Shirley Shaker Village relates that during the procession they "threw love" to each other by throwing both hands forward, and the recipient drawing the hands back to the heart. In their day-long (and occasionally night-long) meetings, the eighty to ninety Harvard Shakers would dance round and round the Fountain, spinning and whirling rhythmically. They would march and sing for hours, swaying in unison.

Whirling like a top, a "chosen instrument" would fall to the ground, then arise speaking in unknown tongues. Before long, the entire meeting would be in violent ecstatic throes, where they believed that spirits thronged among them. Recorded here on Holy Hill were the spirits

Processional Path

of Christ, the Virgin Mary, Noah, Abraham, Jeremiah, Isaiah, Mother Ann, the two angels that drove Lot out of Sodom, and the Angels of Truth, Repentance, Peace, Prophecy, and Victory.

The New Era ended around 1844 almost as abruptly as it began. The practical Shakers realized that they could not abandon their farms for day-long revelries, and although Shaker headquarters in New Lebanon never issued a decree, the communities made a unilateral decision to end the Holy Hill experiment and return to the land. The last mention in Shaker diaries of meetings there is the semiannual feast on

Harvard Shaker dorm

May 6, 1844, only six months after its completion. Elder Myrick, who had lettered the Fountain Stone, quietly removed the slab one day and buried it somewhere on Harvard Shaker lands. After that there is silence. It has not been seen since, and he left no record of its final resting place.

Today the dancing ground on the Holy Hill is covered in trees, with a new white fence erected around it. Only the slotted footing stone of the Fountain Stone remains. A palpable spiritual power seems to linger, however. I know of people who have whirled the night away here, as the young Sisters did one hundred and fifty years ago. Others come to meditate. Some have attempted recordings of the so-called spirit voice phenomena at the site of the Fountain Stone, but with what results I do not know.

One thing is certain: This is holy ground of an uncommon and ecstatic type; tread here at your peril lest ye also dance.–*Daniel V. Boudillion*

Granny Squannit

In Cummaquid, in a cave among the dunes on Great Neck near the entrance to Barnstable Harbor, lived a powerful witch named Too-quah-mis-quan-nit, or Granny Squannit. Old Granny was short, stout, and kept to herself. In the forest, each year she would plant seeds that grew into small bushes. When the shrubs were mature, Granny Squannit would gather their pods for her magic.

Though Granny Squannit was reclusive and didn't respect any of the tribal chiefs or elders, she served in a rather helpful role to Wampanoag Indian families. When Wampanoag children misbehaved, Granny Squannit would come to scare the little brats back into line.

There was one child, however, who required special attention because the devil was in him. Wampanoag legends tell of a particularly bad boy who couldn't be cured by punishment or any medicine from the chiefs or shaman, so Granny Squannit abducted the boy and brought him to her cave. There she gave the boy a potion to make him sleep for several days. When he eventually awoke, Granny told him to play in the sunshine while she napped. Her only orders were to not touch the hair on her head under any circumstances.

That was all this bad boy needed to hear. He crept up on the sleeping Granny Squannit, pushed her hair back from her forehead, and discovered a single green eye staring back at him. The sight scared the devil out of the boy, and he never made trouble again.

Pukwudgees

The Irish have leprechauns, the Inuit have their Little People, and the Wampanoag Indians of eastern Massachusetts . . . well, they have the Pukwudgees.

These magical mini folk lived in the swamps and around the bays and salt ponds, and hid their homes in the tall marsh grasses. Their chief wore clothes made entirely of green leaves, with a string of brightly colored shells around his neck. He carried a white bow made of oak wood and had more powerful magic than any Wampanoag medicine man. Although he was the biggest of his people, he was no taller than an average man's knee. And he was dangerous. He could order his clan to perform deadly magic on their human neighbors.

What makes the Pukwudgees especially diabolical is that they weren't always bad. When it suited them, they would come to the aid of their human neighbors. The Pukwudgees controlled the Cape Cod version of the will-o'-the-wisp, luminous fairies called Tei-Pai-Wankas. These creatures came to travelers by night and either led them home on the right path—or to their doom in the marshes, as their whims dictated.

The Pukwudgees themselves also made trouble for the Wampanoags. The little creatures could shape shift into animals and trick hunters into following them. When the hunters approached a cliff's edge, they soon found themselves the hunted as the Pukwudgees pushed them over. Between 1616 and 1618, eighty percent of the Wampanoag nation died from a plague. Or did the Pukwudgees perhaps work their horrible magic on them?

Wizard's Glen and Altar Rock

Gulf Road in Dalton is both wild and picturesque, yet beneath its postcard appearance lurk many strange tales of the supernatural. The road follows a tight valley between two steep-sided hills strewn top to bottom with flint boulders. Although the hills around are green with mountain laurels and hemlocks, nothing grows among the stones.

On the north side of the road lies Wizard's Glen, a desolate site marked with two landmarks—a broad square rock called Altar Rock and a talus cave known as Lucky Seven Cave. Altar Rock, once called the Devil's Altar, is marked with crimson stains that local rumor says came from the blood of human sacrifice. In reality, the stains appear to come from iron in the rock, but for centuries it has been known as a sacred haunt for Indian shamans, whose ceremonies there honored Hobbomocco, the Spirit of Evil.

The best-known story of Wizard's Glen comes to us from Joseph Edward Adams's 1852 book *Taghconic: Or Letters & Legends about Our Summer Home*. Adams's source was a ninety-year-old man of "credulous simplicity," who heard it from the eyewitness himself, a certain John Chamberlain of Ashuelot (now Dalton), who took shelter at dusk under boulders near the Devil's Altar during a thunderstorm. Here we will let Adams, who told it first and best, pick up the story:

> This was apparently a gala night with Satan, although none of the guests were yet arrived. He was not now going to battle or to work, but rather to hold a royal drawing-room, by way of enjoying himself and receiving homage. . . . Every ghost, as he came in, made a profound obeisance to the rock

Below, Altar Rock; next page, Lucky Seven Cave

throned Satan, and then took his place in the circle around the altar-stone. . . . Two barbarous looking phantoms presented themselves, leading between them a beautiful Indian maiden, robed only in her own long, black hair. At another moment the beholder might have admired her graceful proportions and regular features but now his senses were too much absorbed by horror. . . .

One of the familiars, seizing her rudely around the waist, placed her upon the altar-stone, before the priest. Then she shrieked—so wildly that the hunter declared the echo never ceased ringing in his ears to his dying day—what part she had to perform then was no longer doubtful. . . . It seemed the sacrifice was about to be consummated; but as the weapon was raised, the maiden's eyes (averted from it) met those of Chamberlain.

The kind-hearted hunter, in whom compassion had overcome fear, could no longer restrain himself; so taking out his Bible, he pronounced the great NAME, —and with a terrific crash of the elements the whole scene vanished, leaving him in impenetrable darkness.

Beneath the trappings of a Dante-esque scene, this tale has real echoes of a native tradition associated with the spot. In Charles Skinner's 1896 *Tales of Puritan Land*, an Indian priest, Tashmu, "proclaimed that he would pass the night in Wizard's Glen, where, by incantations, he would learn the divine will." This implies that the glen was a place of power within their culture, chosen for ritual and communion with their spirits.–*Daniel V. Boudillion*

Modern Mysteries of Wizard's Glen

Is there still a luminous power in the Wizard's Glen, ripe for the modern age? If the bits of magical paraphernalia found among the rocks are any indication, it would appear that the effort to touch the supernatural world is still being made in Wizard's Glen. See for yourself at GPS coordinates 42.4882°N, -73.1854°W, just east of the Appalachian National Scenic Trail. This fabled place may still be attracting modern wizards and witches who perform their rites by the light of the full moon in the glen. Some speak of covens convened under the road in the kivalike Lucky Seven Cave.

A Bewitching History of Salem

Ask someone who isn't from Massachusetts about Salem and it's likely the name will conjure up images of witches riding broomsticks and the infamous Witch Trials of 1692. Salem is a New Age mecca today, but how did this Boston sleeper community gain that reputation? The answer is worth a *Weird* tour through the town and its history.

An important initial point is that Salem Town and Salem Village were two different worlds. The town was a small, thickly populated settlement on the sea, bursting with commerce; the village a large rural area of farms and woodlots. The hysteria took place almost exclusively in Salem Village, renamed Danvers in 1752.

In the 1620s, when Salem Village was first established, the Puritans were on the rise in Europe. They believed people were predestined for heaven or hell and there was nothing anyone could do to change that fate. And they most certainly believed in the devil. One such group moved into Salem Village.

Trials (and Tribulations)

In 1688, one of the village's most influential people, John Putnam, invited a minister from Barbados named Samuel Parris to preach. He came with his wife and daughter (both called Elizabeth), his niece Abigail Williams, and Tituba, his slave.

In January 1692, the Reverend Samuel Parris's daughter and niece became ill with convulsions and screaming fits. They claimed to see ghastly images that no one else could see. The village doctor, William Griggs, couldn't find a cure in any of his medical books, but he had read Cotton Mather's 1689 book *Memorable Providences, Relating to Witchcraft and Possessions*, and surmised that the girls must be under some kind of enchantment. This meant witchcraft was afoot, and in puritanical New England that wasn't just a sin, it was a crime punishable by death.

Soon playmates of Elizabeth and Abigail began to exhibit signs of bewitching. Eleven-year-old Ann Putnam and seventeen-year-olds Mercy Lewis and Mary Walcott started having screaming fits. Once the notion of witchcraft was firmly in place, the adults brought the children together

Roger Conant, founder of Salem

and told them to name names. In seventeenth-century Salem, children had few ways to entertain themselves. The girls had little more than their imaginations, possibly influenced by tales of voodoo from Barbados that Tituba had shared with them. "Sport," the girls afterward said of it. "We must have our sport." But their sport started a horrible chain of events that sent their neighbors to their deaths.

The hysterical girls were told that they wouldn't get into trouble if they cooperated. "Was it Tituba? Was she the witch?" The girls had only to nod to end the questioning, and they dutifully did so. It's likely that Tituba had indeed learned some folk magic in Barbados that would look like witchcraft to a Puritan, and because she was a slave, she didn't stand a chance of defending herself.

The adults led the girls to two others: Sarah Good and Sarah Osborn. Sarah Good was a beggar and transient who went from basement to barn . . . wherever anyone would let her stay. Sarah Osborn was a cranky old biddy who hadn't been to church in over a year. In short, they were easy targets.

The Putnams, who'd brought the Parris family and Tituba to Salem, wanted charges brought against the three women and called on the county magistrates to hear the accusations. On March 1, 1692, hundreds of townsfolk came to the preliminary hearings to listen to the afflicted girls describe their torment.

Claiming to be pinched and bitten by unseen forces, they fell into contorted poses and went through their screaming fits right there in the meetinghouse. According to transcripts from the hearing, the magistrate asked Tituba, "Why doe you hurt these poor Children? whatt harme have thay done ont you?" "Thay doe noe harme to me I noe hurt them att all," Tituba replied. "Why have you done itt?" the magistrate asked. "I have done nothing; I Can't tell when the Devill works."

The Witch House

Sarah Good and Sarah Osborn didn't fare much better. As they denied harming the children, the girls would break out in fits and point at the accused.

There were plenty in Salem Village who felt the ordeal was spiraling out of hand, but when Tituba confessed to being a witch, many skeptics were converted. And when she claimed that Sarah Good and

Rebecca Nurse House built 1636. (She was hanged as a witch in Salem 1692)
Danvers, Mass

Sarah Osborn were in league with her, the witch hunt really began.

Soon others were accused. Some claimed they were nowhere near the afflicted and that others could swear to it. This failed when the girls claimed it was their specters that did the harm. Others, such as the elderly Rebecca Nurse, as a defense, claimed to be Christian and pious. The jury found Rebecca Nurse not guilty, but after the verdict was read, the children went into hysterics, claiming Nurse was attacking them again. An angry Chief Justice Stoughton told the jury to go back and reconsider the case. When the jury returned the second time, they found her guilty.

In Salem, those convicted of witchcraft also lost all their property. Giles Corey had this in mind when he was brought before the magistrates. When asked how he pleaded, he said nothing. Refusing to enter a plea meant he could not be tried, and if he couldn't be tried, he couldn't be found guilty and thus lose his land.

But the magistrates had ways of dealing with the silent. Boards were placed across Corey's chest, and heavy rocks were placed on those boards, slowly crushing him in a torture known as pressing. Stone after stone was set upon him, but Corey refused to enter a plea. He was stubborn to the end; some accounts claim his last words were defiant: "more weight."

As the days passed and the hysteria grew, dozens of others from Salem and the surrounding villages were being accused of witchcraft. If there were no local girls who could go into hysterics and point fingers, the girls from Salem could be brought in to sniff out the witches.

The heat of the summer of 1692 intensified the accusations and speed of the trials. More people were hanged on Gallows Hill, and the jails were overflowing. Not until early autumn did reasonable people such as the Reverend John Hale ask how so many respectable citizens in such a small area could all join in league with the devil in such a short period of time. Finally, Governor Phips ruled that no court could make a conviction on spectral evidence alone, and the madness came to an end.

But before the hysteria died down, nineteen people had been executed for witchcraft, one had been pressed to death, and at least three others (possibly as many as twelve) died while in prison. Anywhere from one hundred to two hundred others had been imprisoned for witchcraft in the region. Two dogs were even executed for suspicion of being a witch's familiar.

As the last significant hunt of a dark period in history and one of the best documented, the Salem Witch Trials have stayed in the minds of many, laying the foundation for the town's future.

The Memorial

On August 5, 1992, a memorial was dedicated to the fallen of the Salem Witch Trials. On the three hundredth anniversary, a rectangular area was carved out in the corner of Old Burying Point Cemetery, just a few yards away from the final resting place of John Hathorne, one of the magistrates who sent many of the accused on to trial. Within the area are stone seats engraved with the names of the fallen and their dates of execution.

Ouija Believe It?

For a short while, Salem was appropriately the place where one of the world's most "spirited" board games was produced.

The story starts with George S. Parker, who was born in Salem in 1867 and published his first game there at the age of sixteen. Five years later his brother Charles joined him and the business was officially named Parker Brothers.

Not long after, a group of game makers from Baltimore started the Kennard Novelty Company and launched a product called the Ouija board in 1891. Within a year, a sharp young game maker named William Fuld became president of the company and renamed it The Ouija Novelty Company. Fuld died in 1927, but the company stayed with his family until 1966, when the estate sold it to Parker Brothers.

Parker Brothers started producing the Ouija board in Salem, and in 1967 it became the first board game to ever outsell Monopoly. The Ouija board called Salem home for more than two decades, until Parker Brothers was sold to Hasbro in 1991, and the company decided to close the Salem facility that same year.

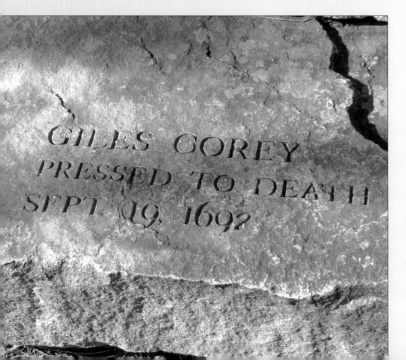

Witch Caves and Salem End Road

During the witch hysteria in Salem, all three daughters of William Towne of Topsfield were accused and jailed. Only one of them, Sarah Bridges Cloyes, made it out alive. She escaped to what is now Framingham in 1692 and spent the winter in caves, where she was joined by others who fled the hangman's noose. Within months, an expatriate community sprang up.

It's a strange thing, but the land where these refugees sought asylum was owned by one of the early judges at the Salem Witch Trials, Deputy Governor Thomas Danforth. In the spring of 1693, he gave Sarah Cloyes and her husband, Peter, permission to build a house on his land. Within a year, Danforth turned over more than eight hundred acres to families seeking asylum and safety from the madness playing out in Salem. The new settlement quickly became known as Salem End Road.

As for the place the Cloyes spent that first winter, local legend has always claimed that they were in a network of small boulder caves in a steep cliff face on the Framingham–Ashland line, at GPS coordinates 42.27630N,-71.46930W. They have always been called Witch Caves.

Anyone who has explored these rocky recesses knows that they are small, cold, drafty, and hard. Even

though the Salem escapees would have blocked the holes tight with snow, built a lean-to of logs in front of the entrance, and made a door flap with birch bark, it would have been little improvement over the stone cell of Salem Town Prison. Except, of course, that they had a chance to survive and build a new life for themselves.

And the houses they later built still stand. Of the original escapees who built in the Salem End Road community, a surprising five of their houses still remain. Sarah and Peter Cloyes's 1693 house stands on Salem End Road, as does the 1694 Benjamin Nurse homestead. Caleb Bridges's house is on Gates Street, John Towne's 1698 home is on Maple Street, and his son Israel's pre-1709 home stands on Salem End Road.

—*Daniel V. Boudillion*

Salem Witch Museum

An imposing structure on Washington Square North, the Salem Witch Museum was originally built as a church in 1845 but became a museum in 1972. Alison D'Amario is the director of education for the museum and has been working there since 1987. She explained that the museum's objective is to give an accurate and succinct depiction of the witch trials and to provide an overview of what witchcraft is today.

Does the museum receive many visitors who are witches? "We do," D'Amario said. "We have an exhibit that talks about the practice of witchcraft. We consulted witches before we did the exhibit, and I think most of them feel this is an accurate portrayal. I think we have been well-received in the pagan community."

The exhibit hall includes various portrayals of witches in folklore, television, and movies. Visitors also learn about paganism today and a brief overview of the belief system. Near the end of the tour, visitors see the most profound point the museum has to offer: that witch hunts continue.

"We give four examples of witch hunts from our history," D'Amario said. "The first is from the Salem trials, the next is from Pearl Harbor and our treatment of Japanese Americans . . . then we have McCarthy and the House Un-American Activities Committee, and then we have the fear of infection and how people were treated after the AIDS epidemic started in this country."

Weird Massachusetts could easily add to this list. Whenever discrimination becomes acceptable, fear can rise into full-blown hysteria. History has repeated itself since the puritanical days of early Salem, and it likely will again.

The Real Gallows Hill

For many unfortunate victims, the 1692 Salem witch hysteria ended with a hangman's rope on Gallows Hill. You would think such an awful location would live forever in infamy, yet today the exact location of Gallows Hill is not precisely known.

When I visited Salem as a young man, the directions I had led me to a park near Proctor Street named Gallows Hill Park. I walked up the hill to the official hanging spot and looked around. The view was magnificent, but it simply did not line up with the facts I had learned from my reading.

The hill was steep, and the thought of the accused being transported to the top in a cart seemed ludicrous. Also I had learned that Benjamin Nurse had rowed a boat from a creek near the Nurse Homestead, out into the North River, and then to the base of Gallows Hill to recover his mother's body. The closest water was a canal over a quarter mile northeast. This hill simply did not square with the historical record.

Twenty years later I bought Salvatore Trento's *Field Guide to the Mysterious Places of Eastern North America* and was intrigued once again. Trento proposed a nearby hill as the site, complete with a gallows footing stones. So off I went in July 2003 to locate this hill. I found it south of the playing fields in Gallows Hill Park, and about two hundred yards southwest of the water tank. This hill even had easy cart access up the south side from Colby Street, but it was even farther away from the closest waterway, over a half mile to the canal in fact. So I went back to the books and refreshed my grasp of the known facts.

Several things immediately invalidated the Trento site. The footing stones for the gallows are still visible, but the accused were hanged from the branches of trees, not on a gallows. Also, the condemned went over Town Bridge at what is now the intersection of Boston and Bridge streets. The Trento site does not fit with this fact.

The official Gallows Hill site was chosen by the Reverend Charles Upham as the probable hanging site in his 1867 book *Salem Witchcraft,* even though he admitted, "There is no contemporaneous nor immediately subsequent record that the executions took place on the spot."

The most thorough and convincing presentation was made by Sidney Perley in 1921. Perley reconstructed the landscape and land ownership of Salem at the time of the hangings, making a number of maps. He also used this passage from a letter written by a Dr. Holyoke in 1791:

> In the last month, there died a man in this town by the name of John Symonds, aged a hundred years lacking about six months, having been born in the famous '92. He has told me that his nurse had often told him, that while she was attending his mother at the time she lay in with him, she saw, from the chamber windows, those unhappy people hanging on Gallows Hill, who were executed for witches by the delusion of the times.

Perley located the house Symonds was born in and found a low hill nearby. He believed that the sheriff of Salem took the immediate left after the bridge onto Proctor Street, at that time only a cart road skirting a low hill, and deposited the condemned for execution. At the time, the North River extended in a large bay all the way to Town Bridge, which fits with the story about Benjamin Nurse's boat ride. An interesting side note is that there was a so-called Witch Tree on the Perley site as late as 1793. It was the custom among some Salem residents to pass newborn babies through a hole in its trunk to protect them from witches. *–Daniel V. Boudillion*

GALLOWS (Proctor St.)

Gravel Bank

Town Bridge
(Blubber Hollow)

NORTH RIVE

Probable Place
of Executions ×

Probable Site of
Graves of Witches

HILL

Bickford's Pond

North R.

Causeway

(Pope St.)

(Proctor St.)

Norman's Rocks

George
Hacker

Joshua and Caleb
Buffum

#11

Joseph
Boyce

John and
Rebecca
Bickford

Hannah Gill

John McCarter
of Robt. Wilson

Edward Flint

Thomas
Flint

Gallows Hill, Salem, Mass.

Sea Witch of Billingsgate

Back in the eighteenth century, when the Cape Cod town of Wellfleet was still called Billingsgate, one resident of this coastal town instilled fear in the oystermen, fishermen, shipbuilders, and whalers who lived there, and earned her place in the annals of infamy.

The Sea Witch of Billingsgate was said to stalk the shoreline, taking the souls of lost sailors, but she could also head inland and be just as fearsome in town. The only way you could tell that this beautiful woman was a witch was to glimpse the high, red heels beneath her swishing dress. Some theories said the witch was an Indian, or European, or both, but those high, red heels are consistent, as are her familiars: a cat and a gray goat with one glass eye.

The legend of the Sea Witch began one spring evening in 1715, when an older man seduced and impregnated fifteen-year-old Goody Hallett of Eastham. Some have said the man was the pirate Black Bellamy, but regardless of who was responsible, the following winter Goody Hallett was found in a barn with a dead baby in her arms. The assumption was that she murdered her love child.

The young girl was apprehended, taken to the whipping post in town, and repeatedly lashed for the crime of murder. This was simply a prelude to more torture, leading up to a trial to determine her guilt. Goody Hallett pleaded with her captors to let her die, but they wouldn't oblige her. Instead they imprisoned her in the Eastham jail, where she beat at her cell window bars and wailed in torment.

Local legend says a well-dressed gentleman approached the cell window. He had a gold-tipped walking cane that he used to flick the cell bars away as if they were straw. He eloquently convinced the young girl that she was the victim, and the more he spoke, the more her rage grew, until she agreed to sign the contract he held in front of her. Once Goody Hallett made her mark, she was free to crawl out the jail's window to her freedom. She left Eastham for the next town over, and the Sea Witch of Billingsgate was born.

The Sea Witch took up residence inside a whale. She would hang a ship's light on the whale's tail and lure vessels in toward land. Once the ships were stuck, the Sea Witch struck, taking the lives and souls of the stranded sailors that she fancied. Her other mischief included inflicting horrible wind and rain storms, even the occasional hurricane, on the mariners off the shores of the Cape.

As decades passed, the Sea Witch continued to make her presence known through storms and disappearing sailors and townsfolk, but she remained hidden to those who went looking for her. What may have made the Sea Witch even more elusive is that the title may have passed on from one woman to another. Goody Hallett was simply the first. There may have been many more.

As the industry of Wellfleet slowly changed from fishing and oysters to tourism and other forms of commerce, locals believed the Sea Witch simply moved on. Others think she's still patrolling the coast inside her whale, waiting for just the right man or moment to come along so she can make her return to Wellfleet.

Cape Cod's Mermaid

Wampanoag folklore speaks of Squant the Sea Woman: a mermaid-like creature who spins her magic along the shores of Cape Cod. She is described as a square-eyed giantess, with webbed fingers and a head covered with slimy locks of seaweed . . . a real knockout if you're into that. But what makes Squant most alluring is her singing. She can push storms back out to sea, and ride the tides right up to the shore near the cliffs of Gay Head. When she's angry, she can also make the storms rage against the shore.

Squant rides the rising tide each day and shines a flirty smile to those she wants to seduce. If they don't respond, she brings the wrath of weather down upon her would-be lovers and forces them into the sea.

Legend says that Squant eventually lured Maushop the giant down to her undersea cave, where she lulled him to sleep with her singing and bound him with her green locks of seaweed. Maushop is said to be resting there today. During the winter months, Squant fears Maushop will awaken and leave her, and the waters above the undersea caves churn and whirlpools form. But so far, the giant remains asleep in the depths below.

Old Betty of Witches' Hollow

Salem isn't the only Massachusetts town that whispers of witchcraft. Plymouth has its own tale, set in a hollow outside town. "After you pass Carver Green on the old road from the bay at Plymouth, you will see a green hollow in a field," wrote William Root Bliss in his 1893 book *The Old Colony Town.* "It is Witches' Hollow, and is green in winter and summer, and on moonlit nights witches have been seen dancing in it to the music of a fiddle."

Near the green was a little cottage, and inside lived a witch named Old Betty. Some say they saw her dancing in Witches' Hollow with the devil himself. Old Betty was a begging woman and counted on handouts to get by. One particular old man, a neighbor, often gave her food and firewood. But one day he grew tired of giving handouts, so he told her not to come around anymore. But Old Betty didn't listen. She came sneaking to his place looking for food and firewood to steal, and the old man caught her at it.

"I told you to go away, old witch," the man said.

Old Betty said nothing. She just stood there, and this angered the man further. He went to his closet and grabbed a large sack. Quick as you please, he tossed Old Betty in to the sack and locked her in his closet. Then he went back to work for the afternoon.

Old Betty may have been old, but she was still spry. She wormed her way out of the sack and then went to work on the lock. Some say she cast a spell that opened the door, others that she used a hairpin. Either way, Old Betty escaped. She gathered the old man's cat, dog, rooster, and pig, tied them all in the sack she had just escaped from, and locked the whole menagerie back in the closet.

"Now I'll hide and wait for the old man to return," Old Betty said.

That afternoon the old man came home to an awful noise coming from the sack in the closet. "I've had enough of you, Old Betty," he said. The old man unlocked the closet, dragged the sack outside to his front steps, and slammed the bag over and over against them until all of the noises stopped. Old Betty jumped out from behind a nearby bush, cackling a hideous laugh. "You'll not be rid of Old Betty so easy, old man," she said, and she disappeared into the woods with her cackle still echoing around the hollow.

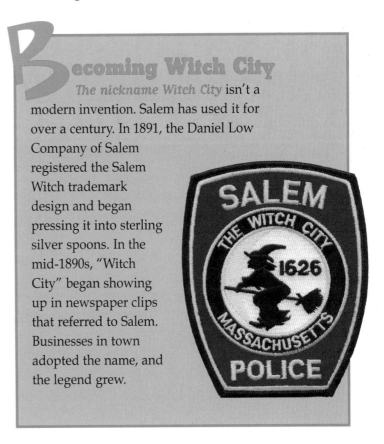

Becoming Witch City

The nickname Witch City isn't a modern invention. Salem has used it for over a century. In 1891, the Daniel Low Company of Salem registered the Salem Witch trademark design and began pressing it into sterling silver spoons. In the mid-1890s, "Witch City" began showing up in newspaper clips that referred to Salem. Businesses in town adopted the name, and the legend grew.

Unexplained Phenomena

The idea that there are things in our world that science can't explain is both terrifying and hopeful. It's terrifying because what we don't understand can be very frightening. And yet it's hopeful because things beyond our understanding also offer limitless possibilities—for good or for evil.

The people of Massachusetts know this. They believe miracles can happen because they've seen them. And they most certainly know that people and places can be cursed by some entity beyond our knowledge. They've seen that too. In some cases, the unexplained leaves physical evidence, maybe a reflection on a window, perhaps some tracks in the mud, or just a permanent memory for a few select eyewitnesses. But no matter what your pleasure is, from divine intervention to UFOs, the unexplained has a home in Massachusetts.

Milton Madonna

Have you ever seen a Rorschach test? You know, those blots of ink on cards that seem to take on various shapes? Some people see a butterfly; others see a two-headed monster eating little children in a meadow. The test uses the human tendency to look for patterns—the familiar in the unfamiliar. "Normal" adults usually find human features in inkblots (faces, body parts, and so forth) because from birth we're programmed to look for faces and to remember them.

In June of 2003, international attention focused on a strange image formed in mildew between two panes of glass at Milton Hospital. Hundreds of visitors came each day to gaze at a third-floor window on Highland Street in an otherwise nondescript brick building. For many believers, the image was that of the Virgin Mary holding a baby Jesus. Was it a miracle or an organically formed inkblot?

Cecelia Garvin has been employed at the hospital since 1992. She worked in room 201, right next to 202—the room with the now famous window. "The window was like that for years," Garvin said. "The seal between the two panes of glass broke, and this image came up."

Garvin explained how room 202 was converted into an eye exam room many years ago as the ophthalmology practice inside flourished and expanded. Instead of removing the window and closing it up, the hospital simply built a new wall in front of it to seal off the outside light. So there is no way to access the window in room 202 from the inside without tearing through a plaster wall. The window is made with double-paned glass, and when the seal broke, moisture seeped in. The mildew eventually formed into the shape that can still be seen today.

Could the image have a spiritual connection to Dr. Joseph Michon, the physician who started the ophthalmology practice? He devoted much of his time to mission work, and by 1975 he had left his practice entirely to join a traveling mission that provides medical care to some of the poorest people in the world. Someone must have contacted the local media, because stories about the window began to appear, and soon there was a flurry of activity. "There were tons of people coming to see it," Garvin said. "It does look like the Virgin Mary. Is it something that's a miracle? I don't know."

The mob of people who came to see the window grew to such proportions that the hospital lowered a tarp over it except for a few hours a day to allow for observing. The tarp helped control the mob, until one day a mighty wind (or the hand of God, to some believers) came and blew it and its frame into the window and cracked a corner of the glass. Visitors were crushed and feared they would lose their sign from God forever . . . but the image persevered.

Today people still visit the window, but not in the numbers that they used to. Flowers are left at the site, believers stop and pray, but the donation box that was once there has been removed because people kept stealing the money. Though the Catholic Church's official stand was that this was not a bona fide miracle, even local clergy shrug their shoulders when asked what it means. People will see what they want to see in that window in Milton, and if it gives some hope, that's something the hospital can live with.

Historic Booms of Nashoba

"Near unto this town is a pond, wherein, at some seasons, there is a strange rumbling noise, as the Indians affirm; the reason thereof is not yet known. Some have considered the hill adjacent as hollow, wherein the wind, being pent, is the cause of this rumbling." *–Daniel Gookin,* Historical Collections of the Indians in New England, *1674*

"[The hill] was hollow and the four winds were pent up inside. Periodically they would attempt to escape, and at these times . . . terrible roaring and growls and rumbles would issue forth from within the hill. The very earth would shudder, massive rocks would shift from their beds, trees would sway and creak, and were it not for the intercession of the shamans, the earth might have cracked open and revealed the dark, boiling innards." *–John Hanson Mitchell,* Trespassing, *1999*

For more than three centuries, people have heard rumblings, roaring, humming, and the sound of cannons from the depths of this hill in Littleton. The Praying Indians who settled there in the 1600s named it Nashoba Hill, meaning the "Hill That Shakes." To this day,

you can hear its rumblings and sometimes see strange lights in the area too. But what's behind this strange sound?

This rocky hill is a strange and inspiring landscape indeed. The bare bones of the earth are exposed in bleak gray ledge and strange long humps of granite bedrock that look like beached whales. Narrow trails wind between them, and stone walls of inexplicable origin abound. Traces of the old village remain: acres of corn-planting mounds, three worked-stone springs, a hollowed and smoothed rock surface, and artifacts unearthed on the western slopes. A retired professor told us that the fire-blackened rockfaces are the marks of Indian fires. Also seen are veins of white quartz, a crystal structure prized by the shamans of old.

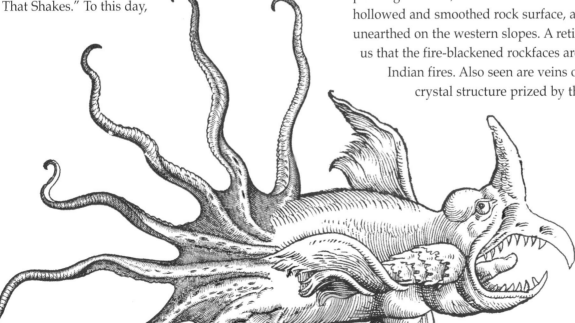

At one time, the local Indians believed that Nagog Pond, which lies near Nashoba Hill, was home to a water monster named Ap'cinic that lived deep in the pond. It had horns and a "gnashing beak," and would "reach up out of the waters of Nagog at certain times and draw the entrails of passing villagers down into its depths." Its tentacled arms would feel along the shore for victims. The hill itself, according to some historians, was supposed to contain the four winds, pent up and buffeting the mountain from the inside in an attempt to break free.

Some people believe that Nashoba is haunted, specifically the five-hundred-acre Sarah Doublet Forest on the rocky hill squeezed between Nagog Pond and Fort Pond. And some of the English settlers who called the phenomenon the "shooting of Nashoba Hill" were convinced there was an army trapped inside trying to blast its way out.

Strange aerial lights accompany the sounds. Following a 3.1 magnitude earthquake in Nashoba on October 15, 1985 (described as the "rumblings of a freight train"), there appeared yellow-orange, brightly glowing pockets of air in the Woodchuck Hill and Oak Ridge area on the Harvard–Boxborough border. After a 2.5 earthquake on November 23, 1980, I observed at night from the vantage point of Nagog Pond a bright welling-up of intense white light out of the top of Fort Pond Hill in Sarah Doublet Forest. This welled up like a dome of light, about 350 yards wide and about 200 yards tall at its peak. After about three seconds, the light collapsed back into the earth. Perhaps the sound in the hill is a combination of seismic activity and the local geology. The area is a three-mile island of granite in a sea of sedimentary schist and gneiss. The makeup is the same as the Moodus region in Connecticut, which also gives off strange sounds. –*Daniel V. Boudillion*

To Weigh a Soul

Yes, Virginia, there is a soul, and it weighs three-quarters of an ounce. As for your little doggy? Wel-l-l-l . . . don't expect to be playing with little Scruffy in the afterlife.

At least, that's what Dr. Duncan MacDougall of Haverhill concluded in the early twentieth century. In April 1901, the good doctor was working at a consumptives' home located in an estate called Grove Hall, on Blue Hill Avenue in Dorchester. Back then, it was likely that the consumption (tuberculosis) patients who checked themselves into this home were not going to check out, and they may have found themselves participating in unique death experiments.

In the nineteenth and the early twentieth centuries, pulmonary tuberculosis was one of the world's great scourges. Until the development of effective medicines in the 1940s, untreated tuberculosis killed two out of every three people who contracted the disease. Consumptives' homes were set up all over the world to help comfort the sick and dying and to remove the contagious from the general population.

At Grove Hall, Dr. MacDougall saw an opportunity to scientifically prove or disprove a spiritual question he had been pondering. MacDougall hypothesized that if there is some kind of "soul" that leaves the human body after death, its weight can be measured. In his 1907 paper published in the journal *American Medicine*, he wrote, "It is unthinkable that personality and consciousness continuing personal identity should exist, and have being, and yet not occupy space. It is impossible to represent in thought that which is not space-occupying, as having personality; for that would be equivalent to thinking that nothing had become or was something, that emptiness had personality, that space itself was more than space, all of which are

Dr. Duncan MacDougall and Grove Hall

contradictions and absurd."

Thirty-four-year-old Dr. MacDougall's next question was, "Has this substance weight, is it ponderable?"

With wooden supports and hammer in hand, MacDougall customized a large Fairbanks scale—the kind mercantile business used to weigh large quantities of silk. He arranged a cot to hold patients during their final moments. Dr. MacDougall wrote:

> My first subject was a man dying of tuberculosis. It seemed to me best to select a patient dying with a disease that produces great exhaustion, the death occurring with little or no muscular movement, because in such a case the beam could be kept more perfectly at balance and any loss occurring readily noted.
>
> The patient was under observation for three hours and forty minutes before death, lying on a bed arranged on a light framework built upon very delicately balanced platform beam scales. The patient's comfort was looked after in every way, although he was practically moribund when placed upon the bed. He lost weight slowly at the rate of one ounce per hour due to evaporation of moisture in respiration and evaporation of sweat. During all three hours and forty minutes I kept the beam end slightly above balance near the upper limiting bar in order to make the test more decisive if it should come.
>
> At the end of three hours and forty minutes he expired and suddenly coincident with death the beam end dropped with an audible stroke hitting against the lower limiting bar and remaining there with no rebound. The loss was ascertained to be three-fourths of an ounce.

Often the bowels and bladder release in a person who has just died; MacDougall accounted for this. The first subject's bowels did not release, and any liquid he expelled remained with the body and bedding, so its weight was still accounted for. The doctor noticed that the patient steadily lost ounces of weight, but he couldn't account for the sudden drop of three quarters of an ounce just after the moment of death.

MacDougall experimented on five more patients (though he admitted the sixth experiment didn't count, because the patient expired within five minutes of being placed on the scale). In each case, MacDougall measured some degree of unexplainable weight loss from as little as half an ounce to as much as an ounce and a half. Though the good doctor was enthusiastic about his work, not many of his colleagues felt the same. He was accused of experimenting with human life, though he claimed to have gotten consent from each of the patients ahead of time, and his findings were dismissed.

Nevertheless, the doctor from Haverhill believed he had empirical evidence of the soul's existence. Now he just needed a control group, so bring in the dogs. MacDougall's fifteen test mutts weighed between fifteen and seventy pounds, and always the humanitarian, MacDougall felt that "the ideal tests on dogs would be obtained in those dying from some disease that rendered them much exhausted and incapable of struggle." The dogs were euthanized with injections, ensuring there would be no struggle that would disturb the delicate scale. There was no unaccountable weight loss at or shortly after the moment of death; ergo, dogs must not have souls as humans do.

"Is it [the soul] substance? It would seem to me to be so," MacDougall concluded. His findings would also mean that not all dogs go to heaven. In fact, he'd have to say none of them do.

Gravity Hills

Around the country and even around the world, there are legends of strange forces that propel a car in neutral to actually roll UPHILL, with no human hand behind it. Theories on what causes this to occur include geomagnetic fluctuations, optical illusions, and the supernatural. Massachusetts is blessed with not one but two (and maybe even three) "Gravity Hills" where this phenomenon can be tested.

The lesser known hill is in the north-central part of the state. If you drive into Greenfield on Shelburne Road, you'll see a slight hill just after the Route 2 bridge. The magic spot is just before the bridge, where the locals say you should stop your car and put it into neutral (after checking your rearview for traffic, of course). Your car will then roll uphill about fifteen to twenty feet.

Why? According to the story, a long time ago there was an accident on the Route 2 bridge involving some schoolchildren who fell to their deaths on Shelburne Road below. Locals also claim that if you sprinkle powder or flour on your bumper, or if your bumper is dusty, after your car is mysteriously pushed up Gravity Hill, you'll find tiny handprints on your bumper. These are from the spirits of the children who perished, who have pushed your car out of harm's way.

The better-known hill of magnetic mystery can be found on Lowe Street in Leominster. This site is also known as Magnetic Hill, and it rose to prominence in July 1939 after the *Leominster Daily Enterprise* reported that a salesman in town on business stopped his car along the wooded stretch of road on Lowe Street and didn't set the parking brake, because he was at the base of a small hill. Imagine his surprise when he stepped out of his car and watched it begin to roll up the hill. The gentleman reported what he saw, and soon the curious flocked to Lowe Street to try the hill for themselves.

Walter Deacon, a reporter for the *Leominster Daily Enterprise*, followed the developing story over several days. Townsfolk came with their cars and bicycles, and even police chief George H. Smith ran his own test. All were amazed as they watched cars rolling up the hill.

The crowds caused a road and safety hazard, and some Leominster officials were getting their hackles raised by the notion of some magical magnetic hill in their town. The town superintendent came to the site and determined that it was a mere optical illusion that cars were rolling up the hill. There was an unseen dip in the road that made it appear that way. He even went so far as to order fill to be brought in to level the road.

Eventually the hubbub died down, but the legend lives on in Leominster. Even today, you'll occasionally see a car stop on Lowe Street and go into neutral just to see if there's still a little magic left in the hill.

Gravity Sandwich

There's a gravity hill on Route 130, Exit 2 in Sandwich. Go halfway down, stop, put the car in neutral, and it will back up the ramp. *–Don Cressey*

Floating Around Springfield

We hope you've never experienced this kind of neighbor. One who crashes into your backyard unannounced, who smells bad, and is a tad gassy. Who just doesn't know when to leave. Sometimes this neighbor damages your property, taking out a fence or the occasional tree. You might even have to use force to get back some personal space.

Thankful this isn't part of your home life? Now, imagine that this neighbor is actually a floating island.

This is the case for some people who live in Springfield, where a ten-thousand-square-foot island

floats in the ten-acre Island Pond. According to an article on Boston.com, the floating island is "one of few in the country and perhaps dates back centuries."

The article said scientists believe the island's base is "made up of a webbing of tree roots and other organic material." The trees on the island "act as sails and routinely send it on a slow careen around the pond." Scientists think that methane gas keeps the entire thing afloat and also contributes to the "funny smell" residents say it has.

In its travels around the pond, the island confused at least one resident who has waterfront property into thinking he had woods behind his home. And it's probably the only island that's ever been blamed for knocking down trees or fences (try explaining that to your homeowner's insurance rep).

The island gets stuck to the shoreline from time to time. When that happens, it has to be towed back to the center of the pond. When that occurred in October 2005, it took "eight men using two cables capable of pulling 45 tons three hours to 'refloat' the island."

The pond and its delinquent island are both owned by Cathedral High School, and they don't seem to have any plans to invite the curious to experience what it's like to sail an island. Though it might be a good idea: The October 2005 towing bill came to $5,000.

It Really Floats!

There is a floating island in the pond behind the high school I attended in Springfield. I hear that this is very unusual, and it is one of only two floating islands in North America. What's also odd is that the Catholic Diocese of Springfield owns it. The pond is called Island Pond and it is located close to the intersection of Roosevelt Avenue and Surrey Road. It has been in the news lately because it washed up into a back yard and they are talking about towing it back into open waters.
—Benjamin Murphy

Shaker Medicinal Spring Water

"Moses Smote the Rock.
This Water smites Disease and Death."

So promises the 1880 advertisement for Shaker Medicinal Spring Water. But wait, there's more!

The ad continues, "It is a Cure for Bright's Disease of the Kidneys, Stone in the Bladder and Kidneys, Dyspepsia, Liver Complaint, Dropsy, Salt Rheum, and Scrofulous Humors, Loss of Appetite, General Debility, Indigestion, Constipation, and Diseases of the Urinary Organs, and an antidote for drugs and intoxicants." Sign up the *Weird Massachusetts* team!

In the latter half of the nineteenth century, it was no secret that the Shakers were living much longer lives than their non-Shaker neighbors. Shakers were surviving into their seventies, eighties, and even beyond. The reason? Must be the water.

So what do you do with really pure water that's being drunk by really long-lived people? Bottle it and sell it, baby. The Shakers, it would seem, were more than a century ahead of their time.

"Well . . . not just the water," said Jonathan Feist, the Chair of the Harvard Historical Commission. Feist has lived in the former Shaker Meeting House in Shaker Village in Harvard since 2001. He became interested in Shaker history by default. He's surrounded by it in his home and his neighborhood. "Living in an old house like this has its own built-in hobbies," he quipped.

The Shakers, officially called the United Society of Believers in Christ's Second Appearing (USBCSA), are a religious sect of Protestantism that got its start in Manchester, England, in 1772 under the guidance of Mother Ann Lee. Mother Ann Lee had very strict ideas on how Christ was to be worshipped, and sitting quietly in a church pew wasn't among them. Members of the USBCSA would dance erratically during worship and work themselves into an ecstatic state. Those who looked on from afar in disapproval dubbed the group the Shaking Quakers (also a good name for a band). The disapproval led Mother Ann Lee to bring her band of nine Shakers to Watervliet, New York, in 1774 to start a new life; eventually, they set up nineteen communities in the northeastern United States and opened their doors to new members.

The Shakers had a firm belief in how they should live their lives, the foods they should eat, and the buildings they should live in. They also believed in strict celibacy, so propagating the religion got a little tricky. To grow the faith, the Shakers depended on converts and the adoption of orphans. "The Shakers were always relatively long-lived," Feist said. "It was an easier lifestyle, particularly for women in the days before birth control. I'm not sure if it was the leading cause of death for women, but one of them was certainly childbirth. To have a celibate lifestyle was to extend the duration of your own life. But they were also into nutrition and health care. Shaker buildings were built well, and they were relatively healthy places to live. They were really into cleanliness. So the spring water kind of fed into the whole thing."

Some estimates say the Shakers attracted about 200,000 converts at their peak, though only about 6,000 full-timers. "You had a lot of winter Shakers," Feist said. He explained how during the difficult winter months, converts would come in for the free and clean shelter and communal living, then wander away when spring came.

On Oak Hill in Harvard, just about a mile from Jonathan Feist's house, sat the East Family Shakers and a well of water that was unusually pure. The Harvard Shakers built an aqueduct from Oak Hill to a reservoir in the main Shaker Village. In November of 1880, one of the Shaker elders, Elijah Myrick, sent a sample of the water off to the state's assayer's office to be tested. The results showed that the water was unusually pure, chemically speaking, even purer than that from Poland Spring: the very same water many of us buy today.

So what do you do with really pure water that's being drunk by really long-lived people? Bottle it and sell it, baby. The Shakers, it would seem, were more than a century ahead of their time.

"This is not an ordinary flowing spring," the 1880 advertisement continues, "but is forced up from a great depth and filtered through Micaceous Schist, over a space of several square rods." "We have no hesitation in pronouncing it equal, if not superior to the Poland water, in its therapeutic effects," another physician's testimony reads.

Could this be the reason the Shakers lived so long? Was this the fountain of youth, right in the woods of Harvard, Massachusetts? If that's the conclusion you wanted to draw, it's likely the Shakers wouldn't mind.

The springhouse is still in the woods off a hiking trail right next to a stream. It's a small stone-and-mortar hut with an iron door that's locked shut. No one in town seems to know who has the key. If one were to get inside, would you find dead bodies? "Or maybe live ones, if it's the fountain of youth," Feist said.

The springhouse is the only testament left to the Shaker Medicinal Spring Water enterprise. If the fountain of youth does indeed lie inside, we're just a key away. In the end, Poland Spring may have won the water war, but the Shakers win on mystique.

The Bridgewater Triangle

You're likely to be familiar with the Bermuda Triangle, a giant area between Puerto Rico, Miami, and the island of Bermuda that became infamous after a 1950 Associated Press article mentioned the unusual number of unexplained events and mysterious disappearances that occurred there. But you may not know that Bermuda is not the only scary piece of geometry in the world or that a similar triangular spot of mystery exists right here in Massachusetts.

The Bridgewater Triangle is located in the southeastern part of the state. The towns of Freetown, Rehoboth, and Abington comprise its northern point, and it encompasses Bridgewater, West Bridgewater, North Middleboro, Segregansett, Dighton, North Dighton, Berkeley, Myricks, Raynham, East Taunton, and Taunton (about two hundred square miles in total). Though significantly smaller than its cousin in the Atlantic, the Bridgewater Triangle can match Bermuda in the number of reports and beats it in the diversity of unexplained phenomena found in its swamps and woods. The list includes monsters, Bigfoots, UFOs, strange beasts, snakes the size of stovepipes, ghosts . . . even murders and suicides.

Author and researcher Loren Coleman first mentioned the Bridgewater Triangle in 1980 in a *Boston Magazine* article. "I started hearing different rumors," Coleman said. "One of the wildest rumors I had heard was that a busload of nuns had disappeared in the Bridgewater area. And then I started digging and I noticed that there was a natural triangle there with the three Bridgewaters: West Bridgewater, Bridgewater, and East Bridgewater. I saw that on the

map, and then I started taking all the little reports I was getting of Bigfoot, of giant snakes, of black panthers, of Dighton Rock, of Freetown and the weird human reports from there, and I kind of mapped it all out and saw there was a larger triangle."

The heart of the Bridgewater Triangle is the Hockomock Swamp, a six-thousand-acre wetland located in southeastern Massachusetts. The mystery behind the swamp dates back to the Wampanoag Indians, who felt that the land had an inherent magic. To the Wampanoag, the spirits of the swamp provided both food and protection. Wild game such as moose, deer, or caribou could become trapped in the muck, making an easy kill for a lucky hunter. And the Wampanoag knew the swamp well. If their enemies could be drawn into the area, they clearly had an advantage in knowing where not to step.

This knowledge served them well during King Philip's War (1675–1676), when the Wampanoag rose up against the English settlers and their allies in one of the bloodiest conflicts in American history. One in twenty were either wounded or killed, and more than a few met their end in Hockomock Swamp. Some English went in and were never seen again. Others managed to make their way out and spread tales of the frightful scenes and monsters that lurked inside.

There are still hundreds of acres in Hockomock Swamp that look much as they did more than three centuries ago. And though major roadways like Interstate 495 and Route 24 have sliced it up, thousands of acres are still almost impenetrable. Swamp, wetlands, ponds, underbrush, weeds, and vines allow passersby to look, but not always to step inside.

A well-worn path cuts through the swamp in a northwest–southeasterly direction next to an old abandoned railroad track. This path skirts the backyard of the Raynham Park dog track. For years, witnesses have reported ghost lights, or glowing masses of energy, moving along this path. Loren Coleman writes, "The spook lights are often reported near the power lines that run through the swamp. Additionally, every January the strange balls of light have been seen over the railroad tracks that run beside the (dog track) and through the swamp."

If one follows the path northwest from the dog track, it intersects with a utility road where high-tension power lines run. Strange cat creatures have been reported here along with enormous turtles, and large shadowy dogs with glowing red eyes. (See the next chapter, "Bizarre Beasts," for more about these fascinating creatures.)

Strange Bridgewater Skies

Loren Coleman writes of one of the earliest strange events to occur in the Triangle: "From colonial times comes the report of 'Yellow Day' when the skies above the area shone all day long with an eerie sulfurous yellow light." The first recorded UFO sighting in the Triangle occurred one May morning in 1760 when a fireball in the sky was seen over the swamp. It wasn't the last UFO to be seen here.

Coleman describes a 1973 event that happened in Rehoboth: "Patrons of Joseph's Restaurant on Park Street believed a UFO visited them. There was a short power failure, and after the lights came back on, people could see two large, perfect circles imprinted in the dirt behind the restaurant."

This was followed by another event in December 1976, when two UFOs were reported to have landed near Route 44 in Taunton. Coleman describes more sightings that occurred throughout July and August 1978, and a major flap that occurred during the spring of 1979. That March an object was seen near Taunton giving off a green, cloudlike substance.

Coleman provides more details:

> Jerry Lopes, a radio newsman at WHDH in Boston spotted a UFO he described as being shaped like home plate on a baseball diamond, with a bright red light on its top, a powerful white 'headlight' at the point on the bottom, and rows of white and red lights around the edges. He saw this strange aerial apparition at the junction of Routes 24 and 106 near the center of the Bridgewater Triangle.

In 1991, a green disk was seen moving over the Triangle. Reports continue to the present day.

A Dark Cloud Overhangs It

In the 1970s and 1980s, rumors circulated of a satanic cult operating in the woods of Freetown State Forest, roughly within the cursed triangle suggested by Loren Coleman. In the woods, police found mutilated cow and calf bodies that may have been linked to some kind of ritual sacrifice. The cult rumors grew in 1978 when the body of fifteen-year-old Mary Lou Arruda was discovered bound to a tree in the forest. In the late 1970s, another woman's body was found in the vicinity. This unfortunate had ties to Carl Drew, a lowlife from Fall River who was suspected of murdering three of the girls he rented out to paying customers. Soon witnesses came to police with talk of Drew's being the leader of a satanic cult that was regularly holding a Black Mass in the forest. Part of the Mass, some testified, was human sacrifice. Drew was eventually arrested for murder and sentenced to life in prison.

Over the next twenty years, more bodies turned up. In 1987, the corpse of a transient man who hung out near Freetown was found in the woods. In 1988, two men were shot and killed in the forest over a dispute. And then there's the area known as the Ledge: a cliff of rock where several people have leaped to their deaths.

As recently as 2007, there was a rash of suicides at Bridgewater State Hospital—a medical and psychiatric facility for prison inmates who are in need of medical care or are a threat to themselves or others. While researching the Triangle, Loren Coleman noticed an unusually high suicide rate in the area. Does a dark cloud hang over the Bridgewater Triangle, or is this a case of concentrating on the negative in a given area?

Even Coleman admits his original triangle isn't precise. There isn't a literal line in the sand where one side is safe from the monsters, ghosts, aliens, cults, and suicides. Enter Christopher Balzano, director of Massachusetts Paranormal Crossroads and author of *Ghosts of the Bridgewater Triangle.* Balzano is working on expanding Loren's original triangle to reflect more recent data.

Triangle Comes Full Circle

Where Coleman focuses mainly on the cryptozoological phenomena in the Triangle, Balzano is more interested in the ghostly and the occult. "Looking in that same exact area, I was seeing a lot of paranormal activity in terms of hauntings, famous places that were haunted, and I started to draw the lines based on that. So I looked at it as an area that has many types of phenomena—it crossed over into ghosts, it also crossed over into unexplained hauntings, and even things such as people who were reporting demonic activity."

In Balzano's career in education, he has worked with the departments of Youth Services, Social Services, and

Mental Health. Along the way, he's noticed the unusual grouping of detention facilities in the area of the Triangle—especially juvenile detention facilities. And then there's Bridgewater State Hospital. "I started wondering if there was a connection with that stuff too," Balzano said. He says he receives ten times as many reports of unexplained activity from the Bridgewater Triangle area than from any other part of New England.

"Why this place?" Balzano asked. "If you go down the street and you check out a haunted building, you find there's a reason for them to be haunted . . . or at least there is a backstory like a murder, tragedy, or something else. A lot of these haunted places that fall in the Triangle have no backstory. Why would the Hockomock Swamp—other than the fact that it's a swamp—have so much activity? Why would a place like Freetown or Rehoboth have so much paranormal activity when someplace next to it has not as much?"

Various places, especially secluded and wooded areas within the Triangle, are a draw for several different kinds of groups who are attracted to the energy there, Balzano said. Covens of witches (both light and dark) practice rituals here, and satanic cult activity is still whispered about in the region of Freetown.

But why here and not a few towns away? Balzano says, "You can expand the Triangle and push the borders a little bit farther and a little bit farther, but there is a point where the paranormal activity does seem to taper off just enough to kind of make a line in the sand."

Is it still a triangle?

"I'd say it probably looks a lot more like a circle. It seems to radiate out. The physical center is still the Hockomock Swamp, but Freetown is the emotional center of it."

So the Triangle comes full circle.

UFO Invasion of 1909

Most people assume that if UFOs do exist, they didn't appear until the 1940s and 1950s. The fear of being invaded by a foreign power during the Second World War and the cold war had people watching the skies—and seeing things they couldn't explain. But the postwar UFO boom wasn't the first: The beginning of the modern UFO-spotting era began in 1909 with the appearance of a mysterious "airship" or "aeroplane" in countries all over the world. In July 1909, newspapers in New Zealand and Britain were already theorizing that the lights in the sky were flying machines peopled by creatures from another planet. By the end of that year, most newspaper reports seemed to assume that the epicenter of this activity was Worcester, Massachusetts.

The Worcester sightings began the Wednesday before Christmas, when crowds on the street saw a strange moving light, apparently the searchlight of a dirigible. The following night, similar lights appeared in Marlboro, South Framingham, Natick, Ashland, Grafton, North Grafton, Upton, Hopedale, and Northboro. And in Fitchburg, according to the Christmas Eve issue of the *Fitchburg Sentinel*, "Over the peak of Rollstone Hill a wonderfully bright light glowed, and hundreds watched it with wonder, not unmixed with awe."

The spate of sightings reached a fever pitch on December 23 in Boston's North Station, when the *Evening Limited* rolled northward on the Boston and Maine Railroad. As it approached Ayer, a messenger on board looked out of the window to see a cigar-shaped object descend from on high and hover above the train. The *Fitchburg Sentinel* takes up the story:

> He says the powerful light of the ship played upon the cars of the train, and it followed along until this city was reached. Then it temporarily disappeared

and was not picked up again until the train got up the line, and for some time the light played over and around the cars.

The Christmas issue of the *Springfield Union-News* reported that many passengers also saw the bright searchlight, including a policeman from Springfield:

> The machine kept ahead of the train from Athol until near Miller's Falls when it shot off to the side and went away. The machine was driven ahead of the train and then would wait until the train caught up and would go ahead again. It seemed to be a good height in the air and kept about at the same height during all the time it was following the train.

According to a Connecticut newspaper, the

Willimantic Chronicle:

> From Boston the light passed to the northeast, circling over Chelsea and Revere, through Lynn toward the Salem line, then returning as far as Framingham where it mysteriously disappeared. . . .
>
> Some say there were two men in the craft. One was standing forward near the headlight, which has been seen by thousands of people, and the second man was in the stern, where a much dimmer light was burning. They say the craft at times attained a speed of fully 80 miles an hour, while again it remained stationary for fifteen minutes at a time.

These dramatic holiday-season lights were almost immediately credited to (or blamed on) a businessman from Worcester named Wallace E. Tillinghast. Tillinghast had announced the previous September that he had designed a "heavier than air" flying machine that he would soon unveil to the world. In fact, Tillinghast boasted he had already flown the machine from Boston to New York and back—an unheard-of distance for flight at the time. But three months later he had failed to show a shred of evidence of his machine.

The sight of lights in the sky immediately prompted the local newspapers to mention the Tillinghast machine. But oddly enough the wily self-promoter had not announced the flight and had been seen in Worcester on the day it occurred.

From our vantage point a century later, the trail has gone cold. If there ever was a terrestrial explanation for the lights, it is now lost to history. It's hard to believe that a 1909 businessman, even one from Massachusetts, could design a flying machine capable of crossing the Atlantic and the Pacific to appear in the skies above Europe and the antipodes. There must be some other explanation. But what?–*Matt Lake*

Nantucket UFO

On July 16, 1999, a flying saucer—four to five hundred feet in diameter by one witness's estimate—was seen over Nantucket and across the sound off the shores of the Cape by several different witnesses who had no knowledge of each other. The first sighting happened just before eight p.m. over Mara Vista on the southern part of Cape Cod, according to the following reports submitted to the Web site www.MysticalUniverse.com.

The first witness, "Carl," described what he saw:

> We were flying from New Hampshire to Florida (private aircraft) for a two week vacation. While over Mara Vista, we noticed what seemed to be the landing light of another aircraft approximately 10 to 15 miles east of our location. Since it appeared to be on approach for landing and quite a bit lower in altitude, we did not think much of it. Then, in a matter of seconds, what we thought had been an aircraft, was right along side of us. It kept a distance of about 3/4's of a mile to our east and approximately 1,500 feet higher in altitude.
>
> We were able to clearly see the shape and color of this, now non aircraft, object. Its shape was as if you took two pie pans, inverted one on top of the other and placed a much smaller inverted pie pan on top. It was completely smooth and was dull gray in color. The other peculiar thing we all noticed about this craft, is that it had no windows, and the once prominent light was now extinguished. The plane we were flying is equipped with an aircraft avoidance system, and this object did not set off any of the warnings as it should have. Approximately 30 to 40 seconds later, the craft went straight up and disappeared from sight. It did not tilt back and go up, it remained level

while going upwards, until it was out of eyesight.

Approximately twenty minutes later, Robert M., who was leaving a restaurant on Nantucket, saw something similar:

I accompanied [four other people] to a seafood restaurant on Nantucket Island. As we left the restaurant and headed towards our rental car, we noticed an unusually bright light to the east. At first, it did not seem at all out of the ordinary until it moved from its original position in the sky to another in the blink of an eye. I would say it traveled ten to fifteen miles north in just a few seconds time. It then seemed to either vanish or become transparent. A few moments later, it reappeared in the same position and then moved across the sky at an extremely high rate of speed to the East, near where we had first observed it. The light that beamed from it changed from a very intense white to a blue color that closely resembled that of a power transformer exploding. When the light went out, we were able to see the faint silhouette of a disk shaped object. The shape of this object reminded me of the space ship used in the "Lost In Space" TV series. After the object hovered for a few seconds, it rose straight up and disappeared from sight. My best guess as to the distance from our location to the object would be approximately two miles. The objects size: three to four hundred feet in diameter

Paul H., who was also visiting Nantucket, reported a similar sighting. He estimated the time to be eight twenty p.m. Paul wrote:

I'm not sure exactly where to start, so I'll begin this from the time we left the seafood restaurant on Nantucket Island 16 July 1999. My wife, son, daughter in-law, and I had just walked out of a local seafood restaurant. When we saw a group of four to five well dressed young individuals pointing at a very bright light in the eastern part of the sky. My first thought was they were just waving to a friend who was about to land at a local airport. As I fumbled with my keys, my son and daughter in-law said in unison, "Did you see that!" When I glanced up to see what all the fuss was about, the aircraft had moved . . . to a location approximately fifteen to twenty miles north. At its new location, it hovered for a few moments, then as if someone had flipped a light switch, the light went out. A few seconds later, the light reappeared and moved back [to its original location].

The aircraft covered the distance in a matter of seconds. Seconds later, the bright light again went out, giving us a clear view of its shape. Its shape resembled two pie pans, one inverted and on top of the other. Having flown several missions in Vietnam, and a military career of twenty years, I have seen many of the "Top Secret" aircraft our military has, but none that have the capabilities to move as silently and quickly as this object did. I have to disagree with the others on the distance and size of this object. Distance from our location: Approximately one mile. Size: Four to Five hundred feet in diameter. The light did change from a bright white to a bright blue in color. As stated by Robert, the color did in fact resemble an electrical transformer exploding.

Otis Air Force Base is less than eight miles from Mara Vista; however, Otis is not known for its secret aircraft testing—the area is simply too heavily populated. Clearly SOMETHING was in the skies over Cape Cod and Nantucket that night. The question remains as to just what it was.

Bizarre Beasts

On the surface, *Massachusetts* doesn't seem to be a state populated by strange monsters and bizarre beasts—except for maybe some of the fans in the stands at Fenway. If we dig a little deeper, though, we find that Bay State folklore, history, and eyewitness accounts are full of unusual creatures stalking us on the shore, in the woods, and along the side streets of the state. For example, there's the bizarre demon that lurked in the small town of Dover during the late '70s, freaking out local teens. And in Barnstable, people say there are a shadowy people, as opaque and unknowable as the marsh mud from which they rise. Even Bigfoot has been sighted here, on October Mountain and in the Clay Banks in Bridgewater. And if you happen to see a hulking creature with six eyes that move around its head, enabling it to see in front, behind, and sideways all at the same time, look out. You've just spotted the long-lost Herring Cove sea monster.

Monster of Coca-Cola Ledge

North Adams is home to an unusual number of unique landscape features and weird legends. One rocky bluff that overlooks Route 8, just south of the city's downtown area, combines both. A hairy monster is said to stalk Witt's Ledge—or Coca-Cola Ledge, as locals refer to the area.

In the 1940s, the Coca-Cola Company had its logo painted onto the cliff walls, making for one large billboard that could be seen for miles. Over the last several decades, the Coke logo has been covered up many times by various fraternities and sororities from the local college who have taken to painting their Greek letters on the rocky face.

But the billboard isn't the only monstrosity in the area. A Bigfoot-type creature allegedly walks along the cliff walls and in the nearby woods. The Monster of Coca-Cola Ledge may have been a ploy by generations of parents eager to keep their children away from the dangerous drop, but many locals today can still recall hearing about the beast that lurks around the ledge.

Dover Demon

Most mysterious creatures that frequent the byways, forests, and swamps of the world grow into legend over many years. As generations come and go, folklore combines with further sightings to propel these "monsters" into our collective conscious. Not so with the Dover Demon. A few brief sightings in the late '70s are all it took to make this creature legend, though nobody seems to have seen it since.

It was Thursday, April 21, 1977, a clear early spring evening. Seventeen-year-old Dover resident Bill Bartlett was driving along Farm Street in his '71 Volkswagen Super Beetle with two of his friends, Mike Mazzocca and Andy Brodie, both also seventeen. They were on spring break and ready for fun, but something strange happened that evening that Bartlett would never forget — probably because local media and fans of the unexplained just won't let him.

"I do remember it was around ten o'clock at night," Bartlett said. "My friends and I were out hunting around looking for people to hang out with — you know, looking for the party. We couldn't find anybody, so we were heading back toward Sherborn. I'm driving down Farm Street, and I see something ahead on a stone wall. I wasn't really sure if it was a cat or a dog. My headlights were hitting this thing, and the eyes were glowing — just like when your headlights hit the eyes of an animal, they glow. These eyes were glowing bright orange. I didn't think that was so unusual, but when I got closer, I got a real good look at what this thing was, and it turned toward me and I saw these spindly-like hands grabbing onto a rock. And I still didn't believe what I was seeing. . . . I was like . . . what the heck is that?"

What the heck WAS that? For more than three decades, that question has intrigued not just the residents of Dover and the surrounding towns, but those interested in cryptozoology — the study of creatures unknown to mainstream science — and in the paranormal. In 2006, paranormal investigator and author Brad Steiger polled various researchers internationally to determine a top-ten list of real monsters, and the Dover Demon came in at number 10.

Today Bill Bartlett is a fine arts painter who has had his work displayed on both coasts of the United States. Like many visual artists, he has a keen perspective on size and proportion. What exactly did he see back in 1977? "It looked like one of those kids who are from Biafra, with the distended bellies and the long, spindly arms and the big eyes, except it was very pale, really gaunt, and its cheekbones were sunken in — you really couldn't see the features of the face."

Growing up in the small town of Dover, Bartlett is familiar with the various critters that roam the neighborhoods — animals like raccoons, skunks, foxes, and deer. "It wasn't any animal that I've ever seen from around here," he said. "I could judge the size of the creature, and I knew that this was larger than a raccoon and definitely larger than a fox. This was a good-sized creature. And its hands. . . . I've seen a raccoon's paws up close — they're small — and this creature had large hands. And it wasn't large like the size of an adult human; it was large like a kid with long fingers. And the eyes. . . . I don't know if human eyes glow in headlights, but I've never seen it."

When he got home, Bartlett sat down with pen and paper and drew what he had seen. Sadly for the painter, that rough sketch doodled long before years of academic training and practice may be his most famous work to date. He told his parents what had happened, but aside from the two friends who'd been in the car with him, no one else knew.

Enter John Baxter.

Around midnight that same evening, fifteen-year-old John Baxter had just left his girlfriend's house. He was walking home along Millers Hill Road—just over a mile from Bartlett's sighting on Farm Street—when he spotted a strange creature. It was lurking near the side of the road, about one hundred feet away from him.

At first, Baxter thought it could be a kid from the neighborhood, but as he drew closer, he saw that it was neither the right size nor proportions for a kid. He was only twenty to thirty feet away from the creature when it scurried off into the woods and up a small hill. Baxter said he could hear the thing as it plodded through the leaves and underbrush. When this strange beast stopped, it molded its spindly toes over a rock and wrapped its spindly fingers around a tree. This is where John Baxter got his best look at the biped. When he got home about an hour after the encounter, Baxter also drew the creature that he had seen. He described the head as a figure-eight shape on its side with very large eyes.

On Friday, April 22, there was one last sighting, again around midnight—just twenty-six hours after Bartlett's experience. Fifteen-year-old Abby Brabham was being driven home to Sherborn by her friend Will Taintor. They were driving along Springdale Avenue, just two miles from the Bartlett sighting, when Brabham claimed she saw the headlights illuminate an apelike creature with glowing green eyes perched on the side of the road. Will Taintor didn't get as good a look at the creature, but he later described something about as big as a goat or large dog.

Bartlett, Baxter, and Brabham were aware of each other's existence before April 22, but they didn't consider themselves even so much as acquaintances. Once a few people in town heard about the incident, word quickly spread. Within days, the eminent cryptozoological researcher Loren Coleman began his interview and investigation process. After speaking with the witnesses and interviewing the parents, friends, and teachers of Bartlett and Baxter, Coleman determined that the accounts were genuine. It was Coleman who coined the term Dover Demon.

There have been myriad other supernatural and preternatural labels slapped on this thing back in 1977. The witnesses themselves may have their theories, but they haven't reached any conclusions.

More than three decades later, the Dover Demon lives through the accounts of these three witnesses. Bill Bartlett is currently hard at work trying to ensure that he is ultimately known for his work as a fine arts painter rather than an eight-second witness to an event that has risen from regional to international infamy.

. . . they told me of a seas-serpent or snake, that lay quoiled up like a cable upon a rock at Cape Ann and a boat passing by with English aboard. . .

Gloucester Sea Serpent

At this time we had some neighbouring gentlemen in our house, who came to welcome me into the country; where amongst variety of discourse, they told me . . . of a seas-serpent or snake, that lay quoiled up like a cable upon a rock at Cape Ann and a boat passing by with English aboard, and two Indians disswaded them, saying, that if he were not kill'd out-right, they would be all in danger of their lives.

So wrote the English naturalist John Josselyn on June 26, 1638. His account was later published in his book *An Account of Two Voyages to New England*. Since his report, hundreds of other sightings of a giant sea serpent—up to one hundred feet long, with a head the size of a horse and a snakelike body as wide as a barrel—have poured in from all around New England. But if there is one hot spot for these sightings, it's Cape Ann and Gloucester's bay.

Between the mid-seventeenth and early nineteenth centuries, reports of the sea serpent were sporadic, but in August of 1817, the great beast visited Gloucester harbor almost daily for the entire month. When a skipper from a coasting vessel claimed to see a sixty-foot serpent at the bay's entrance on August 6, he was laughed at, but not for very long. On August 14, a ship's carpenter named Matthew Gaffney not only saw the creature but also fired at him. Gaffney wrote, "I had a good gun, and took good aim. I aimed at his head, and I think I must of hit him. He turned toward us immediately after I had fired, and I thought he was coming at us; but he sunk down and went directly under our boat, and made his appearance at about one hundred yards from where he sunk. . . ."

By several accounts, just about all of Gloucester saw the eel-like creature during August of 1817. David Humphreys, a former aide to General George Washington, wrote, "[The serpent] was seen by two hundred, at one time, sporting the whole afternoon, under Wind-Mill Point." Those who saw the creature move claimed it swam with a vertical motion—like a caterpillar in the water, with the humps of its back forming hills.

The newspapers were in a frenzy printing stories culled from eyewitnesses. But then, eventually, the Gloucester Sea Serpent stopped making the news. Editors considered the creature's existence to be fact and weren't interested in debating it any longer.

In the twentieth century, giant sea serpent sightings have basically ceased. According to J. P. O'Neill, author of *The Great New England Sea Serpent*, the reason the beast no longer comes around is because humans have overfished the coastal bays and banks, and the giant creature has simply moved on to more hospitable feeding grounds.

The most recent sighting of a sea serpent in Massachusetts occurred on July 25, 1962, off the coast of Marshfield. The Associated Press covered the story and told of witnesses on two separate fishing vessels (the *Vincy* and the *Carol Ann*) who saw the creature. The Marshfield serpent was described as having the head of an alligator and a body shaped like a nail keg. One of the fishermen, Archie Lewis, was quoted as saying that the critter had a healthy appetite. It was, he said, "gulping up the fish in the area and did not concern itself with fishermen in the way. I have seen all types of whales, but never one that resembled this creature."

Herring Cove Sea Serpent

Gloucester isn't the only harbor to hold a giant sea creature. Herring Cove, in Provincetown, at the very tip of Cape Cod, has its own monster, witnessed in 1886. What makes the Herring Cove Sea Serpent unique is the theory behind it. Scientifically minded locals believed that recent underwater earthquakes awakened a prehistoric creature from its slumber and scared it to the surface. This monster was described as being over three hundred feet long. And unlike that of the Gloucester serpent, which was mostly depicted as a huge snake, the description of the Herring Cove serpent doesn't resemble any creature ever seen by man before—a true monster. A local newspaper reported in 1886:

> Mr. George W. Ready, a well-known citizen here, was going from the town to the backside of the Cape and in crossing one of the sand dunes, saw a commotion in the water about a half a mile from the shore in the Herring Cove. It looked like a whirlpool and from his standpoint appeared to be about 20 feet in diameter from the center of which jets of spray, looking like steam, were ejected to the height of fifty feet.
>
> Intently watching this strange phenomenon, he presently saw a huge head above the surface and pointed for the shore. The head was as large as a 200-gallon cask, concave on the under side and convex on the upper.
>
> Mr. Ready saw the creature coming towards the shore and secreted himself in a clump of beach plum bushes, where he got a good view of the monster. The creature swam to the shore with a slow and undulating motion and passed within about 30 feet of where Mr. Ready was secreted. It was about 300 feet long, and in the thickest part, which was about the middle, he judged as it passed him to be about 20 feet in diameter. The body was covered with scales as large as the head of a fish barrel and were colored alternately green, red and blue. . . .
>
> The most curious feature was the head. The open mouth disclosed four rows of teeth which glistened like polished ivory and were at least two feet long, while on the extreme end of the

head or nose extended a tusk or horn at least eight feet in length. The creature had six eyes as large as good sized dinner plates and they were placed at the end of moveable projections, so they were at least three feet from the head. In the creature's moving along, these projections were continually on the move so that the reptile could see before, behind and sideways at the same time. Three of the eyes were of a fiery red hue while the others were of a pale green. . . .

When the tail came out of the water it was seen to be of a V shape, the broadest part towards the body to which it was joined by a small bony cartilage about 20 feet long and only 10 inches in diameter. This tail on the broad part was studded with very hard, bony scales shaped like teeth about one foot long and eight inches at the base and cut everything smooth to the ground as it was dragged over the surface; pine and oak trees, nearly one foot in diameter, were cut off as smoothly as if done by a saw.

The creature made for one of the large fresh water ponds called Pasture Pond. When in the center, the head, which had all the time been raised some 30 feet in the air, began slowly to descend and was soon under water, the body slowly following it. As the tail disappeared, the water commenced to recede from the shore till the pond was left completely dry with a large hole in the center some twenty feet in diameter, perfectly circular down which sounding leads have been lowered 250 fathoms and no bottom found. By standing on the brink of the hole, what appears to be water can be seen at a long distance down.

Preparations are being made to investigate the matter, and thousands are going to see and examine the track of the huge sea monster. For fear that this statement should be doubted, and any one try to contradict it, I here append a copy of Mr. Ready's affidavit and signature:

"I, George Washington Ready, do testify that the foregoing statement is correct. It is a true description of the serpent as he appeared to me on that morning and I was not unduly excited by liquor or otherwise. George W. Ready."

Giant Birds, Cats, Dogs, and Bigfoot: Hockomock Has Them All!

The Hockomock Swamp area claims more than its share of strange occurrences. Because of its long history of evil, bedevilment, and ominous incidents, residents have recognized this area of the state for its strange and often sinister character.

In the skies above the swamp there have been sightings of large unknown birds. The most dramatic sighting of one of these huge birds took place at two a.m. on a late summer's night in 1971. Norton police sergeant Thomas Downy was driving along Winter Street in Mansfield toward his home in Easton. As he approached a place at the edge of the swamp known as Bird Hill, he was suddenly confronted by a tremendous winged creature over six feet tall with a wingspan of eight to twelve feet. As Sergeant Downy drew to a stop at the intersection, the bird flew straight up and, flapping its massive wings, disappeared over the dark trees into the swamp. Downy reported the sighting to the Easton police as soon as he reached home. A patrol car searched the area, but the huge bird was not sighted again. For weeks after, his fellow officers, who called him the Birdman, teased this policeman with the feathery name. Downy stuck to his story.

Of course, he is not alone in sighting these tremendous birds or birdlike creatures. They figure in the Indian legends of Hockomock and of many other areas throughout the Americas. Known as Thunderbirds in Indian mythology, these creatures were large enough and powerful enough to carry off a man.

Thunderbirds are not the only creatures of the nether land to have appeared in the Hockomock Swamp region.

Several other strange animals occur repeatedly in folklore and legend. The most famous of these creatures is the notorious Bigfoot. During the 1970s and 1980s, all kinds of sightings of Bigfoot, ranging from almost certain hoaxes to incidents involving eminently responsible witnesses and organized police hunts, have been reported. In Bridgewater, in 1970, heavily armed state and local police, along with a pack of hunting dogs, tracked what was reported to be a huge bear. Since the creature was not found, police were never certain what it really was. Although bears have not been seen in the Bridgewater area for

many years, they are certain that, whatever the creature was, it was not a hoax. Several very reputable citizens had a good look at the huge animal before it lumbered off into the woods, and definite tracks were found there. In other parts of the country, people trying to make sense of the unexplained have often labeled these large, hairy creatures as bears.

Around the same time, in April 1970, there were several other reports of a big, hairy animal of some kind walking erect in other places in the Bridgewater vicinity. Farmers in the area reported killed and mutilated pigs and sheep. One Bridgewater resident complained to the police that a large, hairy creature walking upright was thrashing about in the backyards and woods of the neighborhood. Police investigated several times. One officer, lying in wait in his patrol car, reported that, entirely without warning, something picked up the rear of his car. When the policeman flashed his searchlight, he saw something that looked like a huge bipedal "bear" running away between the houses. On April 8, police officers reportedly found tracks after a seven-foot-tall creature was seen. Nothing was discovered in further searches.

However, there were several other sightings in the area during 1973–1974. A night security guard at the Raynham Dog Track reported a series of horrible screams and screeches that frightened him and upset the dogs. Huge footprints, fifteen to eighteen inches long, were discovered in the snow south of Raynham. Several residents had reported seeing a tall, furry, manlike creature in the Elm Street–Bridge Street area of Raynham and near the Hockomock Swamp.

In addition to strange manlike creatures, phantom panthers have been sighted regularly in places throughout the region. In 1972, in Rehoboth, local police organized a "lion hunt" after residents of the area had been terrorized by what they said was a large cat or mountain lion. Cattle and sheep in the area had been mysteriously killed, and carcasses were discovered raked with claw marks. Police took casts of the animal's tracks and used dogs and a helicopter in an attempt to track it down. Nothing was caught. Similar incidents involving phantom cats have occurred in other places throughout the swamp. None of these mysterious felines has yet been

captured, but they seem to be out there.

Huge black dogs ("devil dogs"), as well as black panthers, have also been reported within the swamp. Sir Arthur Conan Doyle's *Hound of the Baskervilles* has its roots in the many legends of the hounds of hell and the Irish pooka, those huge, black, ghostlike dogs with eyes of fire. In 1976, a huge black killer dog was reported in Abington. The dog, if that's what it was, ripped out the throats of two ponies. Local firefighter Phillip Kane, the owner of the ponies, actually saw the animal standing over the bloody carcasses. He said that the critter eluded extensive police searches and, for a period of several weeks, terrorized the community. Schoolchildren were kept in at recess, and many homeowners and storekeepers armed themselves with rifles.

The last time this killer dog was seen was when police officer Frank Curran sighted it along some railroad tracks. The officer fired a shot but missed. The creature, whatever it was, merely turned away and walked off slowly in the other direction. And perhaps into another dimension.– *Loren Coleman*

Spotted in Massachusetts: Bigfoot

Bigfoot, or Sasquatch as he is sometimes called, is that large, hairy, ape-man creature that has puzzled crypotozoologists for generations. Usually reported as being covered in brownish or grayish hair, the critter is notoriously shy—which may be just as well, since he's also said to smell VERY bad. Generally, he will flee from any human contact but in some reports has been provoked to violence. He's most usually sighted in the dense woods of the northwestern United States. However, he has made his appearances right here in our fair state.

Bigfoot on October Mountain

The largest state forest in Massachusetts, 16,500 acres, surrounds October Mountain in the bucolic town of Lee, and this green and rural country is home to more than one unexplained phenomenon. Bigfoot is said to wander the hills and paths.

Sasquatch researcher and Southbridge native Corey Alarie said, "The first sighting in October Mountain State Forest took place in 1983. Four friends were having a cookout near an abandoned Boy Scout camp, referred to as Camp Eagle in the initial report. Around ten a.m., they started hearing movement coming from the woods nearby. The strange sounds continued for a couple of hours until two members of the party decided to investigate the source." Alarie said, "When they were about one hundred yards from the campsite, they saw a creature about fifty yards ahead of them on a trail. The creature was silhouetted by the moonlight." The two went back and told their friends what they saw, and the

group decided that leaving the area was better than contending with whoever or whatever owned the silhouette.

"As they were leaving," Alarie said, "they swung the car around, and the headlights picked up the creature standing behind some bushes. They stopped the car, and one of the witnesses got out for a better look. This person stated that the creature was about seven feet tall, had brown hair all over its body, and had red eyes. As the witness approached, the creature fled back into the woods."

The 1983 account wasn't the only Sasquatch sighting on October Mountain. There is also a 1989 report, involving a woman who was hiking

along a trail on the mountain. She saw something out of the corner of her eye, and according to Alarie, "She kept walking, but also kept noticing this movement. At one point, she took out a pair of binoculars and saw what she described as a Sasquatch in a clearing a ways off from where she was standing. She described it as large and hairy. She also stated that it seemed to her that the creature was rooting around on the ground for food. It would crouch down. Its hand would go to the ground and occasionally lift to its mouth. Being a bit scared, she headed back down the trail."

Alarie has investigated the two claims and has been to October Mountain several times. He's an avid hunter and outdoorsman and uses all of those skills when tracking this elusive creature. He hikes the trails where Bigfoot is said to have been, with his video camera perched on the end of a tripod and cradled across his shoulder the way a soldier carries his gun. If Alarie does cross paths with Sasquatch, he'll be ready to shoot— video, that is.

Big Hairy of Cedar Swamp

Cedar Swamp lies in the central Massachusetts town of Westborough. Interstate 495 and the Massachusetts Turnpike intersect at the eastern edge of the two-thousand-acre preserve, and over the last several decades, industry and residential areas have also encroached upon the area. Perhaps the resulting noise and bustle has finally scared off a creature one local man calls Big Hairy.

"Dave" (not his real name) grew up in Westborough and spent many days hiking, hunting, and camping in and around the area of Cedar Swamp. In the late 1980s, he and a friend were walking along some train tracks when Dave's friend said he saw a large manlike creature bound across two sets of tracks in three strides. Dave didn't see the beast himself, but they went to look at where it had crossed and found a very large footprint.

Several months later Dave and two other friends were camping overnight in Cedar Swamp. They heard some rustling. Then the rustling grew louder and seemed closer.

Even though Dave had his 12-gauge shotgun with him, he was nervous. But he decided to take a flashlight and head down the path. He was just a short distance away when he heard the rustling louder and closer this time.

At that moment, Dave's fear gave way to something else. "I don't know why, but I suddenly got some [courage] at that point and said, 'Wait a minute here.'" He turned and walked toward the sound as his friends dashed by him. "I shined the flashlight at where the sound was coming from, and I saw these two hairy legs—they were like tree trunks." He shined the light even higher until it came to rest on the creature's face. "I saw its face. I had my rifle with me, but I didn't want to shoot it. It looked at me and raised its eyebrow—like it was curious about me."

The encounter lasted only a few seconds before fear took hold of Dave again and he turned to run.

Over the years, Dave shared the story with only a few people because he was tired of being laughed at. He is particular about not labeling the creature he saw as Bigfoot, because of the stigma that witnesses subject themselves to. He and his friends have instead nicknamed the Cedar Swamp creature Big Hairy.

Giant Lizard of Dismal Swamp

In June of 1922, multiple witnesses spotted a giant lizard in the town of Ware. Some claimed that the creature was an alligator or crocodile that escaped from a circus train. Others theorized the saurian was an escaped pet that grew to huge proportions once it reached Dismal Swamp via the Ware River.

According to a *Boston Globe* report, the first sighting occurred on the morning of June 6, when Stephen Faerykiewicz was driving his Gilbertville Bakery truck along the highway next to Dismal Swamp. The driver thought he saw a log about six feet long lying in the road. He slowed down to avoid hitting it, and then realized the object was an animal. Faerykiewicz pulled his truck over and shooed what he later described as an alligator off the road. He followed the reptile until it snapped at him. Faerykiewicz reported what he saw in Ware, and by the afternoon, many young men and boys were out in the swamp trying to spot the creature.

Later that month, Mr. James J. Toomey, a World War I veteran and avid hunter, was telling folks in town he thought it must have been a giant turtle of some kind. But Toomey's opinion changed when he was out by the swamp and saw something in the water. In the June 27, 1922, *Boston Globe*, Toomey was quoted as saying, "I am satisfied there is an alligator inhabiting the swampy section along the river near Dismal Swamp. I saw more than four feet of this freak out of water and was close enough to see its snout and eyes plainly."

Toomey went home, grabbed his rifle, and headed back to Dismal Swamp, but the creature didn't show. It had slipped beneath the surface and into legend.

Vampire of Plymouth

"There are such beings as vampires, some of us have evidence that they exist. Even had we not the proof of our own unhappy experience, the teachings and the records of the past give proof enough for sane peoples," said Dr. Seward's diary in Bram Stoker's classic, *Dracula.*

Bram Stoker may have immortalized vampires as sexy creatures that prey on the bare necks of their beautiful victims, but real vampires from folklore aren't so pretty. In fact, they're the walking dead. And one of these horrible creatures was said to reside in Plymouth.

During the 1800s, consumption, or pulmonary tuberculosis, caused one out of four deaths. Consumption came in many flavors: There was the galloping kind that could turn a healthy person into a corpse in a matter of weeks, or a slower-moving form of the disease that slowly squeezed the life from its victims over the course of many years. Entire families were wiped out as the affliction wormed its way through households.

When medical science couldn't provide answers, some families turned to the supernatural. On May 4, 1822, the *Old Colony Memorial and Plymouth County Advertiser* ran an article called "Superstitions of New England." It highlighted an 1807 vampire case of Plymouth and the folklore remedy that followed:

In that almost insulated part of the State of Massachusetts, called Old Colony or Plymouth County, and particularly in a small village adjoining the shire town, there may be found the relics of many old customs and superstitions which would be amusing, at least to the antiquary. Among others of less serious cast, there was, fifteen years ago, one which, on account of its peculiarity and its consequence, I beg leave to mention. . . .

There was, fifteen years ago, and is perhaps at this time, an opinion prevalent among the inhabitants of this town, that the body of a person who died of the consumption, was by some supernatural means, nourished in the grave of some one living member of the family; and that during the life of this person, the body remained, in the grave, all the fullness and freshness of life and health.

This belief was strengthened by the circumstance, that whole families frequently fell prey to this terrible disease.

Of one large family in this town consisting of fourteen children, and their venerable parents, the mother and the youngest son only remained—the rest within a year of each other had died of the consumption.

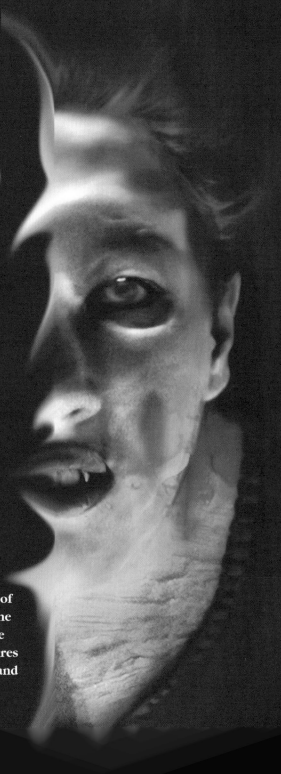

Within two months from the death of the thirteenth child, an amiable girl of about 16 years of age, the bloom, which characterized the whole of this family, was seen to fade from the cheek of the last support of the heartsmitten mother.

At this time as if to snatch one of this family from an early grave, it was resolved by a few of the inhabitants of the village to test the truth of this tradition which I have mentioned, and, which the circumstances of this afflicted family seemed to confirm. I should have added that it was believed that if the body thus supernaturally nourished in the grave, should be raised and turned over in the coffin, its depredation upon the survivor would necessarily cease. The consent of the mother being obtained, it was agreed that four persons, attended by the surviving and complaining brother should, at sunrise the next day dig up the remains of the last buried sister. At the appointed hour they attended in the burying yard, and having with much exertion removed the earth, they raised the coffin upon the ground; then, displacing the flat lid, they lifted the covering from her face, and discovered what they had indeed anticipated, but dreaded to declare. —Yes, I saw the visage of one who had been long the tenant of a silent grave, lit up with the brilliancy of youthful health. The cheek was full to dimpling, and a rich profusion of hair shaded her cold forehead, and while some of its richest curls floated upon her unconscious breast. The large blue eye had scarcely lost its brilliancy, and the livid fullness of her lips seemed almost to say, "lose me and let me go."

In two weeks the brother, shocked with the spectacle he had witnessed, sunk under his disease. The mother survived scarcely a year, and the long range of sixteen graves, is pointed out to the stranger as an evidence of the truth of the belief of the inhabitants.

Dr. Michael Bell's book, *Food for the Dead*, he explores many of the [mo]re cases throughout New England. The Plymouth case is unique. "One of [in]teresting things about the Plymouth example," Dr. Bell said, "and it's the [o]ne I found in New England, is that all they did was just turn the corpse [fac]e-down. Face down. And then rebury it. It shows just how dumb vampires are [*he laughs*]. Like it's just going to dig itself deeper into the ground and [ne]ver going to get out."

[W]ith the gentler Plymouth treatment, somewhere a vampire still rests [al]though facedown in her grave, alongside fifteen others from her

Local Heroes and Villains

Oh, we got heroes, starting with those rabble-rousers in Faneuil Hall. Names of great historical importance have been born right here in the Bay State: John Adams, Paul Revere, Ben Franklin. (Yes, Ben Franklin was born HERE, not in Pennsylvania.)

But Massachusetts has other heroes to celebrate, ones with an odd twist to them. The kind that settle in Salem and don't stand trial when they declare themselves witches. The kind who write a novel of 50,000 words and manage to complete it without once using the most commonly used letter in the English language—the letter e.

And we have those with a darker side. There's the famous whack job in Fall River and a strangler in Boston—who may still be at large.

Yes, we got heroes, and we got villains. Both have left their mark on Massachusetts.

Twenty-nine Whacks Later . . . Lizzie Borden

Lizzie Borden took an axe
And gave her mother forty whacks;
When she saw what she had done
She gave her father forty-one.

Examination of the evidence and court documents tells us that this verse simply isn't true. Mrs. Abby Borden was killed with only eighteen blows of an axe (thirteen of them to her skull), plus she was Lizzie Borden's stepmother, not her mother, and Mr. Andrew Jackson Borden received only eleven blows to the head. Though their spinster daughter, Lizzie, was arrested for the heinous crime, she wasn't convicted. But if Lizzie didn't do it, who did?

It was hot and sticky in Fall River on the morning of August 4, 1892. Temperatures reached over one hundred degrees. It was the kind of summer day where you try not to move or breathe more than you have to because of the stifling heat. The Borden family was at home on 92 Second Street—a rather quaint and simple home, considering who owned it. That morning thirty-two-year-old Lizzie was there, as was her father, seventy-year-old Andrew; her stepmother, sixty-four-year-old Abby; and Bridget Sullivan (whom the Bordens referred to as Maggie because that was the name of their previous maid), the Irish immigrant domestic worker who lived in the house and worked for the Bordens.

Left, Andrew and Abby Borden; next page, Lizzie and the Borden house

Around eleven a.m. that fateful day, Andrew Borden lay down for a nap on the sofa in his sitting room. Borden may have been dreaming about his business interests in town. He was eighth-generation Fall River and one of the wealthiest men around. He got his start as an undertaker, but after inheriting a moderate amount of money and a good amount of real estate, Andrew Borden began to amass serious wealth. His résumé was both long and impressive. He sat on the boards of several banks and businesses in town, including Union Savings Bank, First National Bank, Globe Yarn Mill Company, and Troy Cotton. However, he was a frugal man, and not very well liked. Folks in town thought Borden had taken quite a bit from Fall River but hadn't given much back.

Upstairs from the snoozing Andrew, his wife, Abby, went into the guest room. She may have been looking for some sewing supplies, or maybe she was tidying up, but what she certainly wasn't doing was expecting to die. The time was approximately eleven ten a.m. when someone entered the guestroom and took an axe to Abby's skull and upper body. Eighteen blows later, Abby lay in a pool of her blood on the side of the bed opposite the entrance to the room.

Then the assailant went downstairs to the sitting room. Clearly there would not have been too much of a struggle, because Andrew Borden never had the chance to wake up from his nap. With crushing force, the axe came down on his face. Eleven whacks later, Andrew was also dead, his face split open.

According to her testimony, Lizzie walked into the house from the backyard and then to the sitting room, where she discovered the body of her father. She called up the stairs to Maggie, "Go for Dr. Bowen as soon as you can. I think Father is hurt."

What soon unfolded turned into the trial of the century. All the evidence pointed to someone familiar to the victims being the culprit: There was no sign of forced entry, nothing stolen from the victims or the house, and no sign of struggle—and people were home during the murder. As witnesses were interviewed and then reinterviewed, Lizzie became more of a suspect.

Throughout her questioning, Lizzie seemed confused. She was hazy about details and had a curious lack of memory. The part of her testimony that's most significant is when she said, "I asked him [her father] if he wanted the window left that way. Then I went into the kitchen, and from there to the barn . . . up stairs."

When asked how long she would have been in the oppressively hot second story of the barn, she said, "I don't know, fifteen or twenty minutes." A long time, considering what she was doing. "Trying to find a lead sinker," Lizzie testified. She claimed she was looking for the sinker for a fishing trip she was planning in the coming week. Lizzie unhooked the back screen door when she went outside. When she came back in, she discovered her father's body.

Bridget Sullivan was also brought in to testify, as was John Morse, Abby's brother, who had been lodging with

the Bordens. Everyone had motive—get to Andrew's wealth. But there were a few problems. First, no murder weapon was found, though it was probably an axe. Investigators found an axe in the basement, but they didn't believe it was the instrument used. If Johnnie Cochran was around in 1890 to defend Lizzie, he might have said, "Can't find the axe that gave the blows? Then you must let Lizzie go."

Let her go is just what the jury did after over an hour

of deliberation. There were plenty of holes in time and in the case. Lizzie was reported to have burned a light blue dress shortly after the murder because she said she got paint on it. Why didn't Bridget the maid hear or see anything that day? Who could have come and gone in those twenty minutes when Lizzie was just a few yards away in the barn?

These questions are still unanswered. The most popular theory is that Lizzie and Bridget were in on the crime together for some reason. Some have theorized that spinster Lizzie and Bridget were lovers. Others said it was out of friendship that they stuck together. No matter the reason, both Andrew and Abby were dead and no one would ever be punished for the crime.

Though some newspapers, such as *The New York Times*, praised the jury for reaching the correct

Around eleven a.m. that fateful day, Andrew Borden lay down for a nap on the sofa in his sitting room.

conclusion (after all, the prosecution's case rested on the single tenet that if Lizzie didn't do it, who else could have?), a black cloud hung over Lizzie for the rest of her life. After she was cleared of the murder, she and her sister, Emma, purchased a house on the hill that they called Maplecroft, where Lizzie lived out the rest of her days. It is worth noting that the Bordens' maid, Bridget, on her deathbed allegedly confessed to her sister that she gave false testimony on the witness stand in order to protect Lizzie.

Even with the acquittal so long ago, today Lizzie Borden is the Bay State's most infamous axe murderer.

The Official Witch of Salem

Laurie Cabot was born in Oklahoma in the 1930s while her parents were on the road to someplace else. They were just passing through when baby Laurie came into the world, and they stuck around for only three months afterward before they picked up and continued on a road that would eventually lead Laurie to Salem.

"All my life I had psychic experiences," Cabot says. "My dad said it must be a science. You've got to look toward science for the reason for whatever is occurring."

After the age of eleven, Laurie spent a great deal of time in the Boston Public Library with her mom, looking for books to explain these psychic experiences. One of the librarians there was from England, and after a few months she whispered that she was a witch and that she recognized an affinity for the craft in young Laurie. "In those days, it was illegal in America to be a witch," Cabot said.

Cabot began studying the craft with the librarian and was initiated at age sixteen. As she got older, she tried to fit herself into a traditional life, but something didn't feel quite right to her. She resigned herself to wearing her ritual black robes and looking the part so people

would always know where to find a witch.

In the 1960s, Laurie moved to Boston's North End, where she met a young divorced woman with two children. They found that both of them wanted to get out of the city and move to the suburbs, so the two decided to pool their money and see what they could afford.

"I said the one place I will not go would be Salem, Massachusetts," Cabot recalled. "They have the wrong definition of the word witch, they don't have a clue of what one is or isn't. And they have a history of hanging people. I don't want to impose myself and my black robes on these people." But then Cabot's friend found an ad for an appealing place in Salem. Cabot promised to look before passing judgment. The address turned out to be 18 Chestnut Street. "It was a gray house with black shutters, and it was so charming," she said.

Salem of the early 1970s was nothing like it is today. Many businesses were boarded up, some houses were falling down, and there was nary a witch to be found. Cabot says she moved in with the intention of lying low, until her cat got stuck in a tree in her front yard. After receiving no help from the fire or police departments, she called the local newspaper and said, "My cat's in a tree. They won't help, and I'm a witch, and I want my cat down now!"

The fire department, police, animal rescue, and the press showed up and got the cat out of the tree. The photo of the rescue and the idea of a real witch in Salem spread to other newswires and services. Cabot had learned the public relations power of being a witch in Witch City.

"I'm trying to think of some way to earn a living and wear my robes," Cabot said. "I couldn't go to IBM or work in a bank dressed like this." So she opened her first witch shop at 100 Derby Street and moved into the apartment upstairs: the first witch shop in America, she claims. With little capital, she gathered up flowers, herbs, roots, and other supplies from the Salem woods to mix potions to sell. And she began giving classes on witchcraft.

She also went to the Salem city council and asked to be named the official Witch of Salem, but they refused. Cabot said, "Then Governor Michael Dukakis gave me a Patriot's Award, and on it, it says, 'I proclaim Laurie Cabot the official Witch of Salem for her work with children with special needs.'" With Official Witch as her title, her legend grew.

Within a few years of Laurie's opening her first shop, other witches saw the value of living in Salem and began to trickle in. Cabot says, "Because they think I'm rich, and because I got a lot of publicity around the globe for years and years, because I've written books, they think there's either a sacred piece of land or a throne somewhere by which they could rule Salem and make a lot of money. So there are people here who call themselves witches who are definitely not. And at Halloween, they all show up with green faces and pointed hats."

Now in her seventies, Cabot is a permanent fixture in Salem and almost as much a part of the witch history here as the trials of 1692. Though some witches love her and others despise her, the witches in town acknowledge that she started it all here in the 1970s.

First Lord of America

Since the Pilgrims first arrived at Plymouth Rock, Massachusetts has been a land of opportunity where the poor and downtrodden can find their fortunes. Some of the Bay State's most obvious examples of poor folk who became fabulously rich folk are the eighteenth-century son of a tallow chandler, who became Founding Father Benjamin Franklin, as well as the entire Kennedy clan. But one of the lesser sung poor-boys-made-good was Timothy Dexter, who went to work on a farm in 1756 when he was just nine years old and died fifty years later in his mansion as Lord Timothy Dexter, one of the richest men in the state.

The thing is, Lord Timothy wasn't actually a lord at all. He was just extremely eccentric. And after a slow start, he made enough money that he could afford to be any way he wanted. After graduating from his apprenticeship as a leatherworker at the age of twenty-two, he settled in Newburyport and married a widow with four children. He was pretty much uneducated and semiliterate at best, but he worked hard and somehow saved up several thousand dollars in gold. In a move that looked insane, he blew his entire stash on Continental currency right in the middle of the War of Independence. Trading gold for paper currency during a revolution was crazy behavior, but it paid off after the United States was formed. When Alexander Hamilton persuaded Congress to establish a national bank to back the Continental currency, Timothy Dexter became a fabulously rich man.

The mansion of Lord Timothy Dexter in High Street, Newburyport, 1810.

Pickle for the Knowing Ones
Plain Truths in a Homespun Dress

By Lord Timothy Dexter

By Lord IME the first Lord in the younited
States of A mericary Now of Newburyport
it is the voise of the peopel and I cant Help it
and so Let it goue Now as I must be Lord
there will foller many more Lor[d]s ... M soune
for it dont hurt A Cat Nor the ... r the
son Nor the water Nor the Ea... ue on a
ll is Easey Now bons broake... ll al...
Love Now I be gin to Lay th... to
the kee ston with grat Reme...
father Jorge Washington the gr... hei
...treys past

In the following years, Dexter entered into a series of crazy-looking schemes, such as exporting bed-warming pans to the always warm Caribbean islands and sending ships full of Virginia coal to Newcastle, England, which was at the time fueling the Industrial Revolution out of its own enormous coal mines. Both of these contrarian ventures were absurdly successful. The warming pans were perfect for rendering-down molasses, a primary industry in the West Indies, and Newcastle's coal production had stalled because of a prolonged miners' strike.

It was then that Timothy Dexter's eccentricities began to enter a new phase. Newburyport society barely tolerated this uncouth nouveau riche man, and refused to accept his money for public works projects, because they didn't want to have streets and public buildings named after him. So he skipped town for New Hampshire. When he returned to Newburyport the following year, he was calling himself Lord Timothy Dexter, because, he insisted, the honor had been thrust upon him by the will of the people. He commissioned life-size wooden statues of famous world leaders, including the Emperor of China, Benjamin Franklin, King George IV of England, and, naturally, himself. In fact, he commissioned two statues of himself, which were inscribed with the modest claims I AM THE FIRST IN THE EAST, THE FIRST IN THE WEST and I AM THE GREATEST PHILOSOPHER IN THE WESTERN WORLD.

As if this behavior weren't strange enough, he published a book of philosophy called *A Pickle for the Knowing Ones* (subtitled *Plain Truths in a Homespun Dress*), in which he used the most bizarre and inconsistent spelling. Even in a time before Noah Webster published the first American dictionary, people had some consistency in the way they spelled words. Not so

Lord Timothy Dexter. He declared that he was "the first Lord in Americake" or "the first Lord in the younited States of A mericary," and went on to include the following nuggets of philosophy:

> A sitteson must doue sumthing in the Com younity
> Everyeye annemal will doue for sumthing
> a good laff is beter than crying
> Renoue brotherly Love Dont brake the Chane
> Amen Amen All is well All in Love

To add luster to the eccentric spelling, Lord Timothy included no punctuation at all in the first edition of his book. The second edition made up for this by including a page full of commas, periods, exclamation points, and question marks, with instruction for his readers to "peper and solt it as they please."

The Dexter household now included a New Hampshire fishmonger as official poet laureate, whose poetry, though terrible, was at least spelled correctly.

> Lord Dexter is a man of Fame
> Most celebrated is his Name
> More precious far than gold that's pure
> Lord Dexter shines forevermore.

But Dexter's strange behavior concealed the fact that he had become a sick man. His health had been failing for some time when, three months short of his sixtieth birthday, he died. His will revealed that he had blown a fair amount of his considerable fortune, but had left behind enough to show his snobby neighbors how to die with style: He was to be buried in a plain grave (which still stands on the Old Hill Burying Grounds near the Bartlett Mall in Newburyport), and a portion of his money should be used to establish a fund to aid the poor. In the end, despite his odder side, perhaps he did prove himself a great philosopher after all.–*Matt Lake*

The Great Gadsby

The Bay State has produced more than its fair share of brilliant and celebrated authors, ranging from Henry David Thoreau and Emily Dickinson to John Updike and Dr. Seuss. But few people have heard of Ernest Vincent Wright, the man who achieved a massive literary feat. He wrote a novel called *Gadsby*, a work of 50,000 words, none of which contains the letter *e*.

A piece of writing that deliberately avoids using a letter is called a lipogram, and the hardest type of lipogram is the one that avoids *e*. This letter appears in English words five times more often than any other. So who is the towering man of letters (or at least twenty-five of them) who managed to pull off this strange work of art?

Little is known about Wright's life. We do know that he entered M.I.T.'s School of Mechanical Arts in 1888. The few articles we have dug up describe him as a retired navy musician. He's known to have been born in 1872 and died in 1939, the same year that *Gadsby* was published, and he wrote several whimsical books beforehand.

Apart from that, the details are pretty sketchy until the last year of his life, when, in his own words, his "somewhat balky nature" was roused by constantly hearing people claim "you cannot say anything at all without using *e*, and make smooth continuity, with perfectly grammatical construction." He chose to prove such blowhards wrong, and in the introduction to his book (the only part that he allowed to contain the letter *e*), he described the challenges he faced:

> The greatest of these is met in the past tense of verbs, almost all of which end with "—ed. . . ." The numerals also cause plenty of trouble, for none between six and thirty are available. . . . Many abbreviations also must be avoided; the most common of all, "Mr." and "Mrs." being particularly troublesome; for those words, if read aloud, plainly indicate the E in their orthography. . . .
> Many may think that I simply "drop" the E's, filling the gaps with apostrophes. A perusal of the book will show that this is not so. All words used are complete; are correctly spelled and properly used. This has been accomplished through the use of synonyms. . . .

And the synonyms were not always elegant ones. For the first time in centuries, a face is invariably called a physiognomy. Eyes are regularly orbs. But Wright claims up front in his introduction that this book was not an "attempt to attain literary merit," just to prove blowhards wrong. The story itself is pleasant enough and revolves—like *The Great Gatsby*, the novel to which the author was clearly alluding—around youth in a particular town.

So how did this literary giant manage to stick to his *e*-less challenge? Well, he reveals his secret at the end of the book's introduction, and it's a simple mechanical trick as befits a practical Massachusetts man who graduated from the School of Mechanical Arts:

> Of course anybody can write such a story. All that is needed is a piece of string tied from the E type-bar down to some part of the base of the typewriter. Then simply go ahead and type your story. Incidentally, you should have some sort of a bromide preparation handy, for use when the going gets rough, as it most assuredly will!

Despite the simplicity of this approach, few have attempted to produce a lipogram of this length and still fewer have come close to achieving it. Of course, the book's hard to find these days. In a neat twist of irony, the best place to track it down is on-line. That's right—the best way to find the most famous *e*-free book is through e-commerce, possibly on eBay. Go figure.—*Matt Lake*

Albert DeSalvo— the Boston Strangler?

Frustrated women
Have to be in by twelve o'clock
But I'm wishin' and a-hopin', oh
That just once those doors weren't
locked.

—from "Dirty Water" by The Standells

This eerie lyric is from a hit song written from the perspective of the Boston Strangler. The Strangler was the serial killer (or killers) who terrorized Boston between June 14, 1962, and January 4, 1964.

The first victim was fifty-five-year-old Anna E. Slesers, who lived on Gainsborough Street in the Back Bay section of Boston. On the evening of June 14, 1962 Anna had just taken a bath and was getting ready for a church service. She was waiting for her son to pick her up. A few minutes before seven p.m., Slesers's son knocked on the door. When she didn't answer, he shoved the door in with his shoulder. Anna's naked body was lying on the bathroom floor with the cord from her bathrobe tied in a lethal bow around her neck. Though the apartment had been ransacked to look like a robbery gone bad, obvious items like a gold watch and other pieces of jewelry were left behind. There was no sign of forced entry, which led police to believe that Anna knew her killer—or at the very least, she trusted the person enough to let him in.

About two weeks later, sixty-eight-year-old Nina Nichols was killed in her apartment on Commonwealth Avenue in Brighton. Another ransacked apartment, another dead woman found half naked, this time with her nylon stockings tied in a bow around her neck. Later that same day, just a few miles away in Lynn, sixty-five-year-old Helen Blake met a similar fate. She was also found with her nylons tied around her neck. The police now knew they had a serial

If he saw a woman he liked, he'd introduce himself under a false name and claim he worked for a modeling agency.

killer on their hands. The assailant appeared to be targeting older women who lived alone.

Victim number four, a seventy-five-year-old widow, came in August. Greater Boston was now entrenched in fear. Women who lived alone were setting glass bottles up in front of their door to alert them if the door opened. Of course, none of this did much good considering there was never a sign of forced entry.

After a three-month pause in killings, a fifth victim was found on December 5, 1962—an attractive, twenty-one-year-old African American student who lived in Back Bay. This murder created a big problem for police because their serial killer had previously only gone after older white women. The latest victim opened the already enormous suspect field even further and muddied the theory water some more.

Over the next thirteen months, six more single female victims turned up. Bostonians were buying so many deadbolts for their doors that the hardware stores couldn't keep them in stock. The state offered a $10,000 reward for information leading to the Strangler's arrest, and the media was in a frenzy trying to publish as many details as possible—a turn of events that infuriated law enforcement because it opened up the possibility of copycat murders. Thugs and burglars could simply strangle their victim, tie an article of clothing around the body's neck, and

walk away leaving police to think the Boston Strangler had struck again.

Though the police and the special investigative unit called the Strangler Bureau assigned to the case believed there was more than one culprit, the public believed the Boston Strangler to be one man terrorizing the greater metropolitan area. There were a few instances of witnesses' spotting a stranger walking around their apartment building. One woman claimed she allowed a man into her apartment who said he had been sent by the building superintendent to see if it needed painting. When the man made a remark about the woman's being attractive, she got nervous, made a shushing sound, and whispered that her husband was sleeping in the next room. The alleged painter got uncomfortable and left in a hurry, claiming that he was in the wrong apartment. That same day, a Strangler victim was found in the same building, and the woman who had let the man into her apartment found out that the superintendent had not sent anyone that day to see if any apartments needed painting.

The break in the case didn't come overnight. Instead, one really odd individual began to emerge from the depths of strange-crime files.

It seems that back around 1960, a man was going door to door looking for young, attractive women. If he saw a woman he liked, he'd introduce himself under a false name and claim he worked for a modeling agency. "You were referred to us as a potential model who could make forty dollars an hour" was something like the scam he delivered. He said that all he needed to do was get some basic information and take the young woman's measurements. When he left after sizing up the young women, he'd tell them that the agency would be in contact with them. Of course there was no contact, nor any agency—just a pervert.

The "Measuring Man" turned out to be a weirdo named Albert DeSalvo. He was busted on March 17, 1961, while breaking into a house in Cambridge. He confessed to measuring these women because he wasn't a good-looking man, nor well-educated, but he was able to outsmart these "high-class people," as he called them.

DeSalvo was a family man from Malden who worked in a rubber factory by day, and the judge went easy on him, sentencing him to only eighteen months in jail because he was his family's breadwinner. He was released from jail in April 1962 for good behavior. The first Strangler murder occurred two months later.

In November 1964, DeSalvo was arrested after breaking into an apartment and threatening a newly married woman who lay dozing. Before things went too far, though, he apparently felt guilty, begged for forgiveness, and then fled. The witness worked with police to develop a sketch of the man. When the cops saw the sketch, they recognized him as the Measuring Man. After the circulation of his picture, other victims came forward and identified DeSalvo as the "Green Man," an offender who wore green work pants when breaking into women's homes.

Still, police didn't believe he was the Boston Strangler: From interviews with his boss, neighbors, friends, and family, they didn't think he was capable of murder. So DeSalvo was sent to Bridgewater State Hospital for evaluation. While there, he met George Nassar, a man with a genius IQ who had been charged with a horrific murder of a gas station attendant.

Many have speculated that Nassar was the one who convinced DeSalvo to confess to the Strangler crimes. He was looking at a long prison stretch anyway, the theory goes, and one way to help take care of his family would be to collect the $10,000 reward offered for the Strangler. DeSalvo may also have figured he could sell his story and make a fortune to leave to his wife and children. For whatever reason, the guy known as both the Measuring Man and the Green Man now confessed to also being the Boston Strangler.

Police were doubtful at first, but DeSalvo knew an incredible amount of details about each crime. He knew the layouts of the apartments, and he knew how the victims were discovered. Skeptics pointed out that many of these details had appeared in the newspapers, and DeSalvo had a near-photographic memory—maybe he was reciting what he read. But DeSalvo also knew information that hadn't made the papers.

Perhaps because of some weaknesses in the case against him, DeSalvo's attorney was able to negotiate life in prison as opposed to execution. The life sentence didn't last very long for Albert DeSalvo: He was stabbed to death in November 1973 at Walpole State Prison. The night before his murder, DeSalvo contacted a few people, including a reporter, and asked them to come down to the prison the next morning because he was going to reveal who the Boston Strangler really was. He never had that chance to talk. Shortly before his death, DeSalvo penned this poem:

Here is the story of the Strangler, yet untold,
The man who claims he murdered thirteen women,
young and old.
The elusive Strangler, there he goes,

Where his wanderlust sends him, no one knows
He struck within the light of day,
Leaving not one clue astray.
Young and old, their lips are sealed,
Their secret of death never revealed.
Even though he is sick in mind,
He's much too clever for the police to find.
To reveal his secret will bring him fame,
But burden his family with unwanted shame.
Today he sits in a prison cell,
Deep inside only a secret he can tell.
People everywhere are still in doubt,
Is the Strangler in prison or roaming about?

Doubts lingered for decades and in 2001 the family of Albert DeSalvo and Mary Sullivan (one of the Boston Strangler's victims) had Sullivan's body exhumed to run a DNA test. On December 13, 2001, it was reported that the DNA evidence found on Mary Sullivan did not match that of Albert DeSalvo, which means either DeSalvo wasn't the Boston Strangler or he was, but he wasn't working alone.

So is the Boston Strangler still at large? Was the Boston Strangler really criminal mastermind George Nassar, who manipulated DeSalvo into confessing? The debate has been the subject of many books and televised programs. Even politicians in Texas have weighed in on the matter.

Weird Texans Meet the Boston Strangler

In 1971, Tom Moore Jr., a legislator in the state of Texas, introduced a measure to the Texas house of representatives that would officially commend Albert DeSalvo for his service to his country, his state, and his community. Representative Moore wanted to prove a point: that no one in his state's house of representatives actually reads the resolutions they pass.

Tom Moore's resolution said of DeSalvo: "[T]his compassionate gentleman's dedication and devotion to his work has enabled the weak and the lonely throughout the nation to achieve and maintain a new degree of concern for their future. He has been officially recognized by the state of Massachusetts for his noted activities and unconventional techniques involving population control and applied psychology."

After the resolution was passed with a unanimous vote, Tom Moore proved his point by informing his colleagues that they had just passed a resolution honoring the man convicted of being the Boston Strangler.

It's All About Benjamin, Baby

Philadelphia may lay claim to him, but Benjamin Franklin was born on January 17, 1706, on Milk Street in Boston and is arguably Massachusetts's all-time favorite son. The man on the $100 bill made more contributions to art, science, literature, philosophy, and politics than all the other men on U.S. currency combined.

When Ben was twelve years old, he became an apprentice to his brother, James, who was a printer and the publisher of the *New England Courant*, the first independent newspaper in the colonies. Ben asked to write for the paper, and when his older brother denied him permission, he adopted the pseudonym Mrs. Silence Dogood. Under that name, he contributed satirical letters to the paper aimed at the Puritan leaders of Boston. Dogood was actually a cut on Cotton Mather, the Puritan priest made famous during the Salem witch trials and a wordsmith himself who wrote "Essays to Do Good." James Franklin was none the wiser that Mrs. Dogood, whose letters to the paper were stirring up controversy around town, was actually his younger brother.

Ben's Weirdest Invention

Franklin was also an inventor with many creations to his name: the lightning rod, Franklin stove, bifocal glasses, and the flexible urinary catheter, just to name a few. But his weirdest and also his favorite invention was a musical instrument called the glass armonica.

When living in England, Ben Franklin watched Edmund Hussey Delaval playing musical scores on wineglasses filled with different amounts of liquid to produce specific tones. Franklin loved the sound but saw many flaws with making music this way. For one, it was a great deal of trouble to place so many wineglasses in a position for the player to easily get to them, plus each glass had to be a precise size and filled with a precise amount of liquid. The last limitation was that the player could play only two notes at once.

To get around these problems, Franklin had thirty-seven glass bowls of varying sizes made, placed them on a spindle, and rigged the spindle to a foot treadle. The player pumped the treadle to spin the glasses, and with

wet hands could play not only single notes like Delaval, but also chords. He called it the glass armonica after the Italian word for harmony, and claimed, "Its tones are incomparably sweet beyond those of any other."

Composers and great thinkers were captivated by the glass armonica's angelic sound. Mozart wrote music for the instrument, as did Beethoven. Tchaikovsky wrote "Dance of the Sugar Plum Fairy," the famous piece in *The Nutcracker* ballet, specifically for Franklin's glass armonica.

Today there are only a handful of armonica players, among them William Zeitler. He's based in Los Angeles and performs with the exotic instrument about one hundred and twenty times per year. Zeitler said, "When Franklin invented it, we were a little busy with the American Revolution and trying to get started as a country. There was music going on here in the States, but

of course it developed terribly because we were a little preoccupied. And then England, after the Revolution, was not terribly interested in the glass armonica because it was invented by that traitor, Ben Franklin. France was a little busy with their own Revolution, and for some reason, it just really struck the German psyche, and they went crazy over it."

Zeitler is on a mission to introduce the listening public to an instrument that is on what he calls the "endangered species" list. If he has his way, Benjamin Franklin's favorite, albeit weirdest invention, will never stop being played.

The New England Society for the Suppression of Vice

What would a PTA meeting be without that overzealous mom in the back yelling, "Think of the children!" Sometimes enough of these types of people get together and form a larger group with the aim of deciding what is morally right and wrong for every one else. Just such a group met in Boston on May 31, 1878, at Park Street Church. The group decided to call themselves the New England Society for the Suppression of Vice. Their objective: to suppress vile publications and manufactures, and to promote public morality. The group quickly rose to power and prominence, especially in Boston.

Who were some of the ne'er-do-wells that the society had in its crosshairs? Evildoers like poet Walt Whitman, who published a collection of poems called *Leaves of Grass* in 1855. The collection grew more popular with subsequent printings, and more poems were added. In 1882, the New England Society for the Suppression of Vice urged Boston district attorney Oliver Stevens to write a letter to Whitman's publisher, James R. Osgood. The letter said, in part, "We are of the opinion that this book is such a book as brings it within the provisions of the Public Statutes respecting obscene literature and suggest the propriety of withdrawing the same from circulation and suppressing the editions thereof." The society took particular offense to the poems "A Woman Waits for Me" and "To a Common Prostitute."

Osgood, apparently not a man to withstand pressure, caved in and refused to republish the collection again. So NESSV won that war, but not the battle. Whitman received the rights to his poems back and sold the work to publisher Rees Welsh. The publicity from the case fueled sales, and the label BANNED IN BOSTON became almost sought-after — kind of like the PARENTAL ADVISORY label on music sold today. No kid wants to own a CD that doesn't have the warning label.

Under the leadership of Frederick Bayles Allen, the NESSV changed its name in 1891 to the New England Watch and Ward Society, as a nod to the "old Watch and Ward Society . . . a volunteer police force which, here in Boston, patrolled the streets at night protecting citizens from peril, from disorder, and from vice." Their objective became more focused: "The object of this society is to remove commercialized temptations to vice and crime. . . ."

The Watch and Ward Society was a powerful influence in Boston for decades, succeeding in getting the Boston Public Library to keep books they considered subversive in a locked room. But in 1926, the group overstepped itself. It took aim at H. L. Mencken's *American Mercury* magazine for a short story by Herbert Asbury called "Hatrack,"

which was published in the periodical.

Mencken personally and ceremoniously sold a copy of his magazine to John Chase of the NEWWS while the media and police looked on. When the transaction was complete, Mencken was arrested. A legal battle ensued that ultimately ruled that the magazine was not obscene. Mencken then successfully sued the NEWWS for illegal restraint of trade. The lawsuit marked the beginning of the end for the NEWWS.

In subsequent years, the society blacklisted a number of books, including Aldous Huxley's *Point Counter Point*, Voltaire's *Candide*, and Erich Maria Remarque's *All Quiet on the Western Front*, but BANNED IN BOSTON was turning into a badge of honor for authors. The label meant extra attention and extra sales.

Over the years, the society has renamed itself, merged with other like-minded organizations, and changed its mission to include such worthy causes as promoting respect for law and order, integrity in business and the professions, a wholesome social life, and constructive responsibility in civic affairs. Today it is folded into a group called the Community Resources for Justice. Chief Executive Officer John Larivee says of the organization, "We describe our historical mission in current language as public order and safety. We're not banning books anymore."

So Walt Whitman is okay with you now?

"Yes, he is," Larivee said.

In all seriousness, the Community Resources for Justice works to help three groups of people: adult offenders who are coming out of the prison system, juvenile delinquents, and the mentally retarded and developmentally disabled.

"One of our board members has a bumper sticker that says Someone's Gotta Do It," Larivee said.

Personalized Properties

Massachusetts *is the site* of the first Pilgrim colony, and thus afforded the first opportunity for our odd-hatted forebears to customize their new homeland with unique stuff that screams, "Look at me!" But the Pilgrims weren't much for standing out in a crowd and didn't capitalize on the chance they were given in the New World. Too bad for them, but lucky for *Weird Massachusetts,* the Pilgrims' descendants and many others have taken up the cause with typical Yankee ingenuity. So that's why the Bay State is home to the first museum completely and utterly dedicated to . . . thermometers. We've got a house made of paper, one that looks like it's on a diet, and another with a gingerbread castle design that inspires people to go off their diets. The personalization spreads outside too. A proud son of Massachusetts has made it possible for pink plastic flamingos to grace lawns across America. And Harvard Bridge is the only bridge in the world that's measured in five-foot seven-inch increments called smoots, named after a Lambda Chi Alpha pledge. It's really weird everywhere you look around here.

Tour Hammond's Castle

Known as the Father of Remote Control, John Hays Hammond Jr. has more patents filed than anyone on record but Thomas Edison. He also had some decidedly peculiar ideas about some things. Hammond's Castle, the inventor's home and workplace in Gloucester, offers a glimpse into the strange life of this strange man.

The home has an imposing drawbridge out front and the world's largest privately owned pipe organ inside. It also boasts its own dungeon.

Among Hammond's eccentricities were his instructions for his own burial. He was placed in a crypt with a number of mummified cats, and had ordered that the crypt be covered in poison ivy for protection. Despite these paranoid precautions, his crypt was broken into and his skull stolen, although it was later recovered. The next time you are in Gloucester, be sure to check out this very odd place.

Hammond's Weirder Side

Hammond Castle is a medieval-style castle on the coast of Gloucester. According to the website www.Hammondcastle.org, Hammond, ". . . built his medieval-style castle between the years 1926 and 1929 to serve both as his home and as a backdrop for his collection of Roman, medieval, and Renaissance artifacts. In addition, the building housed the Hammond Research Corporation, from which Dr. Hammond produced over 400 patents and the ideas for over 800 inventions. . . ."

That's their politically correct write-up on Hammond, but I have extra freaky info for you. First, the things that are public knowledge about Hammond:

■ One of his most treasured possessions is in the main hall: the skull of one of Christopher Columbus's crewmen.

■ There is an indoor pool, surrounded by a faux medieval village, which can be drained and filled with either fresh or salt water. The room has been rigged up to simulate different weather conditions.

■ One of the guest rooms has doors that effectively "vanish" when closed. Hammond would put passed-out party guests in that room, and in the morning they would be unable to find their way out.

■ His library/office was built in such a way that from anywhere in the room, you can clearly hear a whisper from the opposite side of the room.

■ He invented a full-sized, remote controlled boat, and—in the years before most people had ever heard of remote control—used it to terrorize local fishermen.

■ He hated the damage seagulls did to his castle roof and backyard and often mined the areas to blow up the birds. He overdid it a bit in the back yard and sent a large part of the land falling into the ocean.

■ His tomb—close to the castle and still guarded by barbed wire and poison ivy—looks like a set from a Conan movie and can be easily viewed from the water.

And now for the more macabre bits of info. Reliable sources say that Hammond was obsessed with trying to mix science with magic as a key to immortality. He had a nude, life-sized bronze statue of himself made, and his library was filled with books about occult practices dealing with immortality from different parts of the world. He is said to have built a contraption that was supposed to catch ghosts and reportedly kept his father's corpse in his basement lab for several years, attempting to reanimate it.

I asked the castle's live-in caretaker about this, and he

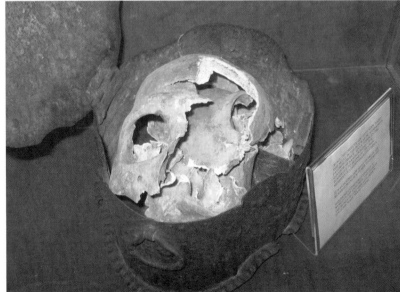

claimed it was all true, but not made public. He said some of Hammond's old associates are still alive and the people who own the castle don't want to embarrass them by publicizing the darker aspects of Hammond's experiments.

Another less-believable rumor regarding Hammond is that his fortunes were withdrawn from the bank mere days before his death, and that no one knows where the money went. Was Hammond anticipating a return visit and decided to put away a nest egg for himself?

It's interesting that author H. P. Lovecraft visited the castle at one point, and then went on to write horror tales about a mad scientist, living north of Salem, Massachusetts, who tried to raise the dead.—*Mike Carey*

Get a Reading on the Paper House

The construction of 52 Pigeon Hill Street in Rockport began in 1922 as a hobby for Mr. Elis F. Stenman, a mechanical engineer from Cambridge who designed the machines that make paper clips. He intended for the Rockport home to be his summer getaway. He built the frame, floor, and roof of the house in the traditional way— wooden studs and joists— but that's about the only part of the construction and house that IS traditional. Stenman built the rest of his summer home out of paper.

For the wall material, Elis took newspaper and other scraps and pressed them together, layer upon layer with glue and varnish, until the material was about one inch thick. The principle really isn't that different from modern-day plywood. According to Edna Beaudoin, who is Stenman's grandniece and the home's current curator, Elis initially intended to cover the outside of the house with clapboard siding, but he was curious about how the varnished paper would fare in the coastal winter. He figured the pressed paper would make for good insulation and nothing more, but when he saw he had no leaks after the house's first season, he stuck with paper.

With the siding up, Stenman got to work on furnishing his cottage. Friends and neighbors gave him their newspapers when they were finished with them, and the raw materials piled up. Elis rolled paper into

READ ALL ABOUT IT!

Amazing house built out of 100,000 newspapers

... And so is the furniture

When it comes to recycling, no one can top Elis Stenman — he built a house almost entirely out of 100,000 used newspapers!

What's more, every piece of furniture in the amazing house in Rockport, Mass., is also made of newspapers, including chairs, tables, a cot, lamps — even a grandfather clock.

One desk is built entirely of papers with headlines trumpeting Charles Lindbergh's historic first flight across the Atlantic.

A bookshelf is constructed only with foreign newspapers, sent to Stenman from embassies around the world.

The grandfather clock is made with newspapers from capital cities of 48 states.

Stenman, who died in 1942, used to read five newspapers a day; but the thrifty Swedish immigrant hated to throw them away.

"I always resisted the daily waste of newspapers after people read them for a few minutes," he once said, rolling them until he had a stiff paper for his project.

"He'd wrap the sheets of paper around a piece of fine wire, tightly

WHAT A PAD — OF PAPER! House is built entirely of newspapers except for frames, floor and chimney. Vivian Curtis, late builder's niece, plays on paper piano in living room. At left is grandfather clock, made up of tightly rolled papers.

---

dowel-shaped logs about half an inch thick and sealed them with glue and varnish. Using a knife, he cut the rolls into the lengths he wanted and built chairs, tables, and a desk. There's even a piano—though the instrument isn't fully constructed of paper, it is covered in rolls of the stuff. Stenman also covered a grandfather clock with paper from forty-eight states (at the time, Alaska and Hawaii weren't states yet).

The house always had electricity and even running water, but there were no bathrooms—which is a shame because there was always plenty to read.

Curiosity seekers asked to come inside as early as the 1930s, but it wasn't until Mrs. Stenman died in 1942 that the building opened as a museum. The cost was ten cents to visit. Today admission will set you back a buck and a half, but it's worth every penny to see what one man can do with so much free time.

THE PIANO IS COVERED WITH ROLLS OF PAPER

Black Church of Salem

One particular tourist draw that's not supposed to be a tourist draw in Salem (as opposed to the many wacky museums) is the former church that was bought a few years ago, painted black, and turned into some sort of home base for the black arts. All I know is that the owner drives a hearse, has placed two very large gargoyles on front of the door, burns red candles on the steps at Halloween, and has a plaque that says NOT A CHURCH, GET OVER IT near the front door.

This in a town with avowed Satanists (watch your cats every Halloween folks—there have been some nasty cat sacrifices in the not too distant past). It could be a total joke or real, who knows?

It was actually for sale for a while, but unfortunately they had taken down the FOR SALE sign by the time I got there

to take pictures. I'm not sure if they have either sold the place or else got so sick of prospective "buyers" actually just being curiosity seekers wanting to know what the inside looks like.

What can I say? It's Salem!—*Caroline Angel*

"Not a Church" Explained

A friend of mine, whose legal name is Davinya DiVinchi, owned the "Black Church" in Salem for a number of years. She's an antiques dealer and she furnished the first floor with all sorts of period furniture but also had hidden modern appliances throughout. It was simply her house. And although she did purchase a hearse, it was never repaired and rarely driven. She put the NOT A CHURCH—GET OVER IT sign up because people would constantly knock on her door at all hours of the night.—*Script*

Getting the Skinny on One Strange House

Boston's Hull Street is home to the skinniest house in the city. It's four stories tall and thirty feet long but just ten feet wide: so narrow that its entranceway is actually not on the front of the house, but rather on the side. Located across from the Copp's Hill burial ground, the house is most likely just a relic from a past era, when many homes were constructed in a similar fashion. Rumors still persist that it was built for the sole purpose of blocking the view of a family member the builder despised.

Tyringham's Gingerbread House

Sir Henry Hudson Kitson was a well-known sculptor who lived and died in America but was knighted for his work in his native Britain. While his sculptures themselves speak to his legacy, one of his most consuming projects was no sculpture at all, but his very own home. Known formally as Santarella, the building is known more popularly as the Tyringham Gingerbread House, because that's exactly what it looks like. The strange dwelling creates the vibe of a fantasy world, and visitors come from afar to experience it.

While Kitson was quite successful, his house actually came to consume him, and he died penniless in 1947 after sinking his fortune into it. For example, he employed three workers for twelve full years just to complete the incredible roof. Kitson was driven by this project, to say the least.

While that drive may have eventually bankrupted and ruined the man, his final work still stands and is open for tours. To see one of the most magnificent personalized properties in the entire country, make sure you swing through Tyringham soon.

Smooting Across Harvard Bridge

Spanning the Charles River and connecting Boston to Cambridge, Harvard Bridge is better known to Massachusetts Institute of Technology students by its more beloved name––Smoot Bridge. Since 1958, the bridge has been known as such, in honor of the man it was measured by, Mr. Oliver R. Smoot.

A few members of the Lambda Chi Alpha fraternity found themselves consistently angered at having to walk over the long bridge without any indicators of its length remaining. So as part of their pledging process that year, they decided that their incoming members would measure the bridge and mark it for them. And they wouldn't use feet, yards, or meters. Instead, they'd be working in Smoots—five-foot seven-inch-long measures of distance that matched the exact height of their shortest pledge that year, Mr. Smoot.

The pledges sneaked onto the bridge, where Smoot would lay down, and they marked where his head and feet lay with bright paint. They did this three hundred times that night before nearly being captured by police; they returned later to finish the job.

Each year the fraternity repaints the numbers to mark the Smoots. A couple of decades back the police stopped hassling them for it, as even they find the markings useful. The last time the city rebuilt the bridge, they used five-foot seven-inch-long sidewalk blocks instead of the customary six-foot-long ones.

Mr. Smoot is still alive and gets a kick out of being a campus legend. In a 2005 article, he told the *Washington Post* that "the first time I went to an MIT gathering of undergraduates, I introduced myself to this young man, and he said 'Oh, I thought you were dead.'"

The bridge, which is exactly 364.4 Smoots long, is still repainted every year.

Barbie's Garden— Mattapoisett

Most people, when they get a little tired of the Barbie™ dolls they or their kids have accumulated, find ways to get rid of them. The carefully preserved ones go up for sale, perhaps on eBay, and the well-loved ones . . . well, sometimes they linger in storage before hitting the garage sales or taking that last, long trip to the land of garbage. Unless you can find another way to use them.

That's the case in Mattapoisett, where Stefani Koorey discovered the Barbie Doll Garden. Just behind a sturdy fence and to one side of the walkway leading to a well-maintained home, you'll find a plastic flora of not only Barbies but also their must-have accessories like a pink jeep and a gazebo. Mixed in with the dolls are small plastic dinosaurs, snakes, and lizards, all living in harmony in the front yard. And in case you weren't sure what you were looking at, a stone to one side clearly declares it the BARBIE GARDEN.

As Stefani told us, the Barbie Garden is "odd and wonderful at the same time."

Is It Hot in Here? The Thermometer Museum

Dick Porter, of Onset, has been building his collection of over 5,000 thermometers since the mid-1980s. They're all located in his home's small basement, which he calls the world's largest and only thermometer museum. He's certainly passionate about his collection, and he's been an invited speaker at more than a few thermometer and weather related events, like the christening of the world's largest thermometer in Baker, California.

Porter values the collection at about four dollars per piece. Visitors should expect him to be an active docent. He has stories about many of the thermometers, even some memories of the day the scientific community decided to honor Anders Celsius by eponymously renaming his centigrade scale.

A visit here conjures first the amusement at Porter's passion for thermometers, then a little bit of fear as you contemplate the confined quarters of his basement museum and his refusal to accept your polite excuses to leave.

You can find the Thermometer Museum at 49 Zarahemla Road. It is strongly recommended that visitors give Mr. Porter a call at (508) 295-5504 to confirm he'll be home to host you.

–Casey Bisson

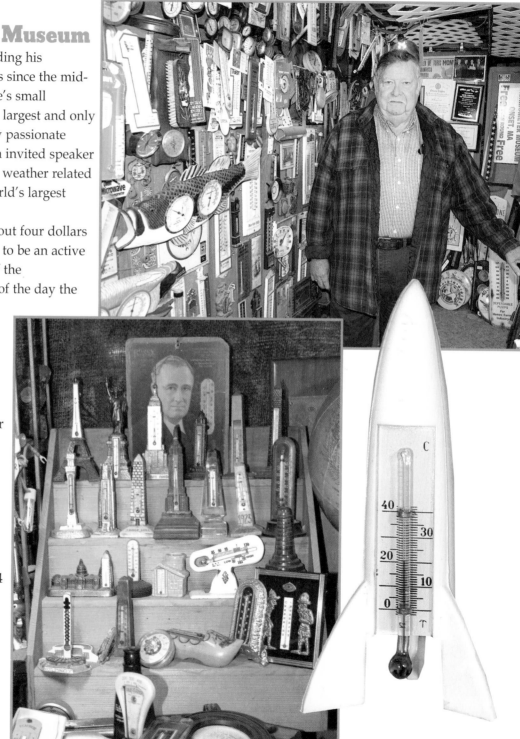

Tacky Yard Art Born in Leominster!

The Bay State's past is both proud and storied, serving as the birthplace of the American Revolution, Benjamin Franklin, and the telephone. And not for nuthin', but we're also the birthplace of the plastic pink flamingo lawn ornament—an object that can class up even the white-trashiest of front yards.

Inexpensive lawn ornamentation is a direct result of the rise of suburbia. After World War II, neighborhoods of affordable housing popped up on the outskirts of cities and large towns all over the United States. Developers built streets where every house was identical to the one next to it, but it was a place to park your Chevy and raise your 2.5 kids. The only way to express your individuality was with decoration, and a company called Union Products of Leominster responded to that need.

Union Products did a moderate business of selling flat plastic lawn ornaments, but the public demanded more. In 1956, the company asked recent art school graduate Donald Featherstone about creating the next big thing in lawn novelty.

"Everybody was graduating, and you had to do something," said Featherstone. "You had the choice of going in the attic and painting and starving to death, you could go out and become an art teacher, or be an industrial designer of some sort. And even before Mrs. Robinson thought of it, everybody was saying, 'Gee, plastic is pretty good right about now,' and the technology was just getting to the point where you could actually make some nice things out of it."

The company asked Featherstone if he could sculpt and do three-dimensional work, which he could. His first three-dimensional creation for them was a duck named Charlie, but it is his sophomore design effort that we remember him for. Union Products had a flat silk-screened flamingo that it wanted to turn into a three-dimensional piece. Featherstone turned to images in *National Geographic* and made a clay model that the company used to churn out its version: yellow beak with a black tip, pink body, and Don Featherstone's signature under the tail. The real thing is sold only in pairs.

The original set of pink flamingo lawn ornaments wholesaled for about $1.98. Oddly enough, the product was not the company's best seller, but it was the item everyone knew them for. Featherstone, who rose through the ranks at Union Products and eventually became its president, estimates that the pink flamingo sold between 250,000 and 400,000 units per year when they were in production. "Back in 1990, we figured there were at least 20 million sets out there— and that's on the conservative side."

Featherstone didn't realize just how big a hit his plastic product was until 1987—the thirtieth anniversary. "I was surprised that people were having flamingo parties," he said. "People would have the yard full of flamingos and about one hundred fifty of their best friends over, and then I started getting calls that they wanted me to go and attend these parties. We had a lot of fun, and the publicity helped the company out."

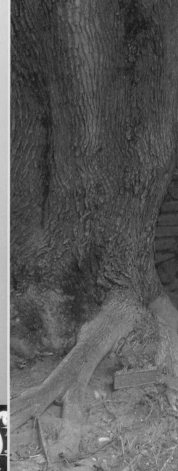

Even today there are fund-raisers that involve the plastic pink flamingo lawn ornaments. For example, a church in Pittsburgh recently began planting dozens of flamingos on the lawns of their church members. They call it being "flocked." The homeowner then pays the church for their removal.

Featherstone retired in 2000, but his famous flamingos were still produced after he left the company. A few years ago, the manufacturer briefly removed his signature from the birds, and fans were outraged. They called for an international boycott of any flamingos that didn't bear the creator's name. The public outcries were heard, and the signature was restored.

Some of the other honors Featherstone has received include Harvard's Ig Nobel Prize from the humor magazine *Annals of Improbable Research (AIR)*. The award goes to achievements that "first make people laugh, and then make them think."

Featherstone and his wife, Nancy, still live in central Massachusetts. For many years, Don would set out fifty-seven flamingos on his lawn to commemorate 1957—the year the product was introduced. Sadly, 2007, the fiftieth anniversary, marked the year he had to stop. Union Products had closed its doors, citing the high cost of production and financial problems. Because the Featherstone pink flamingo had been discontinued,

people were stealing them and selling them on eBay. But today a new company has acquired the molds, and like a pink plastic phoenix, Featherstone's creation looks ready to rise again.

There is one large version still standing on the Featherstone property. Don calls it the Estate Flamingo for people with large lawns and grand front driveways, so visitors can see it from a distance and through the iron gates. His tongue is often firmly in his cheek when he talks about lawn decorating. "With our plastic products," he says, "we brought poor taste to the poor people."

The Passion of Noel Dube

A personalized property in Pepperell was inspired by motives more noble than individual vanity. In fact, Mr. Noel Dube was divinely inspired. It began with one of those inexplicable things, one of those unanswerable questions: Why does the Virgin Mary come a-calling? And when she does, why does she call upon the most unlikely people?

series of devotional paintings. By 1991, tucked away behind a hedgerow, giant vibrantly colored scenes began to appear. The most conspicuous may be the twenty-two by sixty-foot mural reproducing the miraculous visions experienced in Fatima, Portugal, in 1917. There, witnessed by thousands of people, the sun—or possibly a UFO—went streaking across the sky. This alleged miracle gives Mr. Dube's shrine its name: the Our Lady of Fatima Community Shrine.

There is an assortment of religious statues, walkways, benches, grottoes, and gardens at the shrine. On the far side of the yard, you can see a twelve-by thirty-foot, gold-framed portrait of Jesus. It's as tall as a three-story house. And in between, in lurid comic book colors, there are fourteen stations of the cross in which the gory events at Calvary are graphically depicted.

Although none of this can be described as subtle, there is a certain visionary quality about it. After all, Mr. Dube did anticipate Mel Gibson's *Passion* by over a decade.

Today a twenty-four-foot blue cross also adorns the property. It is brightly illuminated by lamps comparable to those used on motion picture sets. Neighbors can see the light clearly. In fact they can read by it inside their nearby houses.

When she spoke to Mr. Dube around 1990, she asked him to build her a community shrine. He agreed, of course. Who could refuse? But like the rest of us, he was inexperienced at shrine building. Also, due to age and a World War II disability, he was not wealthy. Still, he decided to give it his best shot: He would attempt to perform a miracle.

The only property he owned was his house at 47 Heald Street, so it was there that he'd build the shrine. First, he commissioned an artist, who went to work on a

So why a twenty-four-foot illuminated blue cross? Mr. Dube, who was born on Christmas Day in 1919, explains, "Jesus asked for it."

Our Lady of Fatima Community Shrine receives about four thousand visitors a year. We hope Jesus and His mother are as happy with Mr. Dube's work as we are.—*Joe Citro*

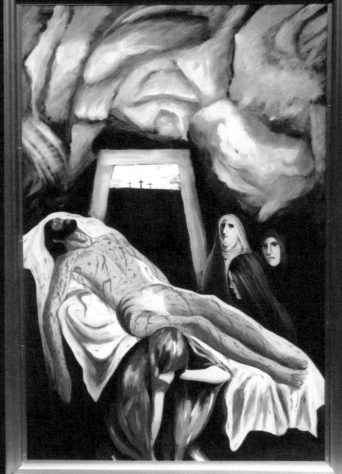

Roadside Oddities

Some people might think of Massachusetts as a stuffy place, full of historical landmarks and things your teachers made you learn in school. These people don't know the other side of the Bay State. From national landmarks that leave visitors with a sense of aw (as in: "Aw, where's the rest of it?") to some very odd museums that save things like burned food, old toilets, and retro plastic—there's no shortage of strange things here.

Massachusetts is proud to be home to some really bad artwork, some quintessential, yet very tacky Americana, and a lake with a name so long we don't dare write it out in the chapter introduction because there simply isn't space. And that's just for starters.

So let's explore. Strap on your seat belt, keep your eyes open and your hands and feet inside the Weird-mobile at all times. Some of our roadside oddities might stop you in your tracks!

Plymouth Rock

"That's it?" a modern-day passing tourist asked.

"That's it," his companion said.

"Huh."

Plymouth Rock could well be the most underwhelming national landmark in the United States. Why? Well, because it's just a rock. Even its scientific name: *Dedham granodiorite*, a form of glacial erratic rock, can't make this thing sexy. You can add a columned monument over it and fence the boulder within wrought iron, but you still have a rock. But damn it, it's our rock, and it's the country's first national landmark.

On December 11, 1620, William Bradford and a group of a few dozen other Separatist Puritans from England left the comfort of the Mayflower for the New World (read: The captain more than fulfilled his charter and kicked his passengers off after taking them south to the Hudson River in New York, north to modern-day Provincetown on the tip of Cape Cod, then finally into Cape Cod harbor to what would become modern-day Plymouth).

The only account we have of those early days comes from William Bradford's journal: "On Munday they sounded ye harbor and found it fitt for shipping; and marched into ye land, & found diverse cornfields, & little running brooks, a place fitt for situation. At least it was ye best they could find, and ye season, & their presente necessitie, made them glad to accepte of it. So they returned to their shippe again with this news to ye rest of their people, which did much comforte their harts."

They named their home Plymouth Colony after the port in England from which they had embarked. Someone noted a large rock near that first settlement as the first solid ground they stood on in this continent. For over a century, this nondescript rock at the foot of Cole's Hill fell into obscurity, until 1741 when the town began plans to build a wharf. The reason we still have Plymouth Rock today is that Thomas Faunce, a ninety-four-year-old church elder and town record-keeper, made a point of finding the actual rock his father had shown him as a boy.

"That's it?" the town surveyor asked.

"That's it," Thomas Faunce said.

"Huh."

In 1774, Plymouth decided to move the boulder to a more prominent location, but in doing so, they broke the rock in half. The bottom half was placed behind the wharf, and the top was moved to the town's meetinghouse. Then Plymouth shopkeepers, with their alchemical ingenuity, turned *Dedham granodiorite* into gold. With chisels and hammers in hand, they chipped away at Plymouth Rock and sold off egg-size chunks in their stores for $1.50.

In 1835, French historian Alexis-Charles-Henri Clérel de Tocqueville wrote of Plymouth's famous boulder: "This Rock has become an object of veneration in the United States. I have seen bits of it carefully preserved in several towns in the Union. Does this sufficiently show that all human power and greatness is in the soul of man? Here is a stone which the feet of a few outcasts pressed for an instant; and the stone becomes famous; it is treasured by a great nation; its very dust is shared as a relic."

Over the years, the rock was hauled around to various places in town. What was left of it ended up at a waterfront monument where a very Washington, DC-esque Roman Doric portico was added over the structure. During the rock's many travels, it had split in half again, and today visitors can plainly see the cement job that was used to piece the two sections together.

Yup, those first outcasts were set ashore right about on this spot. They walked on that rock to help found a nation of outcasts, throwaways, tired, poor, and huddled masses yearning to be free. The site may not be awe-inspiring, but the story is. Stand by the monument off Water Street long enough and you'll see tourists come and go. What the rock means to each will be different, but there is one conversation you'll hear again and again.

"That's it?" a tourist will ask.

"That's it," his companion will say.

Wall of Bones

I want to share with you the most astonishing moment of my vacation, which luckily I have photos of. While traipsing around a woods in northeastern Massachusetts I stumbled on one of the most breathtaking murals I've ever seen, partly so for its design and message, partly for how difficult it must have been traversing the rock face, but more so because it's hidden away, something found only by chance—the artist simply put their mural where they wanted and left it there to be noticed or not. The subject is rather intense: it's a 30-foot-high wall of multicolored bones and skulls, with a message to one side: "Take the knowledge that you will someday be these bones, and enjoy now all that is precious." —*Jim Moskowitz*

The Wall of Bones is located at the Kallenberg Quarry off Ledge Road in Lynnfield.

Lake Chargoggagoggmanchauggauggagoggchaubunagungamaugg

We bet we can make you talk Indian. How? Read this name out loud: Lake Chargoggagoggmanchauggauggagoggchaubunagungamaugg. While it may not be the deepest, widest, or coldest lake in the United States, no other lake in this country has a longer name. In fact, only five other locations in the world can boast more letters in their monikers. At a carpal-tunnel-inducing forty-nine letters, this lake has earned the town of Webster a spot on the international map. How is it pronounced? If you're going to say it like the locals do, it sounds something like this: *Web·ster Lake,* though *Web·stah Lake* is also acceptable.

Lake Chargoggagoggmanchauggauggagoggchaubunagungamaugg holds another etymological record. It has 17 *g*'s and 10 *a*'s. No other English word has so many. It was originally called Chabanaguncamogue, Chaubanagogum, or Chaubunagungamaug by the early Nipmucs. This word roughly translates to "Fishing place at the boundary." Later, the Monuhchogoks tribe began fishing at the other side of the lake. There was peace between the Nipmuc and the Monuhchogoks, and both fished the waters.

Around 1811, a third tribe entered the picture. Samuel Slater, who is considered the father of the American cotton industry, went searching for the perfect site to build a new mill. There had to be plenty of water and enough population nearby from which to draw labor. Slater had his associate purchase all the farmland and water flowage rights necessary to place his mill and have no questions about who had the right to the waterpower. When the textile plant broke ground alongside the lake near where the Monuhchogoks fished, the town of Webster was born. At Slater's request, the area was named Webster after Massachusetts Senator Daniel Webster. The Native Americans called Slater and his workers Chargoggagoggmanchauggauggagogg, which meant "Englishmen at Manchaug." Add the early name of the body of water and an extra *g* to the end of it all, and you have Lake Chargoggagoggmanchauggauggagoggchaubunagungamaugg, which roughly means "Englishmen at Manchaug at the Fishing Place at the Boundary" (though you can purchase bumper stickers at local gas stations that translate the phrase to: "You fishum on your side, I fishum on my side, nobody fishum in the middle").

The lake has long been neutral ground, where fishing was plentiful. Tribes from various nations would gather here for powwows, until the English came and settled along the shores. Though the official name is a mouthful, it's also a point of pride for Webster, as it can be found on overpasses, atop strip malls, and on other signs along the lake.

The welcome sign with one of many alternate spellings of the lake's name.

Where's the Beef?

On November 14, 1995, a cow named Emily jumped a gate at a slaughterhouse and ran for her life. For forty days, the cow was on the lam as various folks hid her and shuffled her to greener pastures. Soon international media was covering the bovine fugitive, and the cow caught the attention of Meg and Lewis Randa, the co-founders of the Peace Abbey in Sherborn. The couple invited Emily to live on their property.

Emily became a huge draw for the Peace Abbey.

Folks came to see the cow who escaped slaughter. Meg Randa claims that more than a few visitors swore off meat forever after staring into Emily's eyes.

Emily died of cancer on March 30, 2003, but that wasn't the end of her story. The Randas commissioned artist Lado Goudjabidze to create a life-size bronze statue of Emily—complete with blankets and flowers over her back, which is a Hindu sign of respect. The statue was dedicated on June 23, 2005, and today visitors are still drawn to this sacred cow in Sherborn.

The Former World's Largest Earth

Atlas was said to be able to lift the world on his shoulders. How does one get that strong? Lifting smaller worlds first, of course. Atlas may have gotten his start in Wellesley, on the campus of Babson College. On the front lawn of the Coleman Map Building is a twenty-eight-foot-diameter, 50,000 pound globe.

Built in 1955 by Roger Babson, the giant metal ball cost $200,000 and actually rotated on its axis and base to show not only day and night, but also the seasons. The ball held the record as the world's largest rotating globe until 1998 when the folks at the DeLorme Mapping Corporation in Yarmouth, Maine, eclipsed Babson's baby with a 56,000-pound, forty-one-foot-diameter rotating and revolving monster they call Eartha.

For decades, the Babson Globe was a true marvel, but in the 1980s, the ball started to deteriorate. The painted tiles were falling off, and by 1988 it was simply a ball of rust—a real eyesore. The college announced it would wreck the unsightly ball and remove it.

Students, alumni, and faculty were outraged and so began a drive to raise the funds necessary to restore it. In 1994, the refurbished globe was unveiled. Though it doesn't rotate any longer, it's still an impressive sight when one strolls up Map Hill Drive on the campus.

Apple Doesn't Fall Far from Sir Isaac Newton's Tree

Babson College is also home to a very special apple tree. This tree's roots go all the way back to 1666 in Lincolnshire, England, and a tree that inspired a physicist named Isaac Newton.

One day Newton was walking through a garden, all the while kicking around various ideas on motion and other forces in the universe, when something struck him. Newton's assistant, John Conduitt, later wrote about the incident: " . . . it came into his thought that the power of gravity (which brought an apple from a tree to the ground) was not limited to a certain distance from earth, but that this power must extend much further than was usually thought. Why not as high as the Moon said he to himself." Whether the apple actually hit Newton on his noggin can be left to the imagination, but what was born that day was Newton's theory on gravity.

Babson College's founder, Charles Babson, was obsessed with the idea of gravity. So it's not surprising that he would be very interested in Newton's tree. Near the center of the campus today, visitors will find a lone apple tree fenced in with wrought iron. It is a fifth-generation apple tree that was grown from a cutting of one of Newton's own trees at Woolsthorpe Manor in Lincolnshire.

Have a Seat . . . a Big One

Gardner, right here in the Bay State, is the self-proclaimed Chair City. In 1905, Gardner had twenty factories in town producing four million chairs a year. To celebrate their most prominent industry, the town erected a twelve-foot-tall mission chair with a base five-and-a-half feet wide and built from over six hundred feet of lumber. They called the mighty construct the World's Largest Chair. What the town didn't realize was that their oversized chair and bold claim would spark a war.

Thomasville, North Carolina, the town that proclaims itself the Furniture and Hosiery Capital of the World, soon plunked down a thirteen-foot six-inch chair. In 1928, Gardner responded by building a fifteen-foot mission chair. Gardner replaced the mission chair in 1935 with a sixteen-foot Colonial Hitchcock.

In the 1940s, World War II derailed the chair-building battle for a while, meaning that Gardner got to keep the World's Largest Chair record for a bit longer. But in 1948, Thomasville came back with an eighteen-footer. The town of Bennington, Vermont, jumped into the battle with a nineteen-foot one-inch chair. Morristown, Tennessee, put its flag (and chair legs) into the ground next with a twenty-footer. Gardner responded in 1976 with a Heywood-Wakefield chair that stands twenty feet and seven inches tall, ten feet wide, and nine feet deep. The World's Largest Chair was back in Gardner.

Sadly, other towns and then private companies began jumping into the chair war. Today, the World's Largest Chair is thirty-one feet tall and resides in Anniston, Alabama. But in Chair City, Massachusetts, on Elm Street in front of the Helen Mae Sauter School, you can still find ground zero—the place where the chair wars began, and the twenty-foot seven-inch monster that held the world's largest title for several years.

A Pretender to the Gardner Throne?

There is a second Giant Chair in Gardner. It's at the Chair City Wayside Furniture Company. Their chair was originally built in 1938 and replaced in 1989 with this 14' Ladderback.
—*Debra Jane Seltzer*

How the Cookie Crumbles

In the world of chocolate-chip cookies, there's only one name that matters: Toll House. The world-famous cookie's humble beginning can be found in Whitman in what was the Toll House Inn. Built in 1709, the building was originally a toll stop on the road between Boston and New Bedford. It was a place to get water for your horse and to eat a good meal before moving along.

In 1930, Kenneth and Ruth Graves Wakefield acquired the building and put on an addition to house overnight lodgers. Ruth Wakefield cooked all the meals for the paying guests, and she became renowned for her desserts.

One day Ruth was baking Butter Drop Do cookies—a personal favorite of hers—when she discovered she had run out of baker's chocolate. Like all great chefs, Ruth improvised. A man named Andrew Nestlé had recently given her a bar of semisweet chocolate; Wakefield

chopped the bar into little bits and mixed them into the batter. She expected that the chocolate would melt into swirls within the dough . . . but it didn't. The chips of chocolate held their shape, and the chocolate-chip cookie was born.

The new dessert was a huge hit with guests of the inn. Word spread, and Ruth eventually published her recipe in a few newspapers in the region. Then Andrew Nestlé noticed something peculiar: Sales of his semisweet bar spiked around New England.

Ruth Wakefield and Andrew Nestlé met to discuss an idea. In exchange for allowing Nestlé to print her recipe on the packaging of his semisweet chocolate, Ruth wanted all the chocolate she could use for the rest of her life. Nestlé agreed, and a dynasty was born. Nestlé next manufactured a bar that was molded into many small squares so it could be easily broken for the cookie. Then in 1939, the company introduced Nestlé Toll House Real Semi-Sweet Chocolate Morsels in a bag, and there was Ruth's recipe right on the back, where it can still be found today.

After Ruth passed away in 1977, the building changed ownership a couple of times and ultimately burned down in a fire that started in the kitchen. But near the intersection of Routes 18 and 14 is where this mecca of homemade cookies once stood. In 2007, the sign that read 1709 TOLL HOUSE was taken down to be refurbished, with a promise that it will return, so the bellman's hand can point to an empty space between a fast-food restaurant and a drug store.

BIG INDIAN SHOP
SOUVENIRS - GIFTS

A Big Indian on the Mohawk Trail

We wonder why they call this store along the Mohawk Trail (a.k.a. Route 2) the Big Indian Shop? Wait: Could it be the eighteen-foot-tall colorful statue of a Native American man out in front? We're guessing that yes, there is a connection between the two. You can check him out for yourself as you travel between Shelburne Falls and East Charlemont.

The South Has Risen in Chicopee

If an unholy union between Mr. Peanut and Colonel Sanders resulted in a child, he would probably resemble this debonair roadside gentleman in a tux and top hat. He stands along Burnett Road outside the Plantation Inn in Chicopee, and while he may bring a little southern hospitality to your roadside adventures, those with peanut allergies may want to keep their distance.

Something Fishy at the State House

The State House on the top of Boston's Beacon Hill was built in 1798 on land once owned by the Bay State's first elected governor, John Hancock. Inside the House of Representatives' chamber, suspended above the entrance to the hall in the visitors gallery, hangs a wooden codfish known as the Sacred Cod. It's likely you'd miss the old fish if someone didn't point it out to you. The speaker of the house faces the cod during the meetings.

The four-foot eleven-inch cod is carved out of pine. It is actually the third one to be displayed. The first was destroyed in a fire in 1747, the second during the Revolutionary War. The current cod was crafted around 1784 by an unknown artist.

So how did this whole fish story get started? Well, according to the Web site CelebrateBoston.com, on March 17, 1784, Mr. John Rowe of Boston introduced the following motion: "That leave might be given to hang up the representation of a cod fish in the room where the House sit[s], as a memorial of the importance of the Cod-Fishery to the welfare of the Commonwealth." The motion passed, and a carved cod was placed in the hall.

On the day of the grand inauguration, legislators carried the fish, wrapped in an American flag, into its new digs, which symbolized the commonwealth's growing prosperity.

Not to be out-fished by the house, the Senate has its own sacred fish, the Holy Mackerel, which hangs right above the main chandelier!

Avian Abomination

Long ago, when the country was being founded, there was some debate as to whether the country's bird would be a turkey or an eagle. Around that time, the Massachusetts Senate wanted to hang the national bird in their chambers. Just to cover their bases, they decided to make a bird that was a hybrid of both.—*Andrea Mercado*

The Doctor Was Here

You don't like green eggs and ham? Then stay out of Springfield, because 'round these parts, the name Theodor Seuss Geisel and all his weird and wonderful creations are sacred.

Born on March 2, 1904, on Howard Street in Springfield, Geisel was a writer and illustrator who got his start editing his college humor magazine at Dartmouth. He was forced to resign his editorship after he was caught throwing a party that served alcohol (during Prohibition, no less). To continue to be published, he did what many great writers have done in the past, he adopted a pen name: Dr. Seuss.

During the Great Depression, Geisel kept afloat financially by drawing advertising campaigns for companies like General Electric, NBC, and Standard Oil, but it was his books for children that earned him acclaim. *Green Eggs and Ham, The Cat in the Hat, How the Grinch Stole Christmas,* and *There's a Wocket in My Pocket!* are just a few of the best-selling Dr. Seuss titles. He wrote and illustrated forty-four books for children, and is one of the best-loved children's authors of all time.

After Geisel's death in 1991, his wife, Audrey, authorized the creation of a national memorial to her husband's work. The Dr. Seuss National Memorial Sculpture Garden is at the Springfield Museum on State Street. Visitors can walk by and see some of the good doctor's creations life-size and bronzed: the Cat in the Hat next to Dr. Seuss at his desk; Yertle the Turtle; the Grinch and his dog, Max; Horton the Elephant frolicking with Thing One and Thing Two; a bronze tree stump with the Lorax (who speaks for the trees); and Thidwick the Big-Hearted Moose.

Drastic Leominster Plastic

If you visit the National Plastics Center's museum in Leominster, you'll have to bring your dead presidents to pay the $5 admission because, ironically, they don't take plastic here.

Inside is a tribute to all things synthetic, from false limbs to children's toys, to another plastic invention fabled in the annals of suburban history: Tupperware.

Leominster calls itself Plastic City today, but it was the comb that first put the town on the map. "We got to be Plastic City from the comb industry," said Marianne Chalifoux Zephir, the curator and collections director for the museum.

In 1770, a man named Obadiah Hills had just moved into town from West Newbury, where he had learned the comb-making trade. What drew Hills to Leominster was the proximity to farmland where he could get a steady supply of animal horns. Early combs were carved from the horns and bones of animals, so the central Massachusetts location with all the rural land nearby was ideal for the birth of the industry.

By the mid-nineteenth century, there were more than twenty comb manufacturers in town and business was booming, so booming in fact that the demand was exceeding the supply. Horns, turtle shells, and ivory were becoming scarce. In order to grow, comb makers needed a new raw material, and new developments in celluloid plastics would do nicely.

Many comb makers were switching over to plastic because the material was much less expensive and early

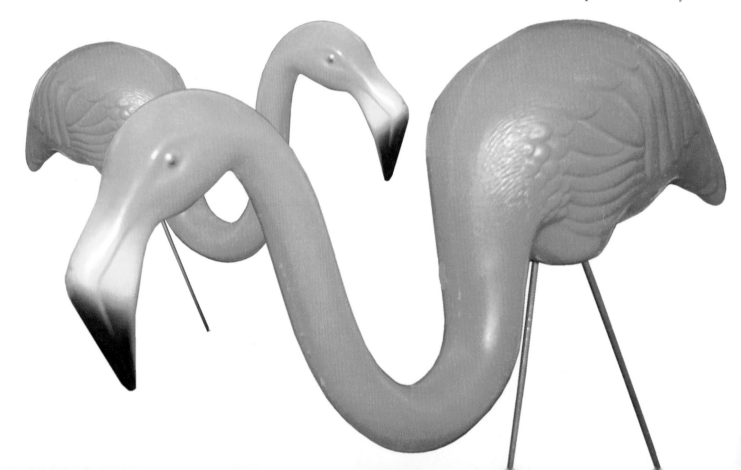

injection-molding machines meant mass production was possible. The comb was just the beginning. Plastics offered the promise of a durable material that could be shaped and molded to fit many other needs. By the mid-twentieth century, there were more plastic factories in Leominster than anywhere else in the United States. This drew to the area inventors and innovators who wanted to learn and improve the trade.

One inventor was a New Hampshire tree surgeon named Earl Silas Tupper, who came to Leominster in 1936 to work for the plastics manufacturing division of DuPont. Tupper tinkered with some of the throwaway material from the manufacturing process and devised containers that were virtually unbreakable, airtight, and after the addition of dyes, pleasant to look at. He formed the Earl S. Tupper Company and brought his product to the masses.

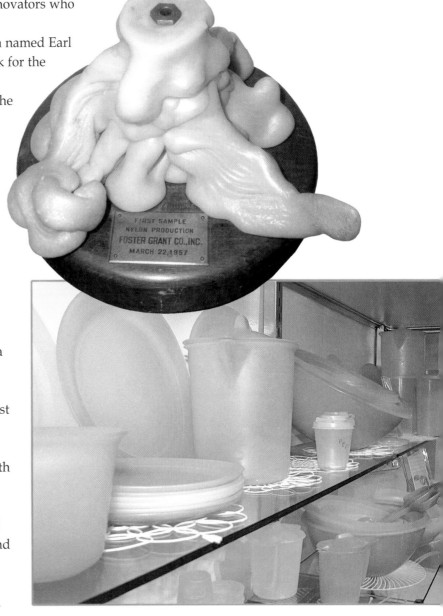

Initially Tupperware didn't sell very well. Consumers trying out the containers in stores had trouble with the lid, and they just didn't get it. But once the company started selling its products via in-home demonstrations, where Tupperware pros could show housewives how to "burp" the lid and seal in freshness, a monster was born.

The National Plastics Center's museum features a display showing some early Tupperware. "It's very collectible," Zephir says. "The collection here dates from the early '50s and even late '40s, when it was first developed."

The museum is also home to the Plastics Hall of Fame, an exhibit that honors some of the pioneers both past and present who contributed to the industry. There's John Wesley Hyatt, the "grandfather of the plastics industry," who invented the celluloid billiard ball; John Grebe, who invented the Styrofoam cup; and let's not forget Wallace Hume Carothers, who is the "father of neoprene." Without him, we would have neither nylon stockings nor the runs to go with them.

Lactose Tolerance

In front of the Boston Children's Museum on Congress Street is a forty-foot-tall milk bottle that is home to an ice-cream stand and snack bar open in the summer.

Built by the Hood dairy company in 1930, the wooden structure was moved here in 1977. The company estimates that it would take about 50,000 gallons of milk to fill the bottle.

Got Milk? Oh Yeah, in a BIG Way!

Both of these milk bottle buildings, one in New Bedford and one in Raynham, were erected by Frates Dairy. They were designed by Les Labrose and were painted white with a cream color close to the brim.

The Raynham Bottle serves ice-cream takeout through the front windows and has a restaurant attached behind it. The bottle is fifty feet tall and twenty feet in

diameter. According to the latest report, it is being repainted. The New Bedford Bottle is fifty-two feet tall and was built in 1930.

Manny's Place in Granby is a twofer, having both a milk can and a milk bottle. In the 1930s, the sheet metal can was produced in Chicopee, and the bottle was produced locally. They were created to draw customers to Dufresne's Dairy Bar, a side venture of their dairy business. Over the years, the business has been known as Marion & Ken's and the Maple Brook Restaurant. It has been Manny's Place since 1987. The milk can, which is attached to the restaurant, contains a few tables. The bottle is used for storage.

Salvador's thirty-foot-tall milk can was originally located in New Bedford and was moved to South Dartmouth next to the owners' house in 1935. There once was a giant dairy building next to the can. In 1967, on-site production of milk and ice cream ended, but the ice-cream business is still family run. In 2005, new owners began restoring the building. They have repainted it and are adding handles to it. There is also a new rooftop cow! *–Debra Jane Seltzer*

When the Smoke Alarm Goes Off, Dinner's Ready

Fine chefs know that presentation counts almost as much as taste. The entire food preparation process is considered art by those who aspire to culinary greatness. Then there's the rest of us, who just want to get through one meal without destroying the food, the pan we cook it in, or the building we live in. This is where Deborah Henson-Conant's story begins. She's a composer and performer, but also the founder and curator of, and primary contributor to, the Burnt Food Museum—a museum that was open to the public for only one day, but whose collection can be found online at www.burntfoodmuseum.com.

Founded in Arlington in the late 1980s, it all began with a phone call, said Henson-Conant. "I was in the middle of making some hot apple cider, which you cook on low heat, when I got a phone call." We started gabbing and gabbing and gabbing, and about an hour later, I noticed a funny smell, and I ran into the kitchen. It was full of thick black smoke down to about maybe a foot off the ground. I plowed my way through it, opened the windows, and when I was finally able to see the stove, I discovered freestanding hot apple cider perfectly preserved in the middle of the pot. So I took it out. I put it on a lovely little plate and kept it in my kitchen."

This wouldn't be her last culinary catastrophe by any means. "About a year later, I went to a barbecue. I was barbecuing Soy Pups, which at that time apparently you couldn't barbecue them, because they became completely stiff. I took it home and put it on another little platter and started realizing, Wow, I do this a lot."

She began displaying the burned pieces, and friends would come over and comment on each one. Some came up with clever titles like Hot Apple Cinder and had the names placed on little plaques near the piece. Her growing museum often got her out of cooking. "So I've often used it as an excuse like, 'Sure I'll be happy to cook for you. Would you like to look at the museum first?'"

The Burnt Food Museum's fame grew because Deborah is a performer and often had journalists come to her house for interviews. The Food Network came to do a segment on Deborah's museum. After she brought her collection to the TV show *The View*, magazines and books began writing articles on the display, and Deborah realized she had a monster on her hands. She was getting e-mails and photographs from all over the world from others who had their own scorched platters. People think the collection is funny, but is it art?

"Each piece is a story; it's a still-life," Deborah says. It's interesting, but at some point it becomes trash when there's just too much of it. I don't think it's art, I think it's more of a museum—like a natural history museum: That's not art. One appreciates it, and the stuff is beautiful.

"When people see the museum, they then see other burnt food differently. And that to me is the most important part of it."

At left, clockwise: Soy Pups, pizza toast, whole wheat toast, before and after, shrimp kebob. This page, freestanding hot apple cider.

Museum of Bad Art

Massachusetts is home to some fine art institutions. Some of the best art in the world, for example, can be found in the iconic halls of the Museum of Fine Arts in Boston. In contrast, we're also home to some of the worst art in the world—a fact one museum prides itself on, being the epicenter of some of the most awful works of art in existence. The Museum of Bad Art (MOBA) in Dedham calls itself "the highly regarded institution devoted to the upliftment of spectacularly bad art." And they mean it. Most of their collection is really bad.

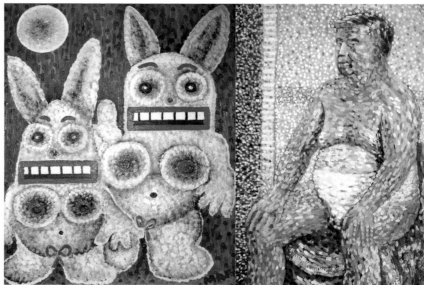

Founded in the fall of 1993 by Scott Wilson, Jerry Reilly, and Marie (pronounced "Mary") Jackson Reilly, the organization had its first show in March of 1994 in the basement of a private home in Boston. The initial response was overwhelming, and within a few years, the museum found itself moving up in the world to new digs. Well, not really up—more like over. They're still in a basement, but this time it's the basement of the Dedham Community Theatre, a 1927 movie theater with enough room to show the kind of art that one would pay others to remove.

The collection is conveniently located next to the men's room in the theater, a site that has a functional reason. According to the museum's Web site, "The nearby flushing helps maintain a uniform humidity."

"Some people just don't get it," says Mike Frank, curator in chief for the Museum of Bad Art. "This is stuff that's just bad. It's not crappy. It's stuff that would not be considered high art, but it's still interesting to look at."

MOBA isn't exactly rolling in dough. At one time, the price limit for acquiring a new piece was $6.50, though Frank admits that over the years he has paid sometimes double and even triple that.

How one defines good or bad art is a difficult question to answer because beauty—as the cliché goes—is in the eye of the beholder. So what makes bad art? "It's kind of like pornography. You can't define it, but you know it when you see it," Frank says. He does have some criteria, however, for exactly which pieces make it into the collection. Poor artistic technique alone wouldn't do it. "But poor technique that results in an interesting image might," Frank points out. "More interesting to me is when there's a piece that looks like there's substantial technique, but there's some kind of over-the-top imagery. We need to be convinced that the person did set out to do something artistic and then stepped back afterward and realized something went wrong.

"Don't confuse this bad art with schlock," he says. "An example of a piece that doesn't belong here is a velvet Elvis painting. Which may be cool, but it's not bad art. It's schlock. Bad taste."

One piece on display at MOBA is titled *Two Trees in Love* and shows a landscape with two trees seemingly embraced in a not-too-affectionate hug in the shadow of a much larger tree. The piece was painted by Julie Seelig

The piece features a knife slash in it that appears to be part of the original work—it forces the viewer to ponder the artist's intentions—destroy the work before it gets out or kill the woman on the canvas staring back at you. The painting had been a real showpiece for the museum, and one day it went missing. MOBA initially offered a reward of $6.50 for any

and was donated by her mother, Sally Seelig. The explanation next to the painting describes how the artist learned she might not be cut out for painting. Apparently, this painting was created for a class. The students left their work in the studio overnight to dry. The next day all of the paintings were stolen . . . except *Two Trees in Love*. Though not good enough to steal, it was good enough to make it into MOBA's collection.

And speaking of stealing, over the years, there have been a few heists of paintings. Mike Frank recalled one case: "There was a painting called *My Self-Portrait as a Bird*. One day I came down here to find the painting missing and replaced by a ransom note saying that they wanted ten dollars or you'll never see this painting again. Of course we refuse to negotiate with art thieves, and when they were convinced of that, the painting returned one day with a ten-dollar bill attached to it."

The museum's most nefarious heist occurred in March of 1996. The piece, called *Eileen,* is an eighteen-by-twenty-four oil by R. Angelo Le acquired by MOBA founder Scott Wilson from a trash receptacle in Boston.

information that would lead to the recovery of *Eileen*. When no information came in, the generosity of benefactors and patrons kicked the reward up substantially. With $36.73 on the line, MOBA waited and waited and waited. A decade went by, and just when all hope was lost, a ransom note came in asking for $5,000. When the museum refused, the demand was dropped to $1,000, then $200. That's when Parker McGurl, MOBA's special assistant to the permanent acting interim executive director, stepped in and developed a phone rapport with the bandit. Through careful negotiations, *Eileen* was returned, no ransom was paid, and no charges were filed.

MOBA is internationally known. They've had showings in Canada, they've had pieces donated from all over the world, and they are a legitimate credit to an aspiring artist. As visitors peruse the gallery, they will notice that Anonymous, one of the most famous painters of all time, has contributed several pieces. Some of them look unfinished, some look like a target was aimed for but missed entirely, and some are just plain weird.

Roads Less Traveled

Massachusetts has so many roads
with so many stories. We have old
byways that were once walked by
famous patriots—as well as legendary humanitarians
such as Johnny Appleseed. Our roads can be lonely
and wooded—a veritable petri dish where legends
incubate, grow, and spread. And our roads can be
treacherous when ice and snow make
for the kind of driving that separates
real New Englanders from the
visitors. It seems that, in some cases,
the less traveled the road is, the more
skeletons there are in its closet and the
more legends are whispered
about its rutted and pitted
paths.

The Mad Trucker of Copicut Road

It's late at night, and you're driving down Copicut Road—a dark strip cut through Freetown State Forest that begins as a paved road, then quickly turns to dirt, then into a desolate strip of potholed, pocked, and partially washed-away trail that is two cars wide but barely navigable. Murder victims have been discovered dumped in the woods off the side of this road, and the forest has its own strange legends of cult activity, killings, and the paranormal, which may or may not be on your mind, depending on how well-versed you are in the local lore.

A truck comes barreling up behind you. You can see that its lights are coming fast, and you can tell the truck is swerving around the road. The truck's horn blares, and now your pulse is pounding. In your rearview mirror you see an angry-looking, twenty-something man at the wheel; below him, nothing but headlights and truck grill. You speed up, and your car bounces as it rolls over dips and hills, and then it jumps as it bottoms out on rocks. You try to hug the shoulder, but the truck behind you edges closer. Then, suddenly and without warning, the truck is gone. Vanished! You've just been the victim of the Mad Trucker of Copicut Road.

The legend of the Mad Trucker is obscure. Even some locals haven't heard it. One person quoted in an October 30, 2006, *Boston Globe* article who lived on Copicut Road since the 1980s claimed to have never heard of the legend. But there are those who have—those who are afraid to drive down the old road at night for fear of the madman behind the wheel. The legend has propagated itself on Internet message boards and has even made its way onto some paranormal talk radio shows. All we need now is for an eyewitness to come forward, and we can see about camping out at Copicut Road.

COPICUT RD

Johnny Appleseed Lane

In the annals of American history and lore, few folks have logged as many miles for the sake of others as John Chapman, who became a legend for walking roads less traveled westward and planting seeds along the way. Better known as Johnny Appleseed, the man, the legend, and the long walk began right here in Massachusetts in the town of Leominster.

John Chapman was born on September 26, 1774, to Nathaniel and Elizabeth Chapman, a poor farming couple. Nathaniel sent his son to be an apprentice in a nearby apple orchard, which planted the figurative and literal seed in Johnny to become the most famous orchardist who ever lived.

In 1797, Johnny headed west with a pocketful of apple seeds. His first destination was Wilkes-Barre, Pennsylvania, where he started an orchard and picked up more seeds from area cider mills. The mills were happy to give away the seeds because more orchards meant more stock of apples and ultimately lower prices.

To say John Chapman traveled light is an understatement. He wore no shoes, not even in the winter. His clothes were ragged because he only picked up garments in barter and kept only the most worn for himself. The rest he gave away to those in need. On his head he wore a tin cooking utensil that could be a cap, a mush pot, or be used to extinguish a fire should the blaze threaten any nearby animals or insects.

Johnny Appleseed held deep religious convictions. He was a missionary for the Church of the New Jerusalem, and he felt he could not harm or even inconvenience any other living thing. There are stories of Johnny extinguishing his campfire because mosquitoes were flying too close and burning up.

From Pennsylvania, Johnny headed west to Ohio.

Many of the children's tales about Johnny Appleseed describe the lanky man as tossing seeds randomly as he went along, but this wasn't true. Johnny set up organized orchards, then left them well tended and in the care of the people in the vicinity. He would return every year or two to collect his portion of the proceeds and then keep moving along. He lived as an itinerant, but when he died in March of 1845, he had amassed quite a bit of land, which he willed to his sister.

Today in the town of Leominster is a street called Johnny Appleseed Lane. Along the side of the road is a small monument that marks the birthplace of John Chapman. It was here that the man and the legend began.

Dudley Road

There is perhaps no street in Massachusetts that inspires more stories and retellings than Dudley Road in Billerica. The small stretch of road, which is hazardous to drive even in the daytime, has been rumored to be haunted for decades and has inspired locals to share their tales of touching the supernatural. The source of the activity there is impossible to uncover, but the stories could fill a few chapters in an encyclopedia of urban legends.

As Dudley Road dwindles down to a one-lane dirt path, people begin to hear cries and screams coming from the woods. They've seen a white, glowing figure move across the road and disappear into the trees, or shadows moving by their car windows. Some claim short, bald people have run up to their car, screamed at them, tried to get in, and then darted back into the darkness. At least one person claims to have taken a picture of a dark figure hanging from one of the trees.

Much of the activity on Dudley is attached to an abandoned asylum back in the woods. It was closed decades ago and forgotten about because of the atrocities that happened there, but its psychic imprint has trapped the souls who suffered there.

Then there is the nun-witch story. People say the convent on the road was the site of bizarre rituals, and the people who discovered the abominations took the nuns to a nearby tree and hung them. Sometimes the story involves one nun, who upon her death placed a curse on the town.

In another variation, a nun and a priest had an affair and the nun became pregnant. To hide his indiscretion, the priest either killed the nun or accused her of witchcraft to soil her name. Or the nun becomes pregnant by some unknown man and kills herself.

The best of the stories combine asylum/convent stories. An escaped patient breaks into the convent, kidnaps the nuns, and kills them.

With little fact to back up the stories, it's hard to take them seriously. All are popular themes in urban legends. Dudley Road is a lonely road void of streetlights, and the low-hanging trees with shadows bouncing from headlights encourages the mind to see what it thinks it is supposed to. The Salem Witch Trials happened only a few towns away, so it is not a stretch that witches play a role in Dudley's tales.

The "convent" is actually a retreat center, and the building does not date far enough back to coincide with any known report of a witch hanging. The order that calls it home was not even founded until after World War I. Of course, people always claim a cover-up to protect the church.

There is no record of an asylum on Dudley Road, and there seems to be some confusion as to whether the building talked about is the Billerica House of Corrections or the old Middlesex House of Corrections, neither of which could be confused with an old abandoned building in the middle of the woods.

Yet there are a few stories from Dudley Road that cannot be explained away. Every so often someone comes forward with a firsthand account. A nearby cemetery is known to experience paranormal activity, and maybe a soul or two finds its way down the street. With so much weirdness brewing on Dudley Road, nothing can be certain or clearly ruled out, and that just adds to the mystery.—*Christopher Balzano, Director, Massachusetts Paranormal Crossroads*

Cape Cod Tunnel

It's a sunny and warm Friday afternoon in July, and the weekend's forecast is for perfect summer weather. So you decide to head out to Cape Cod for the weekend. You get into your car, turn up the radio, don your sunglasses, and hit the road heading east to the Cape.

Then your summer fantasy abruptly ends. Your car's speed diminishes from 65 miles per hour down to 5. Your hands tighten around the steering wheel, and your teeth grit as you prepare to beep and creep for miles up to one of the two bridges that can take you onto this stretch of seasonal paradise.

Three bridges cross the Cape Cod Canal: the Cape Cod Canal Railroad Bridge, the Bourne Bridge, and the Sagamore Bridge. Besides swimming for it or taking a boat, there's no other way on or off the Cape by surface travel.

Or is there? Many people who have driven on or near the Cape have noticed some cars with a small, rectangular bumper sticker that reads something like: CAPE COD CANAL TUNNEL RESIDENT PERMIT. The rest of us suckers sit for hours in the traffic, waiting to get over the bridges, but these lucky locals get to speed right under the canal. So where is this tunnel?

Our crack team of weird investigators consulted the most reliable source for information on the planet: the Internet. One intrepid traveler claims on a message board that the tunnel begins in New Bedford at the steamship dock, runs under Buzzards Bay, under West Falmouth, and comes up in Otis Air Force Base in Bourne—making the Cape Cod Tunnel about 14.5 miles in length, which would make it the sixth longest tunnel in the world.

There's only one problem, of course. There is no tunnel. The sticker is a joke that began around 1994 as another way for Cape locals to mess with tourists who might lose the better part of their day looking for the tunnel to avoid bridge traffic. Since then, several variations of the sticker have surfaced, but the theme remains the same: an official-looking resident sticker to a tunnel that isn't there, never was there, nor is there any plan to make it there in the future.

This Cape Does Not Enable Drivers to Fly

Weird Massachusetts isn't satisfied with simply reporting on the phantom Cape tunnel. Going against most journalistic ethics regarding legend creation, we've come up with a new permit sticker that will test the limits of what tourists will believe: the Cape Cod Jump Permit sticker. This will get you ACROSS the canal in one good flying leap.

The key to the propagation of any good legend is a few details that make it sound at least plausible. To the gullible among us, listen up: The jump starts on Old Bridge Road on the mainland, in Bourne Corners, just south of Route 28/The Bourne Bridge. You'll land in Bourne somewhere near Sandwich Road.

Though the speed limit on Old Bridge Road is 25 miles per hour, there's plenty of room on the ramp itself to build up the jumping speed necessary to clear the roughly 540 feet of water. Good luck!

A Hairy Turn in Clarksburg

Route 2, also known as the Mohawk Trail, is one of the most breathtaking drives in the state. As you begin the gentle climb up through the Berkshires, you pass through towns like Charlemont, Drury, Florida, and then into Clarksburg. The Deerfield River carves through the mountains to create postcardlike views, and just past the highest point along Route 2, you begin your descent into the Hoosac Valley.

You know you're close when you see the sign that reads HAIRPIN TURN 3,000 FEET. A short while later, another sign advises HAIRPIN TURN 2,000 FEET. Then there's the 1,000-foot warning, followed by a sign that says HAIRPIN TURN, and then your last warning: SPEED LIMIT 15. Ignore these signs, and you'll likely become a

permanent part of the impressive scenery ahead.

Located smack-dab in the middle of the hairpin is the Golden Eagle Restaurant. John Morris is its current owner; the restaurant has been in his family since 1980. He's seen it all as far as accidents on the hairpin go.

"I remember it was my dad's birthday," Morris says. "It was about half past eleven in the morning and I heard this funny rumble sound. I happened to look out my parents' picture window, because they lived on-site, and I saw all this fire go right across the whole mountain and down over the embankment. I picked up the phone, and it was dead. [My parents] were in their fifties then, and I said, 'We gotta get out of here.'

"A gas tanker carrying 14,000 gallons of gas scraped the inside ledge out in front of us and just exploded. The gas was going down into the culverts in the road creating gas pockets and then exploding. We had fled to the woods up on the mountain to get away. . . . The driveway was so hot it was melting the blacktop. The fire would leak out of the gas tanker and create streams of fire and run down the length of their hoses. The restaurant was scorched on the outside, but it didn't do any structural damage. And the poor fellow, there, the driver, he didn't survive."

That wasn't the only accident Morris saw, but it was the worst. Anyone who has ever taken Clarksburg's famous hairpin can only imagine what it would be like on a snowy winter's day. Though Morris says it's actually safer than the town roads in the wintertime because it's so well plowed and salted, it's not a place to test your driving skills!

Redheaded Hitchhiker of Route 44

Almost every state has a legend about a phantom hitchhiker. Massachusetts has its own—the Redheaded Hitchhiker of Route 44 on the Seekonk–Rehoboth town line.

According to Seekonk historian and author John Erhardt, the legend goes back to at least the 1950s when the area around Route 44 was mainly farmland. Transients and locals alike would often thumb rides down to Fall River, up to Boston, and elsewhere.

Since the 1970s, talk has gone around town of a disheveled, red-haired, red-bearded man who has been seen walking down Route 44. Sometimes he's hitchhiking; other times he's walking along the side of the road or just on the edge of the woods. Descriptions vary slightly, but usually he's wearing blue jeans and a red flannel shirt. He's believed to be in his late thirties or early forties.

One report from the 1960s claims a driver was motoring along down Route 44 when he heard a sinister laugh. The driver looked over to see the redheaded man looking in the window—even though the car was traveling at more than 40 miles per hour. The face somehow kept pace with the car before disappearing.

Other accounts from later years involve a driver who saw a man thumbing a ride on Route 44. The driver pulled over, the man got into the car, and they drove off. The driver asked where the hitcher was headed but was answered only with silence. The driver asked again, and again there was no answer. Growing uncomfortable, the driver pulled over and insisted that the redhead get out of the car. The only problem was, the mysterious man had already vanished. No car door opened, nothing. Poof!

In the 1980s, the encounters became more extreme. One female witness alleged that she was driving along Route 44 when, out of nowhere, a tall red-headed man appeared in the middle of the road right in front of her. The driver screamed and screeched her car to a halt. When she jumped out to try and help the poor fellow, there was no one lying in the road and no damage to her car.

There are some who believe the red-haired man has kept pace with them in the woods, and others have said they hear his laugh as they drive by the Rehoboth–Seekonk town line.

1877

Forbidden Hoosac Tunnel

In western Massachusetts, a 4.74-mile railroad tunnel cuts through Hoosac Mountain in the Berkshires. Though today only an occasional freighter runs through the tunnel, it's legendary for its air of mystery and haunted reputation. In the Mohawk language, "Hoosac" means "forbidden," and to stand before the mouth of the tunnel is to stare into a seemingly endless abyss.

The original construction of the tunnel was a pretty botched operation that began in 1845 when a group of investors decided to build their own rail line, hoping to connect Greenfield with Troy, New York. After some false starts and slow progress, the state took control of the project in September 1862 and concluded that most of the work done so far would have to be redone. The tunnel the private investors built would have to be widened, and better reinforcing brick was needed to make it safe.

Work started again in July 1863, when miners began to dig a twenty-seven. by fifteen-foot vertical central shaft through Hoosac Mountain. Engineers knew they would need the giant chimney to ventilate the coal exhaust from the locomotives and to bring in fresh air for the workers. With the help of drills that were powered by air compressors that in turn were powered by a mill, the digging went fast. By 1867, work crews were gaining between eighty and one hundred feet of tunnel per month. But there were frequent, fatal mishaps, and the state was uncomfortable with the rising death rate.

Digging the central shaft, although critical, was also wrought with peril. The single worst disaster of the tunnel project occurred there in October of 1867.

Contractors wanted to experiment with a gas lighting apparatus in the buildings at the shaft that a previous engineer deemed unsafe. The first day of their experiment, a gas tank caught fire, causing the building it was in to ignite. The fire made it impossible to save the thirteen men working at the bottom of the then six-hundred-foot shaft. They either died of suffocation or drowned, as both air and water pumps stopped working. Their bodies were not recovered until a year after the accident. After this incident, the central shaft earned the moniker the Bloody Pit.

By February 9, 1875, when the first train was ready to pass through, the Hoosac Tunnel had used over twenty million bricks, cost over $20 million (ten times the initial estimate), and claimed 196 lives. The construction took twenty-two years, but the passage to New York was now open for business.

Strange occurrences were reported within months of the official opening of the tunnel. In the fall of 1875, a fire tender named Harlan Mulvaney was scheduled to deliver a cartload of wood nearby and simply disappeared. His cart and team of horses were discovered in the woods, but he was nowhere to be seen.

Others have reported hearing strange laughter echoing through the tunnel, and then there's the benevolent spirit of the phantom trackwalker who is believed to have saved more than one life by shouting a warning to workers who almost stumbled upon an electrical short within the tunnel.

In the coming years, more features would be added, such as electricity to power a giant fan at the top of the central shaft. The fan was sorely needed to push noxious clouds of smoke out of the tunnel. The area at the bottom of the central shaft became known as Hoosac Hotel, a shanty for hoboes and trackwalkers who wanted dry overnight accommodations.

Today a few freighters operated by Pan Am Railways still pass through the dark and lonely Hoosac Tunnel each day, but it's hardly bustling now that trucks are the primary means of carrying cargo across the country. The dark passage held the record as the longest man-made tunnel in North America until 1916, when the Moffat Tunnel in the Rockies eclipsed it. It's now a curiosity more than anything else, but Hoosac will always hold the distinction of being Massachusetts's first Big Dig.

A Walk Through the Bloody Pit

My friend Andrew and I explored the length of the Hoosac Tunnel in October 2002. We'd heard it was one of the most haunted places in New England, and with all the deaths associated with its construction, we were sure we'd find a spook or two in the darkness. Locals claim to have felt strange winds, seen ghostly apparitions, and heard eerie voices in and around the tunnel. Tape recorders left in the tunnel by paranormal researchers have picked up what sounds like muffled voices — perhaps the long-forgotten, anguished cries from workers crushed, burned, or otherwise extinguished during the many accidents and minor cave-ins. Balls of bluish light and ghost lanterns have been seen, and legends abound of "ghost hands" pushing people in front of oncoming trains, as well as pulling them back to safety.

We entered the tunnel from the east portal, and due to the sunny conditions outside, we found we didn't really need our flashlights to see. There was still a lot to stumble on. Electrical cables were everywhere and often lay in pools of water. The railroad tracks were brutal on our feet, but we walked on them because they were relatively dry and stable compared to the slippery and muddy berms on either side of the tracks. The crumbling brick sections of the tunnel were particularly dangerous. Individual bricks have fallen from the ceiling, and sheets of them have collapsed from the walls.

The Web site of the extreme adventure group IRONFIST points out another danger:

"Large freight trains pass through at random hours, leaving behind them a potentially lethal amount of diesel fuel."

Despite these dangers, we pressed on. We were looking for the Hoosac Hilton, an area where a large section of the tunnel collapsed and killed dozens of workers. It was supposed to be easy to find because the tunnel opened out in a cavernous chamber there. We also kept our eyes peeled for the rumored Hidden Room of Hoosac, a legendary room that was supposedly bricked up to keep an unspeakable horror within.

Central Shaft

Two hours in, we heard a mechanical noise and saw a spark of light far ahead. We debated over whether or not it was a train, because it's really a press-up-against-the-wall-and-hope-for-the-best situation if a train comes through the tunnel. The light didn't get any brighter, so we resumed our journey. Later on, we figured out it was simply sunlight from the other end of the tunnel, which we hadn't been able to see at first.

We were approaching the central shaft, an area where a thousand-foot vertical shaft opens into the roof of the tunnel. A large fan at the top of the vertical shaft draws air out of the tunnel at great velocity. The stiff breeze in the tunnel and the mechanical noise we'd been hearing came from the fan.

The central shaft doesn't open straight down into the tunnel. Rather, there are two dark openings staggered on either side that curve up through the rock to meet in a small cavern that had been blasted out of the rock some feet above the tunnel's ceiling. From the cavern, you can look straight up to the fan in the shaft house on the surface above. Was the cavern the Hidden Room?

Across the tracks from the central shaft opening is a small brick room built into the rock. It has a window that overlooks the tracks, and it perhaps was once a manned station. Now it seemed to be a destination for the heartiest of partiers, with mementos carved into the woodwork and painted on the walls, and various old pieces of smashed electrical equipment lying around.

West Portal

The walk from the central shaft to the west portal was longer than that from the east portal to the central shaft. Water was everywhere too: gushing out of the walls, raining down from the ceiling, and filling both sides of the tracks. We slogged our way to the west portal opening, which features a huge garage door that can roll down to completely close it off. I have heard the door is there to keep snow or bears from getting in, but this seems rather unlikely. It does bring to mind an entry from a ghost-hunting Web site, though, which describes how four ghost hunters—two men and their girlfriends—approached the west portal in broad daylight one winter day. They felt "chills" from the "bad vibes." After much coaxing by the girlfriends, the men went several dozen feet into the west portal. There they heard the sounds of "body bags falling from the ceiling" and ran back out.

More Ghosts?

Our walk back to the east portal was cold and wet. A while after passing the central shaft again, we could see the spark of daylight from the east portal. We also noticed a red light, which we kept an eye on as we found another recess. It was a good thing, as a freight train slowly approached at about 10 or 15 miles per hour. The entire tunnel began to vibrate hideously long before the train got to us, and when it did arrive, even the rock was shaking. I wondered why the bricks didn't all fall as I pressed up against the wall.

After the engine went by, it was completely dark, and quite a sensation to hear car after car slam and rattle by so close. But we had a new development: We could no longer see the light from the east portal. It was like something was blocking the end of the tunnel. It soon cleared, and we realized that black diesel exhaust fumes from the train had completely blocked the light.

We walked out of the tunnel about an hour later, grimed from head to toe. It was a gritty, dirty, cold, and muddy place, and it is no lie that freight trains come through on a regular basis. If you enjoy such adventures, it's one heck of a trip, but it's not for the timid or casual hiker.

Some things remain mysteries. While the little room off the side of tracks is the Hoosac Hotel, I'm not convinced that the cavern at the base of the central shaft is the Hidden Room. The true room remains hidden, and its unspeakable horror sleeps brooding and undisturbed under the mountain. And I was disappointed in the spooks. Even our walking most of the tunnel with no light whatsoever was not enough to entice them out. Still, I hope the Hoosac Tunnel will keep its secrets for years to come.–*Daniel V. Boudillion*

Hoosac Tunnel, West Portal, North Adams, Mass.

The Bay State: God's Country or Devil's Domain?

if the place names the Puritan forefathers chose are any indication, Massachusetts is a devil-haunted land. Rather than leaving the smell of brimstone in his wake, here in Massachusetts the devil simply leaves his footprints behind—in solid rock! These can be seen in Auburn, Easton, Holliston, Ipswich, Medfield, Norton, and Seekonk.

With the demon traipsing so freely around the Bay State, it's good to know that at least ten acres were set aside and actually deeded to God—with a stone engraved to prove it.

With the help of the Berkshire Mountain Man, Jim Moore, who has explored virtually every geological feature in the state, *Weird Massachusetts* has catalogued more than one hundred and fifty devil-named or devil-associated places around Massachusetts. We do not claim that this list is anywhere near complete, but here are a good eighty such places in the state, either named after the devil or where it appears he just likes to hang out. You might think twice the next time you go for a walk in Bay State woods—who knows what you might encounter! *–Daniel V. Boudillion*

Devil's Dens

Seems the devil doesn't live in a mansion or even a house. He lives in a den. Lots of dens. There are Devil's Dens in Arlington, Ashland, Brookline, Martha's Vineyard, Needham, Newbury, Newton Upper Falls, Pigeon Cove, Tom Ball Mountain, Warren, and Williamsburg.

These are small boulder caves that somehow seemed a fit and desirable dwelling to the Prince of Darkness. How this choice of abode was made is not recorded. However, there may be significant clues in the fact that several Devil's Dens are also called Indian caves.

Under Puritan leadership, anything having to do with Native Americans was thought to be associated with the devil as well. Caves, such as the one in Ashland on the Old Connecticut Path, were said to have been used by Indians to store grain and thus became, by association, the Devil's Den.

Satan's Kingdom

In 1692, witch hysteria had Salem in its grip. Witches were everywhere, it seemed, afflicting the innocent and confessing their devilish ways in court. When it was William Barker's turn before the magistrates, he broke the awful news that it was their diabolical plan "to destroy the Church of God and set up Satan's Kingdom."

This floored the Puritans. Their worst fears were realized, and they fought back against the threat by hanging as many of their neighbors as they could. However, unbeknownst to them, the devil had already established two such Satan's Kingdoms in Massachusetts. (Neither of them was called Fall River!)

Topographical maps of Westwood still identify the hilltop site of one of these old Satan's Kingdoms. Out in Northfield, the Satan's Kingdom Wildlife Management Area rather bizarrely commemorates a

second so-named place. This one is out in the Berkshires, so it was probably the devil's summer residence.

Did the demon's administration reside in Westwood, located near the commercial and political centers in the eastern part of the state? It would certainly seem so. The devil had a throne on the premises, a large granite dome of rock shaped like an armchair. This throne is also said to have been used by King Philip, an Indian war leader, who is said to have watched Dedham burn from there.

A recent visit revealed Westwood's Satan's Kingdom to be a steep rocky hill with spectacular views. There are plenty of tumbled boulders, cliffs, ledges, rocky glades, and hidden coves to excite the imagination. At the top is a wizened old tree, appearing much like a gnarled wizard watching over the old stomping grounds.

Hell's Kitchen and Devil's Oven

Any place large enough to be a kingdom would require kitchen facilities, so it doesn't surprise us to find that both the Westwood and Northfield Satan's Kingdoms were so equipped. In Westwood, the culinary needs were supplied by the Devil's Oven, a tunnel in the rock with a cave at the end. This was also known as Indian Cave and was actively used by them for grain storage in Colonial times. Local legend says that the tunnel extends for several hundred feet to Hartford Street.

In Northfield, the cooking was done entirely in Hell's Kitchen. We can assume that wine, women, and song were somewhere on the menu.

Two other locations that served up food for the devil and his league are the Devil's Kitchen in Lynnfield and the Devil's Oven in Sherborn. And for those special party occasions, there was the Devil's Punchbowl in Hampton County.

Devil's Pulpit

The devil's message of indulgence and personal gratification wasn't as easy to spread as you might think. From time to time, he had to get some of the finer points across, and what better way than via the pulpit?

Devil's Pulpits can be found in Great Barrington, Housatonic, Leominster, and Nahant. Feel free to mount these spires of stone and address an imaginary crowd on the most pressing of diabolical topics.

Devil's Brooks, Ponds, and Swamp

The devil has been commemorated in many ways, and it is only fitting that here in Massachusetts he should have a few brooks and ponds named after him. For example, there are Devil's Brooks in Sharon and Stoughton and Purgatory Brooks in Norwood and Sutton. *Weird Massachusetts* spent a lot of time trying to find a reason—any reason—that these brooks were deemed devil-worthy, but couldn't find a single historical reference or folktale to explain it.

To add to his cache, the devil has also collected ponds and swamps. There is the Devil's Dishful Pond in Peabody, which reveals the true size of his Sable Majesty's appetite, if the name is any indication. There is also a Hell Swamp in Hanover and a Hell Pond in Fort Devens, the latter of which was once a hill. Henry S. Nourse, in his book on the town of Harvard, provided this account of what happened to it, which was related to him by an Indian: "A century or two ago before the pale-faced strangers came from beyond the seas, a lofty hill rose where the clear water mirrors the sky in the Shabakin woodlands; one night the earth trembled and in the morning the hill was not, and in its place slept this little lake overshadowed by the gloomy pine forest, its depth equaling the height of the vanished hill."

Devil's Pulpit

Devil's Rocks

With rocks we are back on solid ground, the devil's favorite turf. He was quite fond of rocks, especially big hoary old boulders, and was often found skulking in their vicinity. He was known for hanging around such rocks in Rochester, Sharon, and Swansea, all of which are appropriately named Devil's Rock. In Millbury, he is also said to have frequented games of quoits, a ring-toss game in which the devil preferred to use a large boulder. This boulder can still be seen in Millbury today. No list would be complete without the Devil's Football in Hadley, but whether he played American- or English-style is unknown.

The Devil's Rock in Rochester is noteworthy because history records that there William Harris Sr. was an actual eyewitness to the devil. It was said that Harris discovered the devil making his mark on the rock before the fiend "leaped from the boulder" and scampered off. History does not tell us what the mark was, but we're hoping it was "O.S." for Old Scratch.

What the Devil?

If something could be named after the devil back in the good old days, it was. But the diabolical exploits that led to such commemorations are now largely forgotten—too bad for us! In some places, we have just the names and locations.

For example, there is a Devil's Landslide in Wellesley and a Devil's Hollow in Marshfield. But we don't know why the landslide was diabolical or what was devilish about the hollow. There is also a Devil's Pool in Pelham. This, by the looks of an old postcard, appears positively heavenly. We'll never know what dark deeds transpired here to associate it with Old Scratch.

In Warren there is a Devil's Peak, a stony overlook on an otherwise unassuming hill. Again we are baffled by the silence of history. Warren, however, must have been

a hot spot of devilry. There's a Devil's Den, Devil's Lane, and a Devil's Peak in that town. Perhaps the people here required—or deserved—special attention from the Dark One.

Other Devilish Dwellings

On washing day, which was once a week, the devil visited the Devil's Washtub in Warrick. For lazy summer afternoons, he had a lounger in Cohasset called the Devil's Chair. In Sutton can be found the Devil's Corncrib, where he kept the fruits and grains. He also had two gardens: Devil's Garden in Amherst and Lynnfield's Reedy Meadow.

The term Devil's Garden can also mean a large stand of trees of the same species, especially if the trees are of a type dramatically different from the forest as a whole. So all those orderly stands of red pines planted in the 1930s by the Civilian Conservation Corp are also technically Devil's Gardens. Why was Roosevelt so keen on Devil's Gardens?

Devil's Washtub

The Devil Rocks

Here in Massachusetts the devil really gets around. And where he goes, he leaves footprints—in stone. You can find evidence of his infernal capering in Auburn, Easton, Holliston, Ipswich, Medfield, Norton, Rochester, and Seekonk, to name a few.

The stories surrounding these footprints are all quite similar, as it seems the devil only has a few riffs and sticks to them. He will accost a preacher or try to bargain away a fellow's soul. These encounters never seem to work out for Old Scratch, and he stomps off, leaving a trail of smoking footprints in the living rock.

The best of these tales comes from Ipswich, in Essex County, which is an old New England sea town. It was founded in 1633 by John Winthrop and twelve partners—a witch's number—as a semimilitary post to keep the French away, and its roots are deep in the grim and unyielding Old Testament Puritanism of that early age.

Like all good devil stories, this one takes place in a church, and a famous church at that. When the Winthrop Thirteen came to Ipswich, "upon ascending the hill above the river they found an outcropping ledge of goodly extent, forming a sort of natural platform, and upon this rock they built their church." This church, known as the First Church of Ipswich, subsequently became famous throughout the colony for the learning and piety of its ministers, not to mention their devil-wresting skills.

The story begins on October's eve, September 30, 1740. A traveling preacher, the Reverend George Whitefield, was on a thunder-and-brimstone tour of New England when he made a fate-filled move on that high ledge in Ipswich—unleashing a sermon of unparalleled intensity in First Church.

Some things will never be completely understood. For instance, why was there an enormous curved mirror behind the pulpit in First Church? However it may be, the congregation had no choice but to contemplate their own distorted reflections in the primitive looking glass while the grim words of Puritanism rolled over them every Sabbath. Not a situation to improve anyone's demeanor.

Consider too that the devil, for reasons known only to himself, had previously taken up residence in that particular mirror. Like most monarchs, he liked to keep an eye on things. On that October's eve, our mirror-ensconced fiend sure got an eye- and earful. The Reverend Mr. Whitefield was in rare form and unleashed

Clockwise, the Reverend Mr. Whitefield, First Church of Ipswich and the print of Satan's cloven hoof.

a tremendous sermon, hitting all the high notes. He thundered, gave long dramatic pauses, and issued the direst proclamations on the soul, urging repentance, renunciation, and giving up the ways of the world.

This was apparently more than Old Scratch could take. He burst out of the mirror in a bang and a flash (the mirror went unscathed) and took furious form among the congregation in full regalia of horns and tail and hoofs, much as he was wont to do in those days.

But Whitefield, although a young man, was tough and canny and not taken aback by such cheap theatrics. In fact, the devil could scarcely have found himself a more powerful opponent had he tried. Whitefield, enshrined in history as "the first modern celebrity," was the leading figure of the Great Awakening, the first of several sweeping, dramatic revivals of religion and Protestant reformation in America. With a greater impact than even John Wesley, the English-born Whitefield routinely preached to crowds in the tens of thousands, a fact verified by a skeptical Ben Franklin.

Although only twenty-six years old at the time, the young minister was a veteran of aggressive evangelism and simply grabbed the devil and slammed him to the mat. They wrestled like maniacs on the floor and eventually rolled clawing and punching outside into the churchyard. Squaring off again, Whitefield was slowly forced little by little up the side of First Church and onto the roof.

The two contenders, man and devil, pushed and shoved each other back and forth across the roof, trying to cast each other off while the congregation watched in horror. Inch by inch they fought, with Whitefield backing up the steeple until they battled at the very pinnacle. With nowhere left to go, Whitefield drew on his massively commanding voice, which could carry to crowds in the tens of thousands. No one knows what mighty words he spoke, only that they blasted forth from him like a trumpet and that he emphasized his lion's roar with a mighty push.

Old Scratch was hurled in a flinging leap off the steeple, landing like a cat on the rocky ledge below. He scrambled down the hill in terrified leaps and bounds, never to return. But where his feet had struck the ledge "smoldered the indelible print of Satan's cloven hoof."

The Reverend George Whitefield climbed down and dusted himself off and gave thanks to God, and the meeting resumed. He was a humble man, and all his journal for the day recorded was, "Tuesday, Sept. 30 [1740] Preached at Ipswich about 10 in the morning, to some Thousands; the Lord gave me Freedom, and there was great Melting in the Congregation."

A Pact in Norton

The devil was sticking his foot into things more successfully in Norton, in 1716. This tale starts with a man of God, as is usual in these cases. (The devil doesn't seem to care about the rabble; they get by all right on their own.) This particular man of God was Deacon Major Thomas Leonard, who emigrated from Wales to Plymouth prior to 1662. Deacon Leonard was a vain man and claimed descent from a noble family in England, an unfortunate conceit that was passed on to his son, Major George Leonard, born in 1670.

Young George lusted for the wealth and estates rightly due to his alleged noble heritage. So when he met an enticing man one night, a man dressed all in black, in the primeval forests of New England, George was ready to hear his pitch. It was a simple proposition. George would be wealthy beyond imagining for all the days of his life. In exchange, he must pledge his soul, which the man in black, really the devil, would collect upon George's demise.

Now George didn't advertise this little business deal, but what did get around was the sudden and wondrous upsurge of his fortunes. Not only did he marry the beautiful Anna Tisdale in 1695 but he also became "very wealthy and owner of the largest landed estate in New England," according to historian Ellery Bicknell Crane.

Young and wealthy, George Leonard built the first frame house in Norton, the county seat of his new estates, and settled there with his young bride. The house became known as the Leonard Mansion as many additions and renovations occurred over the ensuing years.

Now, the man in black had granted George wealth and estates for all the days of his life. But the actual length of those days was unspecified. George died in 1716, at only forty-six years old, with a scant twenty-one years of living it up under his belt. He was laid out in an upstairs room in the Leonard Mansion. His wife, Anna, and their nine children—the man in black was generous on all accounts—gathered downstairs with friends and relations to mourn his untimely passing.

Amid the sobs and condolences, a horrible racket was heard from the room where George's body lay. The family ran upstairs, and Anna burst open the door onto a truly horrible sight. There in the room was the devil himself, come to collect George. His eyes blazed red, and with a horrible laugh, he tucked George's body under his arm and jumped out the open window. The black-clad figure landed on a large boulder below and

bounded off into the night shrieking with triumph and trailing the smell of brimstone behind him. A single parchment fluttered to the floor of the room. Anna burned it.

The next day it was noted that the boulder was marked with a deep impression of the devil's infernal foot; it remains so marked to this day. George's family put an oak log in his coffin to make up for the missing weight and hurriedly conducted a burial.

By 1960, the Leonard Mansion was in very poor condition. The owner was unable or unwilling to shoulder the burden of its expense and requested that the Norton Fire Department burn it down for practice, which they did. The devil took George's soul in 1716, but fire—and perhaps brimstone—took the house 244 years later.

Witches and Wizards

Now, it was bad enough that there was the devil, but even worse to the Puritan sensibility was the notion that their fellow man (or woman) might secretly be helping him along with the usual shenanigans: inflicting fits, drying up cows, and causing impotence among the clergy.

And what better place to learn these marvelous skills than at the Witchcraft School in Salem? Yes, indeed, check any topographical map of Salem, and you will see clearly labeled a Witchcraft School. We drove over to see about enrolling, only to discover that the full name on the building is the Witchcraft Heights School. The first set of pictures we took didn't come out. Neither did the second set, but on the third time back, we finally got the pictures. I have no idea why this happened, but I suspect . . . witchcraft.

After graduation from the school, witches were sent forth to find jobs ruining local communities. One honors student landed in North Pepperell around 1812 and single-handedly destroyed the mining village of Nissitissit. She apparently enjoyed making dire prophesies about her neighbors, prophesies that had an unfortunate way of coming true. She liked to generally threaten, "No one shall live in this town!" True enough. After the mining industry collapsed, everyone left Nissitissit village. Witch Brook is still there; other brooks with their attendant witches are found in Townsend and West Tisbury.

Ponds also received the attention of witches. There are Witch Ponds in Foxborough, Gay Head, Plainville, Mashpee, and a Witch Pond Swamp in Mansfield. Sadly, no one can now remember why they were named after witches in the first place. It sure looks as if some curse of forgetfulness worked.

Like the devil, witches liked to hang out around large rocks for their meetings. The famous Witch Rock in Rochester got its name because the local Indians would not go near it for fear of the witches that supposedly flew out of a large split in its surface. Recently someone painted a witch on a broomstick on the rock for those whose imagination is too weak to picture the scene.

A lesser known Witch Rock is in Peabody. Here,

according to Salvatore Trento, author of *Mysterious Places of Eastern North America*, are painted sigils, possibly of seventeenth-century origin. Sigils are magical keys that can pull you toward a certain energy. Trento believes that this rock could document actual witchcraft in Salem at the time of the trials. From the sketch in his book, it would appear that whoever did the sigils on the rock had read *The Magus* by Francis Barrett, because the sigils depicted on Witch Rock resemble ones that illustrate *The Magus*.

When they weren't gathering at large rocks, the witches were poking around in caves. There is a Witches Cave in Ashfield and an old gold mine in North Adams called Witch's Cave. There is also a Witch Cave in Ashland where accused witches escaped from the Salem trials and hid. Add to this a Witch Cave in Nahant used by a mother and daughter also escaping the trials, and our spelunking is complete.

The Witch House in Pigeon Cove was so named after a girl accused of witchcraft in the Salem hysteria was hidden there by her brothers. The house fascinated people for years to come and was the subject of at least a half dozen different postcards in the early 1900s.

Out on Naushon Island is Witch's Glen, a little valley on the water's edge. Naushon is the largest privately owned island in Massachusetts, so the nefarious activities in the Glen are a complete secret.

The Witch-Ground in Danvers was also notorious for its goings-on. This is the field behind the Reverend Parris's house where the Salem witches were supposed to have held their meetings in 1692.

Witch Hill, often called Witchcraft Hill or Gallows Hill, is where the town of Salem says the witch hangings occurred in 1692 (see "Fabled People and Places"). It is probably not the actual site, but it is the official one, and has been turned into a park. There is also a Witch-Hang Hill in Newburyport; in Topsfield, Witch Hill is where accused witch Mary Easty was living when she was arrested in the middle of the night and dragged off to Salem prison.

The Witch Tree in Littleton marks the place where the Dudley house used to stand. Abigail Dudley was accused of being a witch in 1720. Some neighbor girls, the Blanchards, had fits whenever she was around, so obviously she was a witch. After Mrs. Dudley died, she still continued to afflict the girls, or so they claimed. The girls' father did the only sensible thing in the situation—he moved his young family to a distant town, and their afflictions ceased. Then he moved them back to Littleton several years later after the Dudleys (and their ghosts) left town.

OLD WITCH HOUSE. BUILT 1692. PIGEON COVE. ROCKPORT. MASS.

Opposite page, Witch Rock of Rochester; at left, Witch Rock of Peabody; above, the Witch House in Pigeon Cove.

Legend of Deed Rock and God's Ten Acres

Once upon a time a kindly old man created one of the strangest sights to be seen in Worcester. High in hill country he dedicated ten acres to God. And just to make sure God got his due, the old man carved into a flat rock on the hillside a 215-word deed transferring the property. It is unknown if God ever took delivery of the parcel, but Deed Rock remains an enduring testament to the man's unique faith.

Just as enduring, rumors of dark curses and hangings swirl around the area. What is the story with God's Ten Acres? And why is it apparently the Devil's Playground today? Let's start at the beginning. . . .

Solomon Parsons Jr. was born in 1800, in Leicester. When the boy was twelve years old, his father bought a farm in Worcester, which Solomon would call his home for the long length of his extraordinary life.

Solomon Junior came from a line of religious men. His grandfather, the Reverend David Parsons, was the first Puritan minister in Leicester. Solomon Senior was one of the original members of the First Baptist Church in Worcester in 1812. The newly formed Baptist movement was very much looked at askance by the Puritan Church, which clashed with its New Testament teachings. Solomon Junior inherited this maverick religious streak, and he was one of the founders and pioneers of the First Methodist Episcopal Church in Worcester.

A preacher named William Miller, also known as the Prophet of Doom, forever changed Solomon Junior's life.

Solomon Parsons Jr.

Mr. Miller was a Vermont farmer turned evangelist who prophesied the second appearing of Christ and the imminent end of the world. His whirlwind tours across New England fired the imaginations of the time. Whole communities were taken with the fervor of the Millerites, as the Second Adventists were popularly known.

Solomon was a man who valued religious liberty above all things. In the free-for-all of the open-air Millerite meetings, he found a home that suited his wide-ranging mind and maverick religious feelings.

Solomon heard the Millerite message at midlife, and many changes ensued. He severed his connection with the Methodist Church and became a pacifist and strict vegetarian for the rest of his life. He used no leather in his apparel or in his equipage, going so far as to harness his team with ropes and chains instead.

In 1840, he bought a ten-acre tract high in the wilds of western Worcester as a sanctuary to God. Reached by a winding footpath, the land was up on a small plateau near the top of the eastern side of Tetasset Hill. Tetasset is a Nipmunk Indian name, but the Colonists soon renamed the hill Rattlesnake Ledge.

Upon paying $125 to William G. Hall for this beautiful property, Solomon had Hall deed over the parcel to God, rather than to him. To immortalize the nature of the transaction, to perpetually dedicate the site to the service of God, he had Sylvester Ellis carve the deed into a flat boulder in the shadow of Rattlesnake Ledge. This 215-word inscription must have taken months if not years to carve. The workmanship and depth of carving was so carefully done that almost 170 years later the inscription is still as clear and legible as when it was first meticulously chipped into the rock.

The deed reads as follows:

> Know all men by these presents that I William G. Hall
> Of Worcester in the County of Worcester and Commonwealth
> of Mass in consideration of 125 dollars paid by the hand
> of Solomon Parsons of the same Worcester the receipt where
> of I do hereby acknowledge do hereby give, grant, sell
> and convey unto God through the Laws of Jesus Christ
> which are made known to man by the record of the New
> Testament recorded by Matthew Mark Luke John the
> Evangelist this land to be Governed by the above mentioned
> Laws and together with the spirit of God the said tract of
> Land is situated in Worcester above mentioned the South
> Westerly part bounded as follows viz beginning at the southwest corner
> Of the lot at a stake and stones by land of E Daniels
> Thence easterly by land of S Perry about 97 rods to a
> Corner of the fence thence northerly by land of L Cates
> About 54 rods to a corner of the fence thence westerly
> By land of the heirs of J Fowler about 24 rods to
> A chestnut tree in the wall at the corner of the
> Land of said Daniels and a heap of stones by the
> Side of it thence southerly to the bound first mentioned.

Was this deed carved in the rock a legal document? Despite its time-consuming and meticulous carving, the deed had legal flaws. For starters, William Hall did not have his signature, execution date, or an acknowledgment chiseled into it. Even if the rock were hauled to the Registry for recording, it would not be transcribed into the record books, because it wasn't a "duly executed and acknowledged instrument," even though Hall apparently relinquished the property.

But those are mere legalities, of no importance to Solomon Parsons. His real purpose in acquiring the site was to erect a temple to God, where He could be worshipped freely and spontaneously. This structure was called the

Forest Sanctuary and was built by hand by Solomon himself. At the height of Millerite-end-of-the-world fever (which Miller predicted would happen between the vernal equinoxes of 1843 and 1844), Solomon began construction of his sanctuary, a building intended, he said, to "escape the wrath to come," and which "should endure even amid a burning and transformed earth."

When the world did not end on the predicted date of October 22, 1844, many Millerites abandoned the religion in shock and disappointment. However, Solomon and his friends continued to revere Forest Sanctuary as a place of worship and continued to meet there for many years to come, if not as Millerites. Solomon Parsons passed away in 1893 at the age of ninety-three. We'll leave it up to the reader to determine if God ever did come by to claim his property.

Ghosts

There are many theories as to why some not-quite-departed soul would be seen hanging around in this realm after death. One is that ghosts are the spirits of people who died before their time, perhaps violently or from illness, and now refuse to cross over to the beyond. They remain here, stubbornly insisting they are still alive, though their former bodies are now nothing but ether. Some people scoff at the whole idea of ghosts. For them, spirits are just the products of someone's overactive imagination.

Whichever camp you're in, the Bay State has no shortage of ghostly appearances. Maybe it's all the history that's been played out here. The old buildings and fields seem to record the past somehow and play it back for a select few. Or maybe it's the dark and cold New England winters; nothing like a good ghost story to get the blood moving. Or perhaps our friends and ancestors who have died in the physical sense simply like it here and have no intention of ever leaving . . . not even in death. These ghosts are a part of Massachusetts and a part of us.

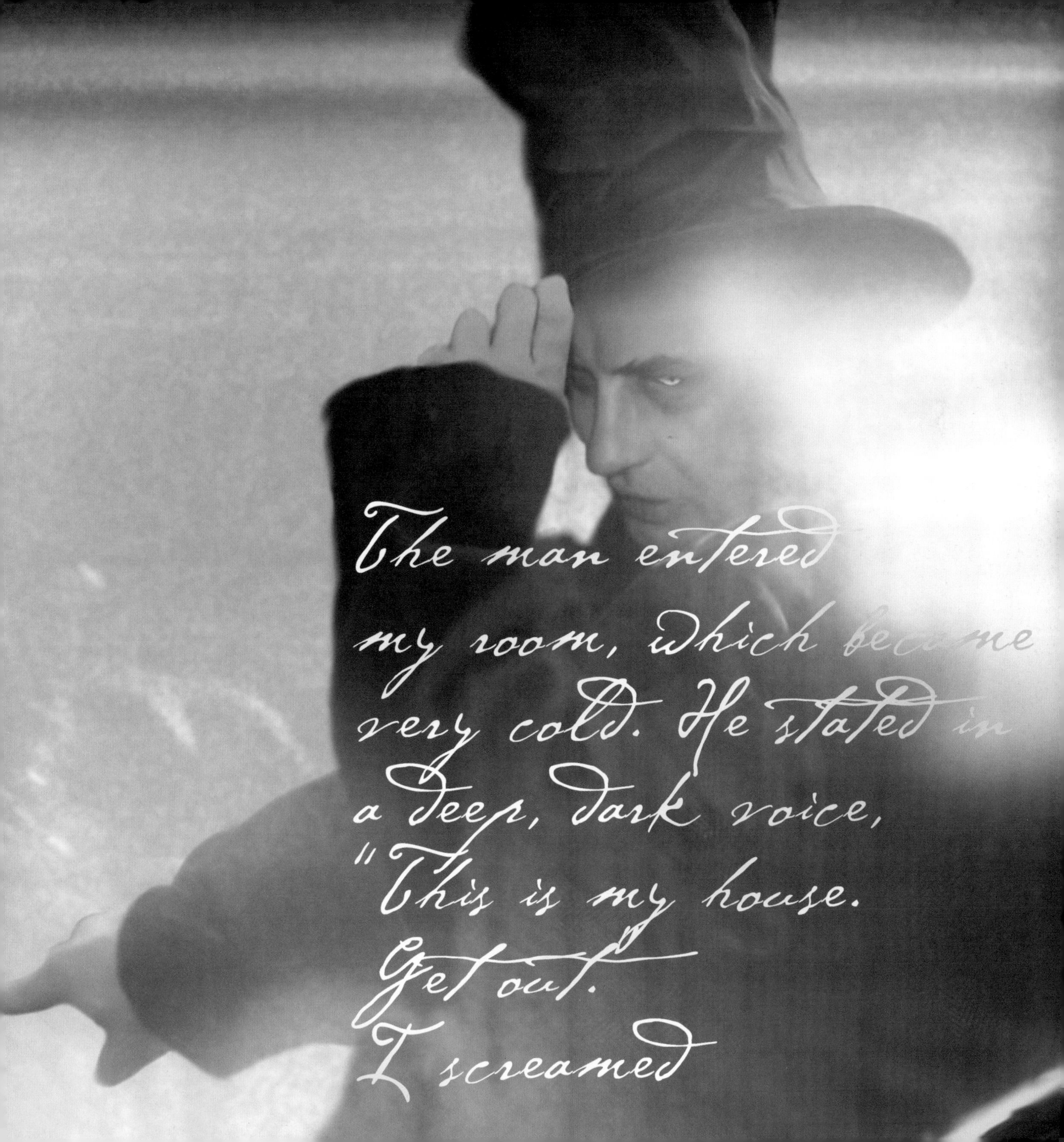

The man entered
my room, which became
very cold. He stated in
a deep, dark voice,
"This is my house.
Get out.
I screamed

House of the Seven Gables

"*Half-way down a by-street* of one of our New England towns, stands a rusty wooden house, with seven acutely peaked gables, facing towards various points of the compass, and a huge, clustered chimney in the midst," begins Nathaniel Hawthorne's 1851 book *The House of the Seven Gables.* The real house that inspired Hawthorne sits in Salem and is both storied and haunted.

Hawthorne's tale mirrors some of the horrors from his own life. His great-grandfather, John Hathorne (the original spelling of the family name) was one of the three judges who presided over the Salem witchcraft trials in 1692. In *The House of the Seven Gables*, Hawthorne explores the idea of paying for the sins of one's kin. Perhaps the real mansion of the same name held some kind of power over Hawthorne, because by some accounts he's still there. But is he forced to remain inside, or does he just visit on occasion?

Built in 1668, the home is the oldest surviving wooden mansion in North America. It sits on the edge of Salem Harbor and has been added on to, renovated, and restored over the centuries. It has been the home of some prominent families, including the Captain John Turner family (who first constructed the mansion), and the Ingersoll family, relatives of Nathaniel Hawthorne. Hawthorne himself spent a great deal of time in this house with his cousin, Susan Ingersoll.

Today the building is a museum with over two thousand artifacts from old New England, and there are tours offering visitors a glimpse into old Colonial life. Various other buildings have been added to the property throughout the twentieth century, including Nathaniel Hawthorne's birthplace home and the Hooper-Hathaway House. Each seems to have its own ghostly legends.

Sean Snyderman was a tour guide at the House of the Seven Gables in the mid-1990s. He spoke about some of the legends he heard while working there. "Hawthorne's mother really fell apart after her husband died, on his first voyage away at sea, when Nathaniel Hawthorne was just a young kid," Snyderman said. "Mrs. Hawthorne kind of lost touch with reality and spent many days weeping on the steps of her house. At that time, there wasn't much a widow could do unless she was rich. Some visitors, especially the psychically inclined, have said when you walk by those steps, you get the sense of sadness, and some say they can hear Hawthorne's mother still crying."

At the actual House of the Seven Gables, others have claimed to see a male and a female figure in one of the first-floor windows. These shapes are presumed to be the ghosts of Nathaniel Hawthorne and his cousin, Susan Ingersoll, still wandering the famed House of the Seven Gables.

Former Bellingham Library

There's a small brick building in Bellingham, on Route 126, right next to the town hall. It was built in 1930, once housed the town's public library, and is currently home to its historical commission. It is also haunted, with ghostly occurrences reported there since 1975.

During the library's tenure in the building, a large unabridged dictionary sat open on a sturdy table. Each evening, the librarians would close the big book before locking up the building for the night. They would come in the next day and find the dictionary open again. Those with a skeptical mind might think this is simply forgetfulness on the part of the librarians, and that may be, but other strange events also occurred here.

Occasionally the staff would come in to find that chairs had been moved from their usual spots, and books would sometimes be lying scattered on the floor. The librarians may have forgotten to close the dictionary or might possibly not have recalled moving a chair, but no librarian would leave books strewn around a floor.

One of the more frightening events happened one evening when only two librarians were in the building—one on the main floor and the other in the lower-level children's room. The librarian upstairs heard a voice clearly say, "Excuse me," from right behind her. When she turned around, no one (living) was standing there. She went downstairs to ask the children's librarian—the only other person in the building—what she wanted, but she replied that she hadn't been upstairs, nor had she said a word. This event would continue to play over and over again, with always the same two words, "Excuse me."

In 1989, the library moved to its new location on Blackstone Street, but the ghost, it seems, stayed behind. The Bellingham Historical Museum moved into the building, bringing with them artifacts donated from around the town.

Mr. Ernie Taft is the chairman of the Bellingham Historical Commission and has witnessed a few unexplainable events in the old building. "A walking cane that belonged to a prominent Bellingham citizen is in our collection," Taft said. "The night before, this cane was in its proper place, but the next morning the top of the cane—which is screwed on—was found lying on the floor at a considerable distance from the bottom part."

That is not the only unexplained event Taft has witnessed. "Back in 1989, someone donated three theater tickets from the old Olympia Theatre in Woonsocket, Rhode Island," he said. "That evening the tickets were left upon the desk. The next morning when I came in, I found the theater tickets ripped to pieces and lying in a pile on the desk." Perhaps the ghost was giving the show a big thumbs-down from beyond?

Though the great big dictionary is no longer in the building, it seems pranks are still played there. Doors that are securely closed the night before will be found open, and books in the historical commission's collection will go missing and then reappear. While it's not known for sure who or what might be causing these events, it definitely haunts the minds of the building's living residents, if only once in a while.

Allen Street House

Everyone knew something was wrong with the house on Allen Street in Salem before Carter and Lucy did. (We're withholding their last name to protect their privacy.) The price of the house was too low, and people looked away when the couple told them the address. It wasn't until shortly after the 2001 closing that the couple was told of the deaths of two little girls there.

It happened on February 10, 1980. The girls were on the third floor when a fire broke out. Neighbors tried to raise a ladder to reach them, but by then, the fire had gotten out of control. The girls could not be saved.

A previous owner first noticed something was wrong when he began renovating the house. Odd things happened, and workers got spooked and left the job site. The girl who lived next door kept her shades down because she said she saw the ghosts of the two little girls in the house.

The activity continued when our couple took up residence. The ghosts appear in the form of orbs, which Lucy can spot clearly, especially in the upstairs bedroom. The orbs are about the size of a silver dollar and bright white, and Lucy sees a difference in them as they dart or hover in the house.

The orbs seem to have a special fondness for Lucy and Carter's daughter, Sarah, and follow her wherever she goes. "You can't take a picture of my daughter in that house without orbs," said Lucy. Sarah's boyfriend has seen the ghosts of the two girls too. They were on the back staircase, climbing to the third floor.

The room where the girls died is now a guest room containing a few old lace dresses hanging on the door and an air mattress with sheets. One day Lucy fluffed up the dresses and straightened out the sheets, then left the room for a while. When she came back later, the sheets were disturbed and the dresses had flattened back out. As she refluffed the dresses, she distinctly saw an impression on the bed that was large enough to be a person. Then the dresses she had just touched flattened out as she watched.

But orbs and ghostly girls aren't the only strange things manifesting themselves in this house. Lights go on and off by themselves, and baffling changes in temperature occur. There are unexplained noises—including banging and voices—that bother the family. One day Lucy came home from work and tried to take a nap. Just as she laid her head down on the pillow, she heard people talking all around inside the house. Their voices were low and muffled, just below her being able to understand them. According to Lucy, the family has stopped investigating every odd disturbance. "I know what is up there. I don't need to check."

Lucy's brother once showered in the bathroom upstairs but came running down a few minutes later, wet and angry. The lights had gone out, and he yelled for whoever shut them off to turn them back on. This happened several times as he tried to shower, and each time, he heard two little girls giggling from the hallway. But he could not blame his niece Sarah and her visiting friend for the prank: They had left the house as soon as he had gone upstairs.

The spirits of the two little girls seem to have opened the door for other ghosts. The family has had several encounters with the ghost of a man in the basement, and their dogs follow commands from an unseen hand. They also tell of a shadowy figure that sneaks into their rooms and walks the house at night. Who these spirits are remains unknown.—*Christopher Balzano, Director, Massachusetts Paranormal Crossroads*

Ghosts on Trial in Plymouth

Only months before he signed the Declaration of Independence in his bold script, John Hancock inherited a haunted house. While there is no proof Hancock ever lived in the house or knew of the alleged hauntings there, the story behind the "finest house on Cole Hill" remains one of the few instances of a ghost's being put on trial.

Decades earlier, in 1733, the house had been abandoned and its reputation solidified in the minds of the local people as the most haunted building in Plymouth. The owner at that time was Josiah Cotton, a prominent member of the community and a strict Calvinist, who did not believe in the paranormal or superstition. He inherited the house from his dead daughter, along with all of her spouse's debts. The husband, a sailor named Thompson Phillips, had died a horrible death at sea, and his will stipulated that his father-in-law was responsible for his dealings. Unable to get out from underneath the debt, Cotton opened the house to renters in the area.

In 1732, he reached an agreement with John Clark, a young blacksmith who decided to use the house as a residence and a workshop. Clark moved in with his family, his business partner's family, and several people who worked for him.

A little over a year later Cotton and his tenants had a falling out. People witnessed the men arguing, and Cotton later testified that Clark claimed he would start unsavory rumors about the landlord and the house.

In June 1733, Clark and his partner moved out, refusing to pay the rent they owed. One by one the remaining tenants left, claiming the house was haunted. It seems Cotton's son-in-law had come back to his earthly home and the devil himself had moved in with him! The sailor had risen from the sea, and in his wake, all sorts of evil followed. The hauntings were so bad, Clark told a friend, "he nor no body allse could live in it because it was haunted with evill spirits." Unseen hands moved furniture or rattled the walls throughout the building. There were unexplained thumps and "a great noise like the banging of a door too and fro."

The haunting also included groans that became so loud they woke other people in the vicinity and forced children in the neighborhood to cover "their heads ready to stifle themselves" when they went to bed. The most disturbing hauntings involved a pale "bluish" light that was seen by people both in the house and in the surrounding neighborhood. The house's reputation grew,

and people began camping outside waiting for something to happen.

Cotton filed a lawsuit against Clark and his business partner, charging them with slander against the house. Their rumors, combined with the large crowds that remained outside looking for ghosts, made the house an

Plymouth Street and the Court House

undesirable investment, he contended, and people refused to rent it. The stories of hauntings also lowered the property value of the surrounding area and tainted Cotton's stature in the community.

By now, the courts and some of the public were weary of the paranormal. Science had entered the picture and started to compete with established beliefs in witchcraft and ghosts. However, the media still had a strong hand in controlling public opinion. Ghosts make good stories, and newspaper accounts of the events served to reinforce old superstitions.

The trial began in March 1734. Originally, Cotton had intended to prove there was no such thing as ghosts and that therefore his tenants' stories about the house were false. Cotton and his family even stayed in the house to show that it was safe.

It may be difficult to verify the existence of ghosts, but Cotton and his lawyer found it equally hard to convince people that there was no such thing as ghosts. They changed tactics to prove that belief in the supernatural was evil and wrong. Superstitions were the work of the "fringe" and undesirable people in society, especially Native Americans and slaves. Tales of ghosts, they said, "receive[d] a ready Entertainment from unthinking People." As young and unestablished people in the community, his former tenants were susceptible to this and then infected their neighbors, who were also eager to believe. This tactic failed as well because people's ideas about the supernatural ran too deep.

Cotton now turned to his last tactic, which was trying to prove the disgruntled tenant's intent. He argued to the court that Clark had known people held these strong ideas and had intentionally started the rumors to hurt his reputation.

None of these tactics worked, however, and Clark and the other defendants were acquitted. The court said it did not matter if ghosts existed, only that people believed it to be true. The paranormal was a subdivision of religion, not a character flaw as Cotton had tried to prove. He was forced to pay all the court costs, but more importantly, the case reinforced the fact that people were not ready to leave their belief in ghosts behind. —*Christopher Balzano Director, Massachusetts Paranormal Crossroads*

Never Got Her Pink Slip

My sister and I used to spend the weekend at my great-aunt's house in Chicopee. She had an old, two-story house with a glass door that enclosed the stairs leading to the second floor. The door was directly across the hall from the bedroom we always slept in.

One night, we both saw a lady in a long, frilly white nightgown walking down the stairs. She raised her hand to turn the doorknob and disappeared, only to come walking down the stairs again. She was glowing with a faint, bluish-white, but we couldn't see her face. It was like it had been smudged out. She walked down the stairs four or five times in a row and then stopped. This activity would be repeated several times over the next three or four years, and then we didn't see her anymore. When we told our mother about her, she insisted we had imagined it all.

In 1998, when my great-aunt's house was being sold, I found the deed to the house and showed it to my father. He told me that his aunt's family had bought the house cheaply in the 1920s because it had been taken by the city for non-payment of taxes. The house had been a bordello, and while the city wasn't thrilled at the activity in the house, they were more concerned about the money they were due in back taxes.

Originally, my great-aunt's brothers slept upstairs, but after they moved out, the second floor was kept closed and became storage space. It was always cold up there, even during the summer. It had a creepy feel to it, and my sister and mother would not go up there alone.

I'm pretty sure that the woman my sister and I saw on the stairs was a "working girl" coming down to get another "customer." My experience gave me an interest in the paranormal and taught me to trust my own perceptions, regardless of what other people say about them. –*Darlene Caban*

The Man with the Tall, Black Hat

When I was about nine years old, I lived in an apartment building located on Buffington Street in Fall River. An evil spirit haunted the building, and he tormented me for as long as my family lived there.

My first sighting happened around 1980. I was in bed one night when I heard someone walking around in the living room. When I called out, "Mom, is that you?" whoever it was stopped, and then started walking toward my room. When it reached my doorway, I noticed that it was a tall man, dressed in black, with a tall, black hat. At this point I became frightened for my life.

The man entered my room, which suddenly became very cold. I could actually see my breath. He walked to the foot of my bed and stated in a deep, dark voice, "This is my house. Get out." I screamed for my mom and threw the covers over my head. When my mom finally entered my room, the coldness went away.

Everything was fine until later on that week, when I was going into my basement to get my bike. I remember that it was somewhat rainy and cloudy that day, and I was afraid to go into my basement due to what had previously happened. But as I walked through the first part of the basement, I felt a cold breeze pass by me. It filled the whole room with its chill.

At this point I stopped. I could see my breath again and I was being held to the spot by something I could not see. I could smell a stench that I can't describe, and then the same man I saw previously appeared at the end of the basement next to my bike. He said in that deep, dark voice, "Get out of my house." At this point I broke free from whatever was holding me and ran screaming out the basement and back upstairs.

—*Bud A. Prater*

My Creepy Apartment

In 1995, I moved into a one-bedroom apartment in Amherst, and everything about it was spooky. There was even a dead tree right in front of my bay window. It was rotten, yet was still growing leaves.

The apartment was okay at first. But there were pencil drawings on the walls that said "Jesus Saves" and "Jesus died for our sins." I tried to get these off with soap and water, but the only thing that came off was the paint. The pencil marks just got darker and more pronounced. And I was cold all of the time, but I figured it was due to the electric heat not working that well. Then the bathroom off of my bedroom kept flooding for no apparent reason. It flooded my bedroom and soaked my mattress, which was on the floor.

I hadn't unpacked most of my stuff. I kept saying to myself that I would unpack when I got to six months of my stay there, but the strange things that kept happening stopped me. It didn't help when I asked my neighbors whom the prior tenant was, because he told me he was a paranoid schizophrenic who had been taken away by ambulance when he blockaded himself in this apartment for three days.

One night I woke up to see a large man standing over me. He was wearing a red plaid shirt and suspenders. When I blinked my eyes, he was gone. This happened two more times.

On another occasion, I had guests over. One worked for the local fire department as an EMT. He said he had been in the apartment before, so I told him that I heard the previous tenant had been mentally ill and had locked himself in the apartment for three days.

My friend said, "Try dead." He then told me the previous tenant had been dead in the apartment for three days. I moved out three weeks later.—*Nina*

A Night in the Funeral Parlor

Some years ago I was a member of the Springfield police force when we received a call from a little old lady who lived above a local funeral parlor. She said there were strange noises coming from the supposedly empty parlor below. (Empty that is except for whatever dearly departed were in residence.) We told her to lock her door and then, with back up, I entered the dwelling on the first floor.

A few lights were still lit, giving the place a very eerie glow. And sure enough, there were two open caskets, with the embalmed remains of two people lying in them. In that light, they didn't look peaceful to me. They looked harsh and kind of sinister. Maybe I was imagining it, but think how you'd feel if you were in an empty funeral parlor at night with two dead people.

But the noises weren't coming from them. Because suddenly I heard a crash down in the basement, where the embalming was done. The hairs literally stood out on the back of my neck, but I drew out my weapon and started down to the basement. There was a strange blue light glowing at the bottom, which cast another eerie shadow over everything. It didn't help that the whole place smelled of formaldehyde and my eyes were burning from the stench.

When I looked around I saw that the caskets for future funerals were also displayed here. And all the caskets were open, to show the lush interiors. Except for two of them. Those two were closed. Something—or someone—was in them.

I lifted my weapon, hoping that whatever I was facing wouldn't be immune to the bullets inside it. "I've got six shots here," I yelled, "And I'm shooting three of them into those closed coffins. If anyone is in there, you'd better come out before I shoot."

With that, two guys jumped out of the coffins

yelling, "Don't Shoot!" I have to say, they were so pale with fright they looked dead themselves. It turns out they were trying to steal the formaldehyde used in the embalming process to make crack cocaine, which was a big problem in Springfield at the time. They were arrested and prosecuted.

When I went back upstairs, it seemed to me that the two bodies still resting in their coffins up there looked more peaceful and benign now. And the threatening presence I'd felt before was gone. Maybe even the dead don't like their home invaded by drug dealers.

—Tony L., Chicopee

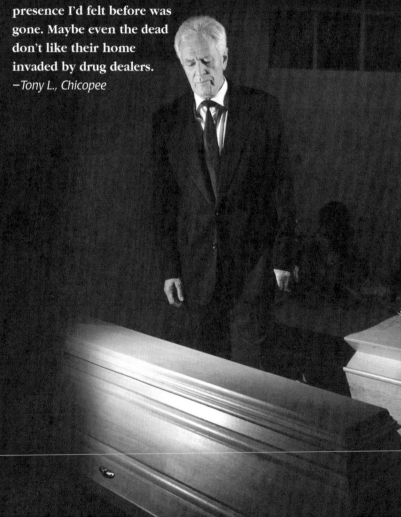

Haunted Houghton Mansion

Many secrets abide in the Houghton Mansion in North Adams, and not just the ghostly kind. Built by Albert Charles Houghton circa the 1890s, the extravagant home was a symbol of his wealth and prestige. He had made his fortune as president of the Arnold Print Works, and he was also the first mayor of North Adams. Not bad for a local boy who made good.

In 1900, Houghton, his wife, Cordelia, and their youngest daughter, Mary, who was twenty-three at the time, settled in the house on Church Street. They lived there contentedly enough, and in 1914, Houghton bought his first car, a beautiful Pierce-Arrow that seated seven. He was very proud of his new possession, but it would bring tragedy to the family.

Houghton put driving the vehicle into the hands of the family servant and chauffeur, John Widders. On the morning of August 1, 1914, with Widders in the driving seat, Houghton and Mary set off for a road trip to Bennington, Vermont. Accompanying them were Dr. and Mrs. Hutton of New York, and their daughter, Sybil, who was a childhood friend of Mary's.

A half hour into the trip, the Pierce-Arrow made its way through the town of Pownal, Vermont, heading up Oak Hill Road—a rocky and bumpy strip of land that was in the process of being repaired. As Widders navigated the car around to the left of a team of repairmen, the car tilted, then tipped down a steep incline. It rolled over several times before coming to rest in a field. All the passengers except for Mary were thrown from the tumbling car. Mrs. Hutton was killed when the car rolled over her. Mary suffered a great deal of trauma and succumbed to her injuries a short while later at North Adams Hospital. The rest of the passengers, except Mrs. Hutton, survived with cuts, bruises, and a broken bone or two.

The incident was immediately ruled an accident by state authorities in Vermont. The report said the soft shoulder of the road was to blame for the car tipping, but it did little to settle the nerves of the chauffeur, John Widders. He blamed himself for the two deaths, and the morning after the accident, he shot himself.

Houghton fell into a depression after the accident and the suicide of John Widders, and just nine days after the death of his daughter he had a stroke and passed away.

The mansion stayed in the family until 1926, when Houghton's daughter Florence and her husband, William Arthur Gallup, sold the home to the Freemasons, who have owned it ever since. The Masons added a lodge to the house where the garden used to be. And by some accounts, Houghton and a few others may still be hanging around.

Josh Mantello has a unique perspective on the Houghton Mansion and its hauntings. He first heard about the ghosts of the building as a teenager, when his father, a member of the Masonic lodge, told him stories about the place. He said members claimed to hear footsteps going up and down the stairs, but found no living person nearby when they investigated. Lights would go on and off by themselves, and the lodge members would smell smoke, especially in the front parlor, even though smoking was not allowed.

In May 2000, Josh Mantello became a Mason and learned more about the ghosts and other secrets the building still holds. In one dusty, dark hallway upstairs, there are a couple of odd Masonic artifacts. The first is a wooden electric chair, complete with exposed copper wires running down the length of it and a small box behind the chair about the right size for a car battery. Next to the electric chair are two beds of nails. "I don't know what they were used for," Mantello said. "I asked some of the old-timers in the lodge about them, and they won't say." These Masonic relics remain mysteries covered in dust in a dark recess of the mansion.

Back to the ghosts . . . in 2004, Mantello co-founded the Berkshire Paranormal Group. He and his team have investigated the Houghton Mansion well over one hundred times now, and they've managed to uncover even more mysteries inside Houghton's old house.

So who is haunting the mansion? "A. C. Houghton, we're pretty sure his daughter Mary, and John Widders," Mantello said. "And then there's something in the basement. . . ."

"I'm not saying it's a little girl," Mantello said, "but it's some kind of small, shadowy creature." Mantello has been on investigations in the basement at night when the only light coming in was from the small cellar windows near the far ceiling. He and others have claimed to see this shadowy figure poke its head out from one of the basement rooms. "It's kind of shy," Mantello said. "I saw it poke its head out, then float out of the room in front of me before going back in and disappearing."

The Phantom Tennis Court

My friend Larry and I got together on a Wednesday afternoon in August of 1997 for a game of tennis. We were driving through North Cambridge, and didn't know where the nearest tennis courts were. I pulled up to a cop on a side street off of Route 2 and asked him for assistance in finding a place to play.

We both thought there was something weird about the cop, though neither of us said anything at the time. I'm not sure if it was the way he was dressed or his attitude. But in any case, he did give us clear directions to tennis courts about two blocks away.

We followed his instructions, turned right into a driveway and, sure enough, three tennis courts were right in front of us. We looked to see if any were available, but all were occupied. It struck us both as odd that all the players were dressed in white, which was a little formal for a municipal tennis court. We both noticed a very attractive young lady in the right court wearing a short, white tennis dress. She was preparing to address the serve.

We decided to wait for a court to come free, and I pulled my car into a parking area immediately on my right. Larry got out of the car first and then said, "Where did the tennis courts go?"

I got out of the car and noticed we were alone. "They were right there!" I said. The tennis courts, the players, and everything we had been looking at were gone! Instead, there was a building in front of us that had not been visible when we pulled in.

Strangely, neither of us was afraid, though we both agreed that what we just experienced was "too weird." We got back in the car and drove off to play tennis elsewhere. Later I did some research into the area. I found out there were indeed tennis courts there—but they were torn down in 1954! Did we "travel back in time"? Did we see "ghosts"? Larry seems to think we viewed a scene from the 1920s. Also, I have to wonder—did they see us? *–Jeff Vachon*

Little Lucy Keyes Lost Forever

Robert Keyes, his wife, Martha, and three daughters—Patty, Anna, and Lucy—moved to the virgin forest on the southeast slope of Wachusett Mountain in Princeton in 1751. The family had purchased two hundred acres of land and quickly set to work clearing trees to build their home.

Though the Keyeses' land was prime, it wasn't a perfect, peaceful paradise for them. Mohawk Indians regularly passed through—a dangerous prospect if a confrontation ensued. But Indians weren't the only problem. Shortly after moving in, Robert Keyes found himself in a legal dispute over land with his hermitlike neighbor, Tilly Littlejohn. Eventually, the dispute went before a local court, and the ruling favored Robert Keyes. Though Tilly Littlejohn felt he had wrongfully lost some of his land in the ruling, he went back to his hermit life, and the Keyes family went back to their property.

Living in Colonial New England brought families close together, as harsh winters compelled them to stay indoors and daily chores forced everyone to pitch in. The Keyeses were no exception. But an incident that took place on April 14, 1755, would forever shatter the serenity of their home and be the impetus for one of the saddest ghostly legends ever to come out of Massachusetts.

It was on that early spring day that Martha Keyes sent her two eldest daughters, nine-year-old Anna and seven-year-old Patty, to Wachusett Lake to bring back some of the fine sand along the shore, which was to be used to scour the floors. Anna and Patty knew the way and set off on their task. Young Lucy was told to stay home because she was too small and would only slow the older girls down . . . but Lucy didn't listen. After her two sisters left, Lucy sneaked off and tried to follow

them. What happened next has been the subject of much speculation, but we do know that Lucy never found her sisters. In fact, she never came home again.

Lucy's frantic parents immediately formed a search party to look for the missing girl. Even the Keyeses' estranged neighbor, Tilly Littlejohn, helped search. As the sun set on April 14, Martha Keyes strolled the acres of their property calling out for her daughter. "Luuu-cy! Luuu-cy!" echoed off Wachusett Mountain. But no little girl came running from the trees to her mother.

After a week of combing the woods and dragging parts of Lake Wachusett, the searchers gave up. When the dust had settled, Tilly Littlejohn decided to move to a small house along the Mohawk River in New York. He left his frustration over the land dispute, the Keyes family, and the desperate calls of Martha behind him and resumed his hermit life.

Martha Keyes died in 1786, never knowing exactly what happened to her youngest daughter. But for her whole life, she had repeatedly roamed through the woods, calling for her—and she continued to call from the beyond. Locals claimed to hear Martha's disembodied voice echoing through the woods every evening as dusk fell.

Fast-forward to August 12, 1815, to the deathbed of Tilly Littlejohn. Littlejohn called his housekeeper to his side and asked her to take down a confession of something that had been eating at him. He told her that on April 14, 1755, he was walking through the woods when a scared and lost Lucy Keyes wandered into his path. He was still furious over the recent land dispute with her family, jealous of the amount of land they had, and blinded by rage. Without thinking, he grabbed a rock and smashed it across young Lucy's head. The girl fell to the ground bleeding and wailing in pain.

Once Littlejohn realized what he had done, he saw

no other choice but to finish what he had started. He smashed the young girl's skull in with his rock, then carried her body deep into the woods and stuffed her corpse into a hollowed-out tree. When night fell, he came back and buried her body under an uprooted tree.

Lucy Keyes's tragic legend continues to inspire, as witnesses still report hearing Martha's voice and some still claim to see little lost Lucy in the woods.

Today, the legend of Lucy Keyes survives through folktales, through ghost encounters in the region, and through the efforts of Princeton resident and filmmaker John Stimpson, who wrote and directed the film *The Legend of Lucy Keyes*. Stimpson moved to Princeton in 1988, where he bought land once owned by the Keyes family. He said, "People used to drive by the house and say, 'Is this the old Lucy Keyes house?' At first I didn't really know what they were talking about."

Once he heard the details of the mystery, he was hooked. He knew it would be a great story to tell on screen.

As part of his research for the film, Stimpson collected several accounts of modern-day witnesses confronting the unexplained around Wachusett Mountain. One witness is Jimmy Dellasanta, a night-shift snow groomer at Wachusett Mountain ski area. He recalled a late evening snowstorm that left him puzzled. "It wasn't a big storm," Dellasanta said.

"We got maybe three, four inches of snow. When I got to the top of the Challenger trail, that's where I came upon the footprints. Had they been there earlier in the evening, say eleven, twelve o'clock, there would have been an accumulation of snow in the footprints . . . but there was no accumulation. They were fresh tracks.

Unexplained fresh tracks. I sat in the machine kind of stunned, thinking, this is a little kid's footprints. What's he doing up here at this time of night?"

Dellasanta called another employee and told him what he saw. His co-worker came up and confirmed that the child's footprints were there. A few weeks later, Dellasanta and his co-worker were having coffee when they happened to mention the footprints to another employee. She immediately thought of Lucy Keyes and proceeded to tell Dellasanta about the legend.

A few weeks later Dellasanta was working near the top of the mountain again when his grooming machine died. He didn't have a radio, and no one else was working up there that evening, so he began to walk down the mountain in the cold, windy darkness. At one point, he says, "I just stopped, and I could have sworn I heard a woman talking. I'd go another couple hundred yards and I'd hear it again."

John Stimpson also interviewed Jean Stratton, a former Princeton resident who encountered a strange voice in the woods while she and her family were living on Mirick Road, a short distance from the Keyes property.

When Stratton was a teenager, she and some friends were walking in the area where the Keyes house once stood when she heard a voice calling. "It was getting late," Stratton said, "about twilight time, and I remember hearing this haunting voice and it really threw me. I mean I stopped . . . it was like a mother wailing. It was the sort of thing that sent shivers. I was quite taken aback."

Lucy Keyes's tragic legend continues to inspire, as witnesses still report hearing Martha's voice and some still claim to see little lost Lucy in the woods. We can only hope that the mother and daughter so cruelly separated in life have been reunited in death.

Old Coot of Bellows Pipe Trail

At 3,491 feet, Mount Greylock is the highest peak in Massachusetts. Located on the state's western border, it's home to chilly winters, plenty of snow, and the ghost of an "Old Coot" who is said to still be wandering a path known as Bellows Pipe Trail, near the town of Lanesborough.

The Old Coot is believed to be a North Adams farmer named William Saunders who left his wife, Belle, and their children at home back in 1861 to fight for the Union in the Civil War. Over a year later, Belle received a letter from a military hospital saying that her husband had been gravely wounded. Days went by, and Belle heard nothing more about her husband's condition. Those days melted into weeks, then months, and still no word came. The Saunders family could only assume that William had perished.

Belle couldn't work her farm alone, so she hired a local man to help run the place. A romance bloomed between them, and they were married.

In 1865, a bearded and war-ravaged man wearing the Union blue showed up at the train station in North Adams. He walked back to his old farm and homestead and saw his wife, smiling and happy; he saw his children playing, and he saw that another man had taken his place.

The old man didn't say a word. He kept on walking past the farm, toward Mount Greylock. Once inside the Bellows Pipe section of the mountain, he built a shack and lived a hermit's life. The Old Coot, as he came to be called, would stroll into town for supplies or for occasional work, but he spent most of his time on the mountain.

Today, Bellows Pipe Trail is a well-defined trail running through the woods of Mount Greylock. Hikers and mountain bikers often traverse it, and some report seeing a bluish apparition wandering ahead. The Old Coot, it seems, is always seen heading up into the mountain.

Concord's Colonial Inn

One April morning in 1775, a gunshot rang out just up the street from the building that today is called Concord's Colonial Inn. It came from the vicinity of North Bridge, and was the shot heard 'round the world, the one that started the American Revolutionary War. The ensuing battle and the casualties of the fighting would play a significant role in one of the Bay State's most historic haunts.

The Colonial Inn is actually made up of three buildings. Captain James Minot had the original structure built some time before 1716. The house remained in the Minot family right up through the Revolutionary War, when the British marched into town looking for the arms and provisions stored in one of the buildings on the property. The Colonial Minutemen stood ready to defend the cache, and between both sides, the resulting battle toll was 122 dead, 213 wounded, and 31 missing.

The wounded and dying from the battle were carried back to the East House, where Dr. Minot tended to them as best he could in his upstairs office. Not every soldier survived his wounds, and some drew their last breath in the doctor's office.

The inn's postwar history is just as noteworthy. In 1799, the Thoreau family from Boston bought the home and moved in. Between 1835 and 1837, the writer Henry David Thoreau lived in the building while he attended Harvard. In 1889, the building became a hotel, and it has

offered accommodations ever since.

With so much history and tragedy in the area, it's no surprise that the inn has a few ghosts lurking. But if there is one hot spot, it would have to be room 24, according to General Manager David Grossberg. "Dr. Minot took care of some of the infantrymen that were injured," Grossberg said. "He performed surgeries up in his office in this corner room, and we suspect many people died from their wounds. Today that's room 24."

In 1966, one overnight guest of the inn found herself in room 24 on her honeymoon. She later wrote to the hotel about her experience:

> I was awakened in the middle of the night by a presence in the room—a feeling that some unknown being was in the midst. As I opened my eyes, I saw a grayish figure at the side of my bed, to the left, about four feet away. It was not a distinct person, but a shadowy mass in the shape of a standing figure. It remained still for a moment, then slowly floated to the foot of the bed, in front of the fireplace. After pausing a few seconds, the apparition slowly melted away. It was a terrifying experience. I was so frightened I could not scream. I was frozen to the spot. . . .

It's not just in room 24 that strange phenomena occur. In the gift shop and front desk area, there are books for sale along the shelves opposite the cash register. One employee was working behind the register when she noticed a book fly off the shelf and hit the floor. At first, she thought this might have been a coincidence, but then a second book flew off right in front of her.

Staff members have reported hearing voices, feeling someone tap them on the back only to find no one there, unexplained cold spots, and the very rare, but very memorable apparition of a soldier from a long-ago war.

Tenney's Flashing Lights

If you're walking down Pleasant Street in Methuen by the Tenney Gate House at night and notice the building is completely dark except for a flickering light in an upstairs window, don't worry. It's not faulty wiring—it's just a ghost.

Richard Whittier had the stately structure at 37 Pleasant Street built between August and November of 1830. The stone farmhouse with its surrounding seventy-five acres of rolling hills was a picturesque spot, and the hand-hewn beams and wide pine floorboards meant the building would stand the test of time.

> **Several families did mention to us that at midnight the lights would flicker on and off in the back bedroom.**

In the early 1880s, this lovely spot caught the eye of Charles H. Tenney, a prominent Methuen businessman who made his fortune producing hats in town. He was moving up in the world, and the house on Pleasant Street would be the perfect temporary dwelling while he built his mansion, Grey Court, behind it. Tenney purchased the house and the land and started building.

Prior to moving in, the Tenneys modernized the stone farmhouse. They added new porches and porticoes, decorative gables to the roof, and a weathervane-topped tower, turning the home into a Queen Anne style. Inside, Tenney updated the look with hand-carved woodwork, colored glass windows, and fancy wallpaper. The Tenneys lived here for three years while their mansion was built behind it. When it was completed, the smaller house became their gatehouse.

In the 1950s, the Tenney family sold the mansion, gatehouse, and property to St. Basil Seminary. "The seminary brothers stayed at the gatehouse," said Joe Bella, president of the Methuen Historical Society. "One of the brothers had passed away up on the second floor bedroom," he said. "He died of throat cancer. And before he died, he was bed-ridden. He couldn't speak. He didn't have any sort of vocal abilities for his wants and needs."

Living in the room next to this dying priest was a nurse who was brought in to care for him. So how did this priest communicate when he needed her? "He used to flick off and on the light switch, which would shine in her room," Bella said. "That light switch was his only means of communication."

After the priest died, the monks moved into the larger mansion and they rented out the gatehouse to local families. Joe Bella has collected various local ghost reports for a number of years, and he's been especially interested in accounts coming from the gatehouse. Since it opened as a museum and meetinghouse back in 1998, various former residents have come back to visit. "Several families did mention to us that at midnight the lights would flicker on and off in the back bedroom," Bella said.

Another visitor explained to Bella that her family rented the gatehouse when she was a little girl. She said that one day her mother was home alone baking in the kitchen. Some flour had spilled on the counter, and when her mom looked over, she saw a fresh handprint in the flour that was too big to be her own. Another tenant came back to tell Bella that they had a dog that hated to be alone downstairs at night. The dog would whimper and bark when it was forced to sleep on the first level.

Joe Bella has also had some peculiar experiences in the Gate House.

I was there in the evening, and we were upstairs with a group. In the back bedroom there are two wall sconce lights, and underneath I saw these two rays of light were shining down at a forty-five-degree angle. Two rays of light for no reason, shone down. They were moving about a foot apart vertically. So I put my hand through the rays of light and nothing happened to my hand or anything, but I broke the beam. Then someone's cell phone went off and those two beams went back into the light and disappeared. Then about a half-hour later they came shooting down again and again they were angled to the left. Some of the people who were there saw what I saw, and some didn't. It was about fifty-fifty. I still to this day don't know what that was. I never saw it before and I've never seen it since that night.

Cemetery Safari

Cemeteries are fascinating places because they're a not-so-subtle reminder of our own inevitable destination. The art and inscriptions on each headstone reflect the sensibilities of the times and the personalities of the deceased. Because Massachusetts was an original colony and the first territory settled by Europeans in 1620, we have some very old graves and monuments compared with the rest of the United States. Headstones range from old bat-winged death heads and obelisks to more modern monuments with sometimes gaudy etchings or funny epitaphs. A walk through more than three centuries of Massachusetts cemeteries is a safari through American history.

WARREN GIBBS
died by arsenic poison
Mar. 23. 1860.
Æ. 36 yrs. 5 mos.
23 dys.

Think my friends when this
How my wife
She
Some
Then
An

A Cursed Headstone

When we think of curses, our mind usually wanders to the ancient past, to medieval sorcerers or Egyptian pharaohs. We don't usually think of the Cape Cod of 1985. Enter Mary C. Dolencie, late of Massachusetts. When Dolencie died in 1985, she wanted to send a message to her neighbors. Her headstone in the Yarmouth Ancient Cemetery has the following passage inscribed on the back:

> MAY ETERNAL DAMNATION BE
> UPON THOSE IN WHALING PORT
> WHO, WITHOUT KNOWING ME,
> HAVE MALICIOUSLY VILIFIED ME.
> MAY THE CURSE OF GOD
> BE UPON THEM AND THEIRS.

Take that, Whaling Port!

Sleepy Hollow

By far the Bay State's most storied cemetery is Sleepy Hollow in Concord. This boneyard is home to some of our most notable authors, architects, and other prominent figures.

In 1855, Concord purchased twenty-five acres of farmland close to New Hill Cemetery and called the area Sleepy Hollow Cemetery. Concord resident and future Sleepy Hollow denizen Ralph Waldo Emerson was the orator at the consecration ceremony.

"Citizens and friends," Emerson said in his 1855 speech, "this spot for twenty years has borne the name of Sleepy Hollow. Its seclusion from the village in its immediate neighborhood had made it to all the inhabitants an easy retreat on a Sabbath day, or a summer twilight, and it was inevitably chosen by them when the design of a new cemetery was broached, if it did not suggest the design, as the fit place for their final repose. In all the multitudes of woodlands and hillsides, which within a few years have been laid out with a similar design, I have not known one so fitly named. Sleepy Hollow. In this quiet valley, as in the palm of Nature's hand, we shall sleep well when we have finished our day. . . ."

Next up to speak was the Concordian, poet, first biographer of Henry David Thoreau, and also a future Sleepy Hollow resident, William Ellery Channing. Channing read his poem "Sleepy Hollow."

> "No abbey's gloom, nor dark cathedral stoops,
> No winding torches paint the midnight air;
> Here the green pines delight, the aspen droops
> Along the modest pathways, and those fair
> Pale asters of the season spread their plumes
> Around this field, fit garden for our tombs.

"And shalt thou pause to hear some funeral-bell
Slow stealing o'er the heart in this calm place,
Not with a throb of pain, a feverish knell,
But in its kind and supplicating grace,
It says, Go, pilgrim, on thy march, be more
Friend to the friendless than thou vast before."

There were a few more stanzas, but you get the idea. Today Sleepy Hollow is the final resting place of such notables as *Little Women* author Louisa May Alcott, Concord grape developer Ephriam Wales Bull, Lincoln Memorial sculptor Daniel Chester French, *The Scarlet Letter* and *The House of the Seven Gables* author Nathaniel Hawthorne, politician George Frisbie Hoar, and philosopher and author Henry David Thoreau.

Sour Grapes

Concord grape developer Ephriam Wales Bull planted twenty thousand varieties of grapes on his Concord farm before he developed the perfect specimen—plump, sweet, early to ripen, and hardy enough to grow in rough New England soil. Early on, he sold his vines for up to one thousand dollars apiece, but the more vines that were distributed, the less he was able to sell, until finally his profits dried up like a raisin in the hot summer sun.

When Ephriam Bull died on September 26, 1895, he was almost penniless. Bull's grave now sits in Concord's Sleepy Hollow Cemetery where visitors can read his epitaph: HE SOWED, OTHERS REAPED.

Who the Hell Is Sheila Shea?

Concord is known for being a very proper upper-class town, but in the famous Sleepy Hollow Cemetery there is one headstone that blatantly thumbs its owner's nose at propriety: the one that belongs to Sheila Shea.

When I was in high school, I became friends with Sheila's daughter, Cindi. Her mom was a rarity to a middle school kid: she was cool. She'd get us pizza on Fridays and we'd sit in her kitchen playing cards, backgammon or other games.

As we got older, Cindi and I drifted in different directions. Years later I heard her mom had died. But the big news wasn't her death: it was her headstone. She had purchased a plot in Sleepy Hollow Cemetery, which is known for being the final resting place of Emerson, the Alcotts, Thoreau, and now . . . Sheila Shea. Being her true irreverent self, she chose the perfect epitaph to let all who see it know she was a woman of great humor, much to the town's dismay! It simply says WHO THE HELL IS SHEILA SHEA.—*Dawn Delsie-Pence*

Spider Gates

Of all the cemeteries in Massachusetts,
Leicester's Spider Gates is the best-known among those interested in things cursed and creepy. Some visitors hike through the woods around Kettle Brook and think they've discovered a lost and abandoned cemetery. But not so—this Friends Cemetery is still active. As of this writing, the most recent burial was 2005. Spider Gates is a nickname that comes from the ornate wrought-iron gates that mark the entrance. (Think twisted metal daddy longlegs, and you're there.) The spider similarities are purely unintentional; the art deco design is supposed to look like the setting— or rising—sun with its rays spiraling outward.

Incorporated in 1737, the cemetery now sits in a remote location in the woods between Worcester airport and the Leicester landfill. "The cemetery is out there because there was a Quaker community there," said Brian Poynton, a member of the Worcester Friends (Quakers) committee that oversees the cemetery. Today there are almost as many mysterious and haunted legends attached to this place as there are headstones inside. Let's begin with the most prominent legends:

- There are nine gates to hell around Spider Gates cemetery.
- There's an elevated area of ground inside the cemetery where bizarre rituals took place.
- People have committed suicide inside the cemetery—specifically by hanging themselves from a tree dubbed the Hanging Tree.

- Cloaked figures regularly perform occult rituals in the cemetery at night.
- The roads around the cemetery appear and disappear.
- Ghosts still roam the grounds at night.

Here is the frightening reality: All these stories are true . . . in a way. Every legend has its roots, and usually those roots are based in fact. The mystery behind Spider Gates begins in a place called Manville.

Manville was a village in the town of Leicester that thrived from the mid-eighteenth century well into the nineteenth century. In the 1800s, Leicester wasn't the quaint and rural New England area it is today. It was a center of industry. There were mills along Kettle Brook, and homes and other businesses soon popped up. Manville prospered until the city of Worcester began coveting its water. "There were seven, maybe eight mill privileges all the way up Kettle Brook, and the city [Worcester] started buying the privileges and diverting the water for public use," said Joe Lennerton, a retired Leicester police officer and chairman of the Leicester Historical Commission. "What Worcester couldn't buy, they started to take by eminent domain— they have never really been kind to the town of Leicester."

As the brook was dammed to create Kettle Brook Reservoir, the mills closed, industry left, and the village withered. What was a center of commerce became a simple neighborhood with a few Colonial houses, some quiet woods, and a Quaker cemetery. A Quaker cemetery

that installed a decorative art deco gate around 1895.

Then another part of the legend fell into place. "In the early 1960s, they extended the runway at Worcester municipal airport," said Joe Lennerton. "They relocated Mulberry Street and tore down about eight or nine beautiful Colonial homes. So what was left of Manville was gone. But the roads were still there. There was Sprague, Howe, Elm, Earle Street, Reservoir Street, and Sylvester Street. And they still are to this day public ways in the town of Leicester."

So by the mid-1960s, you had a network of old dirt roads in a remote part of town behind the airport. The only remaining memory of Manville was the still active

Friends Cemetery. In short, if you were a young person in Leicester or the surrounding towns, and you had a six-pack of beer, Manville was the perfect place to drink it with your friends.

"That's what was happening," Joe Lennerton said. "It's very quiet there. It's a very nice peaceful place to visit. Kids are out there drinking beer, and their imaginations get carried away with them."

The various dirt roads became a haven for the illegal dumping of trash, from construction materials to bags filled with household garbage. Something had to be done, so the town installed a series of gates on the roads (which were starting to look more like trails than roads by this point). How many gates did they install? Nine of them.

Today the area is heavily wooded. Some of the streets look like they haven't been touched in many years. Nature encroaches on both sides, but there are clear ruts where tires obviously still tread on occasion. Other "streets" are scarcely wide enough for two people to walk side by side. Old stone walls mark property lines, and if not for the occasional whine of the airplane propellers from Worcester Regional Airport, the area would be almost silent.

Let's examine the individual legends.

Nine Gates to Hell

This is true . . . sort of. There are nine gates on the dirt paths surrounding Spider Gates. But they don't lead to hell. In fact, they don't lead anywhere. These gates are meant to block off streets and keep kids from parking their cars out of sight on the wooded roads.

The Hanging Tree— Home to Many Suicides

This is true . . . sort of. There is a large tree just to the left after you enter the cemetery through the main gate. And there is a branch that comes out like a bent arm that could be a good place to hang oneself. But there are a few problems. The branch is quite high up, so you'd have to drag a tall ladder into the woods with you. And there's another problem with this legend: The rash of hanging suicides didn't happen at Spider Gates. It happened in Rochdale, one of the other villages in Leicester.

Back in the 1970s, Rochdale experienced a couple of very weird summers. According to Joe Lennerton, there was a suicide every two weeks. "One started, and they all went like dominoes. I don't know what the hell was going on," he says. "That was in Rochdale Park. Of course as the story goes on, it gets switched and now it's Quaker cemetery."

Elevated Area of Ground for Rituals

This is absolutely true. When you walk into the small, square cemetery, there is an area of flat and slightly elevated land just to the left of the main gates. In the corners of this small plateau are four small stone pillars. What rituals took place here? Religious services. Remember, this was once the site of the Leicester Quaker meetinghouse. The January 29, 1739, Smithfield Monthly Meeting minutes read: "Friends at Leicester make report to this meeting that they have agreed upon a Place for Building a Meeting-House at the Burying Place between Ralph Earle's and Nathanial Potter's . . . and Benjamin Earle, Thomas Smith, and Nathaniel Potter are appointed to undertake for Building said House." The meeting-house within the cemetery was taken down in 1791.

Cloaked Figures and Occult Rituals

This is Spider Gates's most intriguing legend, and it too is sort of true. Back in 2004, Ghostvillage.com received the following e-mail regarding the Quaker cemetery:

> The only freaky thing I've heard is when my friend went there with his two brothers about four years ago, when it was easier to get in during the night. Around 11:30 at night or so, they said they were leaving, flashlights off, when they heard leaves rustling. Peering through a few trees, they saw three dark figures with hoods or clothing on to hide features. They let them walk by without alerting them, but I would say I bet it was just weird people who believe in Satanic stuff more than ghosts.

The author of the e-mail wasn't the only one who'd heard about the dark-robed figures. Joe Lennerton saw them for himself when he was still on the police force. "I was working once, when we got a call," he said. "There's thirty-five people all dressed in medieval-type robes holding candles. . . . We used to chase them out of there about once a year. I've seen them with my own eyes."

So who were those folks in robes? Lennerton said he heard that the group belonged to a secret fraternity at Worcester Polytechnic Institute called the Skull. Founded in 1911, the Skull is a society that honors outstanding juniors for their dedication and contributions to the institute. The Skull group was visiting the Friends Cemetery specifically to see the resting place of Ralph Earle, rear admiral of the U.S. Navy and president of Worcester Polytechnic Institute from October of 1925 until his death in February of 1939. Though there's nothing wrong with paying respects to a past W.P.I. president, the group never had permission to go in at night.

Friends Cemetery

The robed figures may have also caused a copycat sensation for other kids who wanted to don a robe, hide out in the woods, and scare the bejesus out of other nighttime visitors.

Roads Appear and Disappear

This is true . . . mostly. If you know where the cemetery is, it's really simple to find. It's located right off Earle Street. However, if you were trying to walk these old "roads" at night, especially when the trees and bushes are full of leaves, it's easy to get lost. This would certainly explain why some visitors would lose their way. Plus, the roads are literally disappearing as trees and brush grow up throughout the trails.

The Ghosts

The ghostly legends are difficult to prove or disprove. Those who study ghosts and legends might argue that any old and self-respecting cemetery in New England would have at least one good ghostly legend. And the remote location of Spider Gates certainly makes it look like a ghostly place.

The legends have caused problems for the Quaker cemetery. Graves have been desecrated, and trash has been strewn about the grounds. In recent years, a sign was put up that reads THIS IS A PRIVATE CEMETERY UNDER THE CARE OF THE WORCESTER-PLEASANT STREET FRIENDS MEETING (QUAKERS). WE HOPE THAT YOU WILL TREAT THIS CEMETERY AS YOU WOULD THE ONE WHERE YOUR RELATIVES AND FRIENDS ARE BURIED.

We hope so too.

Called Up the Wrong Demon!

There is a small town on the outskirts of Boston, and on one side there is a huge forest. If you walk far enough into them you see there are eight gates that look like steel spider webs with locks. If you walk through all of them I heard there is a clearing. Legend has it if you enter the clearing at night and attempt to walk out back through the gates you will be killed by some spirit.

They say that a bunch of Devil worshippers practiced there, and were one night conjuring a demon but they called up the wrong demon and were all killed. So now the Demon protects the clearing and will kill anyone who enters it and tries to leave. I heard this is because the Devil worshippers would sacrifice a person before leaving so the demon they called up for the night would be satisfied and would go back to hell willingly.–*Nate*

Flashes and White Orbs at Spider Gates

Just this past weekend, I decided to take my first stroll down to Spider Gates with a few friends. We didn't see or hear anything at all. We didn't feel weird or get creeped out from being there. But I took my camera there, and took a short video with it as I was walking down the southern path next to the river. On the way home, when I was looking back through my pictures and the video, I noticed a flash going across the screen that I had failed to notice in real life. Also, in my pictures there are a lot of those white orbs that had shown up.–*Glenn D.*

Sagamore Cemetery's Haunted Tree

Sagamore Cemetery is a quaint resting ground in Bourne that is home to some prominent Cape Codders (several members of the Bourne family for one) as well as a ghost and even a haunted tree. Sagamore isn't the oldest cemetery around; its first customer went below ground in 1803. However, it has become renowned because the construction of the nearby Cape Cod Canal forced a few family plots to be relocated here.

There are some universal taboos when it comes to the dead, chief among them a strict "do not disturb" policy, but taboos are not always honored. In 1904, August Perry Belmont put the wheels in motion to slice through the land and connect Cape Cod Bay with Buzzard's Bay, thus avoiding treacherous trips around the Cape's outer banks. Of course there were homes, businesses, and cemeteries in the way of progress, but anyone who has ever sat for two hours on a sunny summer Friday afternoon waiting to get on the Bourne Bridge knows that progress won.

As some of the deceased who lay in the way of the canal were brought to Sagamore, some graves and headstones were inevitably mixed up (another no-no when it comes to the dead). The marker mix-up may account for one unexplained phenomenon that caretaker Jerry Ellis experienced in the cemetery. He discovered that a headstone weighing several hundred pounds had been moved from its base and set to rest against another nearby stone without so much as a mark on it from any kind of lever or crowbar and not a footprint around.

Local psychics believe the cemetery is haunted by Isaac Keith, who died in 1900. Keith was a cigar smoker, and one of the most frequent experiences visitors have is the wafting smell of a stogie. There's also one very odd tree.

Sagamore's most prominently eerie feature is the large tree that greets visitors near the main entrance. From the right angle, the knobby and bulbous branches and stubs resemble a manlike creature yearning to break out of the tree's insides. At night, when the tree is just a silhouette, the effect is amplified, scaring more than a few teenagers off the grounds if they dare to venture in after dark.

Where Rover and Fluffy Both R.I.P.

Pine Ridge Cemetery in Dedham is the oldest continuously operating pet cemetery in the United States. The scenic operation, located on twenty-eight acres, began operations in 1907 and is now the final resting place to more than ten thousand pets, including dogs, cats, a horse, iguanas, rabbits, hamsters, a Yucatán pig, turtles, puffer fish, hedgehogs, many different types of birds, and one human.

Like any old self-respecting cemetery in New England, Pine Ridge also has its renowned residents. The most historic portion of the cemetery can be found behind the barn adjacent to the Humane Society office building. The first notable grave is on the left. Shaped like the tip of an iceberg and noticeably larger than most of the other markers, it is the resting place of Igloo, a fox terrier who once belonged to the famed Arctic explorer U.S. Navy admiral Richard Evelyn Byrd (meaning that Igloo was technically a Byrd dog . . . sorry, couldn't resist).

Igloo was offered to Byrd as a mascot by a woman who read about his plans to conquer the North Pole. At first Byrd protested, claiming that the Arctic cold would be too much for the fox terrier, but Igloo's savior insisted, saying that a dog can handle any weather a man can handle. Byrd agreed to take the dog, and a deep friendship was formed that would last the rest of the dog's life.

On May 9, 1926, Richard Byrd and his pilot, Floyd Bennett, became the first aviators to claim they flew over the North Pole. Igloo was at the frigid base camp, awaiting his master's return.

In 1928, Byrd organized an expedition to the Antarctic to reach the South Pole. He brought with him two ships, three airplanes, and Igloo. At the base camp, called Little America, on the Ross Ice Shelf, Igloo passed the time by nipping at the much larger husky sled dogs and knocking over penguins.

On November 29, 1929, Byrd, his pilot Brent Balchen, co-pilot Harold June, and photographer Ashley McKinley made a successful trip to the South Pole and back. The achievement gave Igloo the distinction of being the only dog to have traveled to the extreme climates of both the North and South Poles.

Igloo accompanied Admiral Byrd through many other adventures—some into the woods of North America, others to remote locales like New Guinea. When Igloo passed away in 1931, he was brought to Pine Ridge Cemetery, where he was laid to rest under the iceberg-shaped headstone. The inscription reads HE WAS MORE THAN A FRIEND.

R.I.P. Lizzie Borden's Dogs

Lizzie's three dogs were Boston bull terriers. Not long after she was acquitted of killing her mother and father, Lizzie and her sister moved into a mansion on French Street in Fall River. During this time period, Boston bulls were all the fashion among Boston's high society, so Lizzie simply had to have one. The dog was the ultimate fashion accessory, and Lizzie would take one along to sit on her lap on her country drives. Lizzie Borden died on June 1, 1927, and the following year her three dogs were exhumed from their graves in the Maplecroft Mansion property and moved to Pine Ridge Cemetery—a resting place of distinction for animals of the day. "On the anniversary of the trial, we had people from all over the world coming by," said Mike Thomas, the caretaker at Pine Ridge Cemetery since 1970.

Humans in the Pet Cemetery

There are even some human remains at Pine Ridge. Some people have had their ashes scattered near their pet's grave, Mike Thomas reports. And there is one unique human story here. In the June 1918 edition of the journal *Our Fourfooted Friends,* writer A. H. Smith explains:

> There is a secluded spot in [the cemetery] where a grave is almost hidden by cedar trees and is marked only by a simple rustic wooden cross. [The woman buried here] wished for no funeral exercises. Life had evidently been very bitter to her, and in her old age she was alone with no companion but a dog that had grown old with her, the only creature that loved her— the only thing on earth she loved. . . .

Pine Ridge averages 250 to 350 burials per year, some for the pets of the wealthy, some for the companions of ordinary folk. A walk among the headstones tears at your heartstrings. Inscriptions like MY LITTLE ANGEL. O, FOR ONE OF THOSE HOURS OF GLADNESS and IF LOVE COULD HAVE SAVED YOU, YOU NEVER WOULD HAVE DIED demonstrate the love and devotion these owners had for their pets. Other graves are simpler—one just says FLUFFY and the years the animal lived. Some bear religious symbols, a Star of David, for example. "We've buried pets of priests, rabbis, and ministers," Thomas said. "We had one little poodle who was an altar boy. His owner was the pastor, and he brought his dog out to sit on the altar while he did the Mass. He could do it because he was the boss."

Last Laugh on Their Epitaph

*Here are some other memorable epitaphs
from around the Bay State:*

CALLED BACK
Emily Dickinson, West Cemetery, Amherst

SACRED TO MEMORY OF ANTHONY DRAKE
WHO DIED FOR PEACE AND QUIETNESS SAKE
HIS WIFE WAS CONSTANTLY
SCOLDING AND SCOFFIN'
SO HE SOUGHT FOR REPOSE
IN A TWELVE DOLLAR COFFIN
Anthony Drake, Burlington Churchyard, Burlington

I'LL SEE YOU IN APPLE BLOSSOM TIME
Thomas Phillip "Tip" O'Neill, Jr., Harwich

OPEN, OPEN WIDE YE GOLDEN GATES
THAT LEAD TO THE HEAVENLY SHORE,
OUR FATHER SUFFERED IN PASSING THROUGH
AND MOTHER WEIGHS MUCH MORE
Mrs. Althea White, Lee

AT LAST, A YEAR-ROUND RESIDENT
*Robert G. Rogers, West Chop Cemetery,
Vineyard Haven on Cape Cod*

BENEATH THIS STONE
A LUMP OF CLAY
LIES ARABELLA YOUNG
WHO ON THE 21ST OF MAY 1771
BEGAN TO HOLD HER TONGUE
Arabella Young, Hatfield

Wyoming Cemetery

I grew up in Melrose in a house across the street from the Wyoming Cemetery on the Lebanon Street side, and I can tell you from experience that that place is creepy day or night. Many a strange thing has happened there.

Here is my story. My friends and I (four of us in total) had just finished watching an under-the-lights fast-pitch softball game at Pine Banks Park. Pine Banks Park borders the cemetery. There was never any question that we would cut through the cemetery after the game. We entered the Grove Street gate, and our walk through was uneventful—full of talk of the game, tomorrow's bike ride, etc. However, as we approached the Lebanon Street gate, we saw a light glowing red near some grave stones along the wall which surrounds the entire cemetery.

We all stopped about 50 yards short of the Lebanon Street gate to check out this light. We could see it flicker, and after a few hair-raising moments, we decided it was a candle in a glass enclosure. We had been seeing them lately during the day. This was a fairly new thing to be seen on graves, but we had much to our relief figured it out. However, just as we were about to start on our way again, we all saw a figure coming toward us from the direction of the light. It appeared to be of a woman. She was small and she was covered from head to toe in a long, black, veiled dress. Needless to say we were dumbstruck. It was late at night, this woman was alone, and in a cemetery. We thought that she must be a widow or something, so out of respect we remained silent. As she passed she almost seemed to float by. She was totally covered in black mourning drape so we couldn't see her face (years later I saw a picture of Civil War widows grave side and they were dressed exactly the same). She continued out of the gate and then proceeded up Lebanon Street toward the old Ripely Elementary School.

We all ran out of the gate and crossed the street. We ran on the opposite side of the street passing her and continuing on to my old house which overlooked the cemetery. As she passed by one of my friends whispered, "She's not touching the ground."

We let out a gasp as she passed by us by no more than 20 feet, and we could clearly see that she was not walking on the ground. It was a moonlit night and we could see her clearly.

She continued past my house and she entered the Ripely School yard, which abutted the cemetery. She walked through the yard and reentered the cemetery by means of an old path which ran from the cemetery to the school yard. We were all looking at each other and we were speechless. She continued on until we lost sight of her in the tree cover. My friends went home and I went inside. I can tell you we were spooked!

Well, that would have been the end of it. But after a few days, I mentioned it to my father in the presence of a neighbor who had lived in the neighborhood her whole life. My father, a police officer, scoffed at the story and told me he would wear me out if he found out I was in the cemetery at night again! My neighbor, a highly respected woman and a teacher at the Ripely School, took me aside. She looked seriously at me and said, "I know what you saw because I have seen her many times over my 70-plus years." When I told my friends what she had said, that was it. We started to believe what it was we had seen. You didn't doubt this woman—she put fear in you with a lift of an eyebrow.—*John Whalen, courtesy www.masscrossroads.com*

It Wasn't the Butler Who Did It

Warren Gibbs of Prescott died March 23, 1860, of arsenic poisoning. Allegedly, he was originally buried in Knight's Cemetery in Pelham, but the stone that visitors find there today is a replica of the original, which sits in the Pelham Historical Society building. Allegedly, supposedly, rumor-has-it . . . what exactly is going on with Warren Gibbs? All the fuss began over the epitaph on his grave. The inscription reads:

WARREN GIBBS
DIED BY ARSENIC POISON
MAR. 23, 1860
AE 36 YRS 5 MOS. 23 DYS

THINK MY FRIENDS WHEN THIS YOU SEE
HOW MY WIFE HATH DEALT BY ME
SHE IN SOME OYSTERS DID PREPARE
SOME POISON FOR MY LOT AND SHARE
THEN OF THE SAME I DID PARTAKE
AND NATURE YIELDED TO ITS FATE
BEFORE SHE MY WIFE BECAME
MARY FELTON WAS HER NAME

ERECTED BY HIS BROTHER
WM GIBBS

In 1906, the *Daily Hampshire Gazette* looked into the strange story from more than four decades earlier. Apparently, Warren Gibbs came down with a fever in March of 1860. Gibbs complained of an unquenchable thirst—no amount of water would satisfy him—which led some to speculate there may have been some poison working through his system. The story goes on to say that a neighbor brought over some hard cider that had almost turned to vinegar, and the acidic drink helped Gibbs feel better. When it looked as if he was on the road to recovery, his wife prepared an oyster stew for him, and he wolfed down every bite. Soon thereafter the horrible thirst returned, and his health quickly declined until he expired on March 23, 1860.

Warren's brother, William, felt that his brother was poisoned by his wife. He had no proof of this, and no matter how much he pleaded to the police, they would not perform an autopsy without any cause. So Warren's body was committed to the ground. The only justice William felt he could get for his brother was one incredibly libelous headstone.

In 1971, the original headstone was moved from Knight's Cemetery to the Pelham Historical Society building, where visitors can ponder the possibilities behind Warren Gibbs's ultimate fate.

Fore John Hall

If you're a golfer with triskaidekaphobia (fear of the number 13), stay clear of the Kings Way Golf Club in Yarmouth on Cape Cod. When you tee off on hole 13—a par three—you'll have to watch out for more than just the sand traps. To the right of the green is a lone headstone for one Mr. John Hall.

You may wonder what a grave is doing on a golf course. A closer look at the epitaph provides the answer:

IN MEMORY OF
MR JOHN HALL
WHO DIED WITH
THE SMALL POX
DECM'BR YE 14TH 1801
IN HIS 64TH YEAR

Back in the early nineteenth century, smallpox meant big trouble for the afflicted. The disease had a death rate of over 30 percent and was highly contagious. If you caught it, you might just find yourself on your own. Even when you succumbed to the disease, you weren't out of its grip. All over the world there are lone grave sites out in the middle of nowhere that hold smallpox victims. This was the case with John Hall. He was buried in the middle of the woods in Yarmouth. When the Kings Way Golf Club cleared the woods to put the course in, they discovered the grave and left it intact near the thirteenth hole.

So what happens if you do hit your ball into John Hall's final resting ground? The pro shop at Kings Way said, "It's a free drop outside the fence." It's probably also bad luck.

Ghostly Groundhog of Old Hill Burying Ground

By Daniel V. Boudillion

Established in 1729, Old Hill Burying Ground in Newburyport has not stood up well to the ravages of time. According to local legend, there is an "intricate tunnel system" under the cemetery that extends down past High Street into the center of town and the old wharf area. If newspaper accounts are to be believed, some old brick tunnels do exist. They are generally referred to as "slave tunnels" from the Underground Railroad era. But some researchers believe they are pre–Revolutionary War smuggling tunnels.

Regardless of what is beneath the cemetery, on top Old Hill Burying Ground is a scenic jumble of old headstones and small crumbling aboveground tombs. It is the final resting place of many Revolutionary War veterans and heroes, including Caleb Haskell.

Recently woodchucks have made a home of Old Hill, burrowing hither and yon in a true maze of tunnels through graves and tombs alike. Indeed, some tombs are so crumbled and woodchuck-dug that even a casual glance reveals human bones.

Sightings of ghosts have often been reported here, especially at the Pierce Tomb, one that has been vandalized all too often. A ghostly head is said to appear nearby at the Titcomb grave.

In his book *Haunted Happenings*, Robert Ellis Cahill recounts how his friend Brian captured a picture of what appears to be Colonel Moses Titcomb's ghostly head poking out of the ground in front of his gravestone for a look-see. This picture is reproduced in the book, along with a portrait of Titcomb. The ghost head and the portrait do indeed resemble each other.

This was too intriguing a story not to check out. And so on October 2, 2005, my nephew Carlton Jablonski and

I packed up the truck and headed out for Old Hill Burying Ground and the Secret of the Ghostly Head. On arrival, I did some preliminary photography of the vandalized Pierce Tomb. Then we got down to work.

We hid behind one of the large stones near the Titcomb grave and waited for the spooks to come out. I savored my Dunkin' Donuts coffee—large regular—while Carlton locked and loaded the camera for ghost, and set the dial on "boo!"

Judging the time to be right, I took the camera and began belly crawling out toward the Titcomb grave. As I inched toward the stone, I saw a sudden movement and froze! Something was stirring at the grave. Lying flat on my stomach and holding the camera out in front of me at ground level, I watched a strange apparition poke its nose out of the ground in front of the Titcomb stone.

First a black nose, then little ears, followed by a furtive brown head and beady eyes. The dark specter started at me. I stared back and frantically snapped away at the camera while reciting the Lord's Prayer under my breath. Then the Ghostly Head, no doubt sensing my prayers, snapped out of sight and totally disappeared!

I crawled back to Carlton, and with shaky hands we brought the pictures up on the digital viewing screen. Success! There it was! The head . . . of a woodchuck! How strange, I thought, the mysterious powers of the cemetery had transmogrified old Titcomb into a woodchuck. It was an awesome realization.

I left the cemetery that day a little more solemn and thoughtful than I had arrived.—*Daniel V. Boudillion*

Abandoned in the Bay State

Yankee ingenuity is credited with the longevity of many New England buildings, institutions, and inventions. We don't abandon much in Massachusetts, but when we do, you can be sure there's a story to be told. Around the state, we have abandoned villages—ghost towns where cellar holes and cart paths hint of the lives lived there; we have buildings that held the outcasts of our society and abandoned work sites where the forest is left to cover the scars men made. Crumbling and hollow-eyed now, these old places possess an aura of history and mystery. Visiting them gives us clues to a time long past when people we'll never know lived and died in our land. Who were they? What happened to them? Often only our imaginations can supply the answers.

Dogtown

The Bay State's most famous ghost town is found in the woods of Cape Ann, where it straddles the towns of Gloucester and Rockport. Originally settled in 1693, the hilltop village then called the Commons Settlement offered a little less bite from the winter winds on the coast, and the higher vantage point gave some protection against raiding pirates, but little else. The rocky soil made farming a challenge, and boulders cast every which way courtesy of the last Ice Age made building difficult. Still, the Commons was the place to be by 1730. The area was convenient since it was central to Sandy Bay (the original name of Rockport), Pigeon Cove, Lanesville, and Annisquam, and many farms managed to prosper there.

But the village's prosperity would be its undoing. Both the livestock population and the Commons's close proximity to the ocean made the area a target for British warships that needed supplies for their crews. The American Revolution and the War of 1812 took a heavy toll on the area. After the War of 1812, the only people left in town were widows and the poor—many of whom kept dogs as pets and for protection, hence the name Dogtown. Some estimate that there were over fifty widows living in abject poverty in town. They survived on the abundant berries they could pick and preserve and anything else they could beg, borrow, or steal.

Some of the buildings left in town were rented out to crews of fishing boats—a raucous bunch to be sure—and Dogtown became the red-light district of Gloucester. There were fortunetellers, witches, prostitutes, and other characters that would be considered unsavory in other parts of town but were right at home here.

One of the village's most colorful characters was

Thomasine "Tammy" Younger. Born in 1753, Tammy was called the Queen of the Witches. She was plump, had two unusually long teeth that protruded from her mouth, and lived with her aunt on the outskirts of the village. Outside her window was the main road that led through Dogtown, and Tammy would often harass drivers into giving her some of their cargo. Thanks to her witchy reputation, the locals believed she had supernatural powers and that if they didn't offer her something—firewood, food, or other goods—Tammy would place a hex on them. She became a kind of supernatural toll keeper.

Whether or not Tammy and others like her were really witches can be debated, but the reputation stopped the "decent" townsfolk from prying too closely into

Dogtown. Around 1830, the residents finally gave up on the place for good, leaving the village to the dogs that once stood watch but now were left to hunt and forage for themselves.

A century later Roger Babson entered Dogtown

history. As a child, Babson would drive cows through town and explore the many boulders and cellar holes there. In 1927, Babson wrote: "There is something inspiring in the huge barren hills and great boulders of Gloucester's Dogtown. At the same time, there are pathos and tragedy in the old forsaken cellars of the original inhabitants."

In 1927, Babson spent a great deal of time researching which cellar holes belonged to which residents. He had numerals (which can still be seen today) carved on a rock near each rocky pit, and in the center of town he had D.T. SQ. (for Dogtown Square) carved into one of the rocks. He published his findings in a pamphlet called *Gloucester's Deserted Village*. Babson is a key reason we know so much about this Massachusetts ghost town.

Roger Babson, who founded Babson College in Wellesley in 1919, believed that if everyone worked, the nation and business would be stronger. During the Great Depression, he hired thirty-six unemployed quarry workers to carve mottoes into Dogtown's many boulders. As you hike through the trails of Dogtown, the carved boulders throughout the forest grab your attention. There are different phrases carved into twenty-four boulders, including IDEAS, USE YOUR HEAD, GET A JOB, and HELP MOTHER.

Modern-day visitors to Dogtown can traverse the well-worn trails that were once roads and imagine what it must have been like to have Tammy Younger threatening hexes and curses in exchange for some of your wares, or think of the rage and rush Commons residents must have felt when the redcoats attacked. Visitors can't mistake the mark Roger Babson left on the woods—his mottoes are etched everywhere. And with so much history, much of it shady, it's easy to imagine why locals still whisper of hauntings or curses plaguing the abandoned settlement today.

Lovell's Island

About seven miles into Boston Harbor is a sixty-two-acre spot of land called Lovell's Island. When the Colonists started to populate Boston, the stretch of water near this island became a busy shipping lane. Lovell's Island was often the closest land to row or swim to in the case of the occasional shipwreck on the nearby shallow shoals.

The most famous shipwreck occurred August 11, 1782, to the seventy-four-gun French warship *Le Magnifique*—at the time, the largest warship ever built. *Magnifique* was trying to navigate Broad Sound when it ran aground near Lovell's Island. The crew carried off much of the cargo, and perhaps some let their greed get the best of them. It's rumored that a few may have buried treasure on the island, intending to go back for it later. Whatever hasn't disintegrated may still be lying offshore in the silt and sand.

The saddest wreck came one winter years later when a sailing ship en route to Maine ran into the rocks near the shore. The passengers and crew dragged themselves onto the island but could find no shelter from the cold. They all died of exposure before anyone discovered the wreckage. The bodies of one young couple who were engaged to be married were discovered in a frozen embrace next to a large boulder called Lover's Rock. Visitors can still see the hallowed stone today. Bostonians were so distraught over the news of the frozen castaways that the Massachusetts Humane Society constructed the nation's first "hut of refuge" on the island so future shipwreck victims would have shelter from the cold.

Old ships aren't the only things abandoned on Lovell's Island. Because the island lies in the outer part of Boston Harbor, it was predestined to be a military installation. In 1825, it was commandeered for military use as Fort Standish. Troops were present here during the

U.S. Civil War, World War I, and World War II. On the north and northeastern parts of the island, the remnants of defensive batteries can be found. The main section of Fort Standish now is mostly ruin, as brush and undergrowth tries to take the island back.

In 1902, two wooden lighthouses were installed to help boats pass through South Channel of Broad Sound. The first keeper (or wickie) of the lights was Alfred G. Eisener from Bremen, Maine. Eisener mostly kept to himself, and his job was a lonely one. One day he was digging in his garden when he unearthed some old European coins dating back to the 1600s. Soon after, the lighthouse keeper was scheduled for shore leave, and his backup came to Lovell's Island to work the wicks. By the time Eisener returned, he discovered the hole he had dug in his garden was significantly larger, and his backup keeper soon resigned from service and moved away, leaving Eisener to wonder if the few coins he discovered were just the tip of the treasure iceberg.

The lighthouses lasted until the 1930s, when Fort Standish was expanded. Obviously, military bases are targets, so lighthouse beacons weren't wanted on the island as World War II approached. By 1958, Fort Standish was closed for good, and the island fell into ruin.

Vegetation is taking back the fort in many places, but the beaches and trails have been opened to tourists during the warmer months. The stories of sunken ships, buried treasure, and an America at war still echo around the tiny island in Boston Harbor.

Chester-Hudson Quarry

If you died in the vicinity of Chester between the mid-nineteenth and mid-twentieth centuries, there's a good chance that your headstone came from a quarry in the small town of Becket.

The Chester-Hudson Quarry opened operations in the 1850s in the granite-rich hills of Becket. The quarry became one of the town's biggest employers, and men hustled to break up the rock, bring it out from the ground with derricks, and move it onto waiting trucks, where it was transported for use as headstones and monuments. During the 1960s, though, something went wrong. Mismanagement led to financial problems, and one day the workers simply walked off the job, leaving the trucks, tools, compressors, and the fifty-foot-high derrick exactly as they were. The rumble of the machines was silenced and Becket became quiet again. Years passed, and no one came back for any of it. The underbrush grew, and the forest reclaimed most of the quarry site.

In 1991, the Becket Land Trust was formed to preserve the wilderness of the town. The people of Becket raised funds to buy the three hundred plus acres of the quarry and donate them to the land trust. The result is a protected forest with a unique "museum" inside. Today visitors can walk through the trails of the old quarry and see everything just as it was abandoned back in the 1960s. The only item the trust rebuilt was the derrick; otherwise, the rusted equipment and broken stones are right where the workers left them all those years ago.

The park is located off Quarry Road in Becket and is open year-round.

Drowned Towns and Villages

By the middle of the nineteenth century, the city of Boston and the surrounding areas were undergoing a population explosion—and folks were getting thirsty. Local ponds and rivers weren't enough to supply fresh water to the growing city and the satellite towns around it. The solution was to head west where fresh water was plentiful, thanks to the rivers that ran down from the White Mountains to the north. The only problem was that there were several towns and a few thousand people in the way of all that water.

The Swift River Valley, in central Massachusetts, was almost preordained to be a watershed. Long before Colonists arrived, the Nipmuc Indians called this valley region Quabbin, which roughly translates to "meeting of

The Quabbin Reservoir is the largest body of water in Massachusetts. Below these clean, clear waters lie the remains of several towns and villages.

the waters." It was a place where rivers came together, where the high hills on the outer parts of the valley were full of deer and other game, and where the land in the middle was lush and ripe for farming.

By the first part of the twentieth century, there were about twenty-five hundred people living in the towns and villages of the Quabbin area. These included the incorporated towns of Dana, Greenwich (pronounced green-witch), Enfield, and Prescott. Other villages in the valley included North Dana, North Prescott, Atkinson Hollow, Greenwich Village, and Doubleday. As in countless other small towns, there were farms, homes, churches, schools, inns, restaurants, mills, shops, and other businesses that make a town run. Unlike countless other small towns, by 1938 all of it, from the people to the buildings, had to go, sacrifices to Boston's ever-growing need for water.

Bob Wilder was one of the people who were displaced. Now in his eighties, he was a boy when he lived in the Swift River Valley. "We grew up on Prescott Ridge," Wilder says. "As you went up Prescott Ridge, we would've been the second house on the

In the village of Dana, all that remains are a few foundations from the buildings that once stood along the main street.

left—that was the Wilder Farm, and it'd been the Wilder Farm since the mid-1800s when my grandfather Josephus came down from Wendell and bought it."

Unfortunately for Wilder and the other residents of the area, the Swift River Valley had been identified as the perfect place to create the largest body of water in Massachusetts and one of the largest man-made reservoirs in the country. To do that, the whole area would have to be flooded. Despite protests and several lawsuits trying to stop the project, it went through and construction began in 1922.

"Prescott dumped out pretty early, and by twenty-eight almost everybody was gone. There were no more schools, no more businesses there, and that was just a mile down the road from us heading north," Wilder says.

The construction and struggle continued throughout the 1930s. Every tree, building, and structure had to be cleared, because the reservoir was going to be used for drinking water. Some people left the Swift River Valley willingly. Some had their homes literally loaded onto flatbeds to be towed to a new town. Many felt they weren't offered a fair price for their land.

Bob Wilder believes his family was not offered nearly enough for their farm. The Metropolitan District Commission initially offered them $1,800 for a forty-acre farm that included a sixteen-acre woodlot valued at $6,000 alone. For years, the MDC tried to buy the Wilder farm, but the family refused each time. Years after the initial offer, the MDC lowered their bid to $1,500, which Wilder's grandfather finally accepted to supplement his pension.

It took well into 1939 to finish construction of the reservoir and to clear out the valley. Over seventy-five hundred graves from various cemeteries in the region had to be dug up and the bodies relocated to Quabbin Park Cemetery in Ware (or other cemeteries if the families requested it), and it's possible not every grave site was actually moved.

"The seventy-five hundred graves removed didn't cover them all," Wilder said. "Because on our farm was another graveyard from the people who built the house back in 1800. That [family plot] disappeared. No one has a record of it. All of the stones and everything else just disappeared. There are many of those throughout the valley."

Near the end, topsoil was dug up and carted off to be sold, and brush, wood, and other debris were placed into piles throughout the valley and torched. One local who witnessed the nighttime burning described the valley as a scene from hell. The area went up in flames, and nothing but a black scar and many foundation holes were left by morning. Within seven years of flooding, the land would be under 412 billion gallons of water.

Many sections of the various towns that were destroyed are still well above water. Today visitors can park their cars near gate 40 just off Route 32A in Nichewaug and hike or bike the 1.7 miles to the former Dana town common. The paved road is still there, though it's cracked and crumbling at best. A stroll down this forgotten street is a walk back in time. There are stone walls edging former properties now filled in with tall grass or trees; there are intersections where once used streets like Tamplin Road, Whitney Hill, and Skinner Hill Road meet up. The only things missing are the buildings and, of course, the people.

In the middle of Dana's town common, a tombstonelike marker is the only acknowledgment of what happened here. It reads:

SITE OF DANA COMMON 1801–1938
TO ALL THOSE WHO SACRIFICED THEIR HOMES
AND WAY OF LIFE
ERECTED BY DANA REUNION 1996

The hitching posts by Dana's town common haven't seen a horse or cart in many decades.

Strange Things at the Kelly Rose House

My friends told me about an abandoned, falling-down house with a strange Irish theme in Hingham, where we live. The house earned its name because of a wooden plank nailed to the front of the house that had "Kelly Rose" skillfully painted on it in old Irish script.

Since it was near my friends' home, I couldn't pass up a visit. We started to walk down an unkempt dirt road in the woods. After about 15 minutes, we crossed a bridge that led across a deep stream of rushing water. And then, it was right there in front of me: the Kelly Rose house.

It was set slightly back from the road, and was falling apart, heavily spray-painted on, and trashed. Absolutely trashed. There were two 10-foot piles of furniture, bikes, and other unidentifiable things lying in the small front yard. As we walked towards it, I saw the plank that gave the house its name. We threw rocks at the plank for a little while, and then entered the house.

We found ourselves in the kitchen, where pans, plates, and even a baby's high chair were strewn everywhere. The sink and dishwasher and other appliances were aging under a layer of dust. One of my friends opened a door that led down to the basement, which none of us dared to enter. Beyond the door it was pitch black: the darkest place I have ever seen.

Taking a left to the family room, we were confronted with an all-round leprechaun theme. There were leprechaun dolls, statues, and posters on the floor. An extremely old-looking television lay atop a beat up, four-foot tall chest. We kept rummaging around the room and found wigs, stuffed animals, and assorted pieces of garbage. The couch was torn up and had some sort of mold growing on it.

On the second floor, we turned then into the "spray-paint room." We could see that many people had been there before us, because foul words and strange, frightening poems were written all over the walls. The room was otherwise empty except for empty spray-paint cans on the floor. A window overlooked the front yard and garbage piles.

The bathroom was the final room we saw as we started walking back down the stairs. It was the smallest, but the most densely trashed room in the house. Planks of wood and trash were piled up six feet high, obscuring the old toilet.

Back outside, we found more spray paint cans, and lots of clothing such as footwear and coats. Once we got home, we searched for info about the Kelly Rose on the Internet but nothing came up. The next time my friends and I went there, the house was boarded up. We think it's going to get torn down soon.–*Chris*

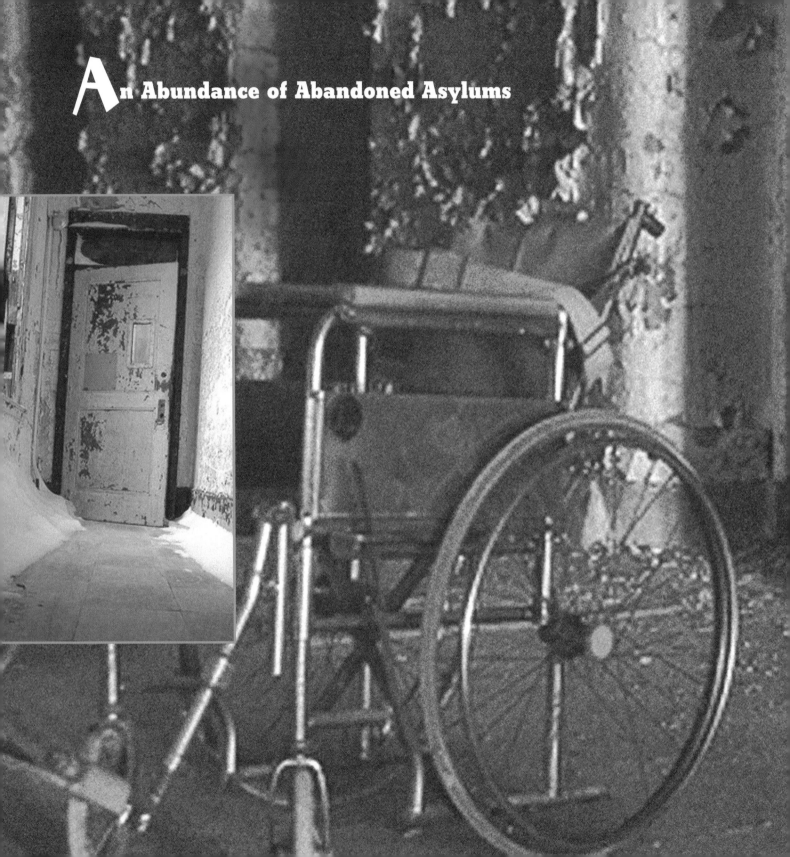

An Abundance of Abandoned Asylums

In the mid-to late-nineteenth century, state-funded mental institutions were popping up all over the United States. Public opinion on how to treat the mentally ill was changing, as people became more enlightened and realized that some conditions were treatable through psychiatry.

The changes were also due to the efforts of a Philadelphia psychiatrist named Thomas Story Kirkbride. Kirkbride argued that locking up, chaining up, or otherwise sequestering the disturbed from society wasn't going to help them. He felt that the proper facility for people with special mental needs would be a building with a center component and staggered wings so that each section received as much sunlight and fresh air as possible. Grounds should be wide and open, similar to some college campuses, and the patients should be given useful work to do: raising vegetables and keeping farm animals to provide food for the facility.

Massachusetts jumped into this new age of treating the mentally ill and constructed a good number of hospitals, many built following the philosophy of Kirkbride. All the facilities were active until advances in psychiatry and medicine outmoded the still primitive techniques employed in Kirkbride's time: lobotomies, electroshock therapy, and other seemingly medieval therapies. As the number of patients decreased, the facilities closed—leaving hulking, abandoned shells that loomed behind gates or up on hilltops, intriguing people for years and years.

Danvers State Hospital

Worcester State Hospital

The original Worcester Insane Asylum opened in January 1833. The site has also been called the Worcester Lunatic Asylum and the Bloomingdale Asylum, and the main building is best known for its stone façade and tall clock tower.

By 1870, the original building was at the limit of its capacity, so architect Ward P. Delano of Worcester designed a sprawling new facility. Construction began on a massive series of buildings laid out in the Kirkbride style—in fact, one of the buildings on the campus was named after Kirkbride. The newly expanded Worcester State Hospital opened in 1877, looking more like a stone prison than a hospital.

On July 22, 1991, a fire broke out in the Kirkbride building and completely engulfed it. Many of the buildings were a total loss and had to be bulldozed to the ground. A newer building was put up near the former Kirkbride structure and still operates as a psychiatric facility, though due to state cutbacks it is in danger of closing, leaving the entire Worcester State Hospital campus abandoned.

The newly expanded Worcester State Hospital opened in 1877, looking more like a stone prison than a hospital.

Danvers State Hospital

Possibly the most notorious of the abandoned mental facilities was Danvers State Hospital, which opened in 1878 and closed in 1992. Fans of weird and urban exploration have let *Weird Massachusetts* know about the place for years, often including a variation on "you've got to see this place before it disappears!" For example:

> The property is shaped like a bat. They kept the most extreme patients on the tips of the wings. The buildings are massive. It is probably the most impressive thing I have seen in my life. There are tons of weird stories and local lore to go along with this building. Unfortunately, the place is scheduled to be torn down in the not too distant future. So if you want to do anything on it you better act now.
> *–Jason Jackman*

> Danvers State Hospital is the scariest place in New England. David Caruso did a movie there called *Session 9,* and he said the place is completely evil. Even the inside pictures of that place make my skin crawl. Apparently the first lobotomy was performed there, and forms of treatment were more like torture.*–Alison*

In April 2006, the Associated Press reported that Danvers was going condo, part of a national trend of renovating abandoned mental hospitals or tearing them down. A big fan of the renovations had to be the Massachusetts State Police. The same AP report said that in the previous five years, the police "charged 150 people and issued warnings to an additional 450 people for trespassing."

And then there was the four-alarm fire in April 2007. North Andover's *Eagle Tribune* reported that the fire took out only new construction, not the remaining hospital buildings. Reader Lauren M. told *Weird Massachusetts,* "It seems something that still dwells (at Danvers) does not approve of the renovations. The condos burned to the ground and they have no idea why!" And the authorities apparently still don't, because in September 2007 various news outlets reported that a cause had not been determined, though arson was ruled out.

A tunnel connects two buildings at Danvers, the protective gates long rusted away.

Northampton State Hospital

In western Massachusetts, the Northampton State Hospital's remains stand on a hill behind Smith College. It's somehow an ominous setting. The red buildings are camouflaged by the brush, grasses, and trees growing up around them. Windows are broken or boarded up, and the grounds are eerily silent.

Like many other asylums around the United States, Northampton was conceived in the mid-nineteenth century to relieve crowding in other facilities. Construction began on July 4, 1856, with the ceremonial laying of the cornerstone atop Hospital Hill. Like Worcester and Medfield state hospitals, Northampton was designed under the Thomas Kirkbride plan.

The Northampton Lunatic Asylum, as it was called, opened in 1858, and by the turn of the twentieth century six hundred patients overcrowded the hospital. Not only was the asylum caring for those with mental disorders, but the poor, homeless, and elderly with nowhere else to turn also poured in seeking care. The Great Depression in the 1930s only exacerbated the overcrowding problem. Even the dead weren't given much regard here. Many were buried in unmarked graves on the hospital grounds. There was simply no other option.

By 1950, the population had swelled to over twenty-five hundred, and the facility was stretched to its limits. Kirkbride's "moral treatment" was no longer possible with so many people to care for. All the staff could offer was the basics: food, a roof, and medicine if time and funds permitted. The mid-1950s also marked a period of more aggressive therapies for treatment of the mentally disturbed: hydrotherapy, drugs, electroconvulsive treatment, and other options that Northampton State simply didn't have. Its reputation suffered, and by the late 1970s the government stepped in. Patients left or were removed from the hospital in great numbers. By 1991, only one hundred and twenty were left. The numbers continued to dwindle until there were only eleven patients left when the doors to Northampton State were permanently closed in August 1996.

Murder at Northampton State

In the late 1960s, I worked for an organization that advocated weight control. Overeating is a serious problem in many mental health care facilities, believe it or not, and one of my company's weight loss programs had been carried out at Northampton State. I was asked to visit the hospital, interview the participants, and write a story about their experiences. So off I went. I sat down with the group in the program, heard about how much weight they'd lost, how happy they were and so on. It was really a sweet little session and they seemed so

happy to talk about their feelings of accomplishment.

When I went a little deeper though, things were not so sweet. The gentleman who had been so courtly, pulling out a chair for me to sit on and offering a cup of coffee, I found out had murdered his wife in a fit of jealous rage. The woman who proudly showed me her new figure suffered from severe depression and had drowned her children. When one of the other participants stood up and said, "I ate my liver!" I actually shuddered, not entirely sure what she meant. Liver was one of the things on my company's eating program at the time, and most people resisted eating it. The world of the severely mentally ill is a place most of us cannot imagine. Weird does not begin to describe it. It was more than thirty years ago that I was at Northampton, but I've never forgotten the experience.—*Marjorie*

At right, Medfield State, once home to the "chronic insane." Long before psychotherapy, electroshock and lobotomies were the cures for what ails your brain.

Medfield State Hospital

In 1892, the town of Medfield broke ground on its own asylum for the "chronic insane." The hospital eventually expanded to over nine hundred acres of land and fifty-eight buildings. The campus included farmland where the institution grew its own produce and raised livestock. It had its own water and sewage system, and by all accounts was self-sustaining.

At its peak, Medfield State Hospital was home to twenty-two hundred patients, but over time, fewer people were committed to mental hospitals, many being treated by drug therapy instead. Only two hundred patients remained at Medfield when the state closed the doors for good, sending whoever was left to Worcester State or Taunton State Hospital.

This led to another problem for Medfield. Its boarded-up windows almost beg teenagers to break in, straining local police resources. Tearing down buildings like Medfield State Hospital can be as expensive as maintaining the empty structures. For now, the hospital grounds are like a ghost town, and the boards over the windows keep out the sunshine and fresh air that Dr. Kirkbride once fought so hard to provide.

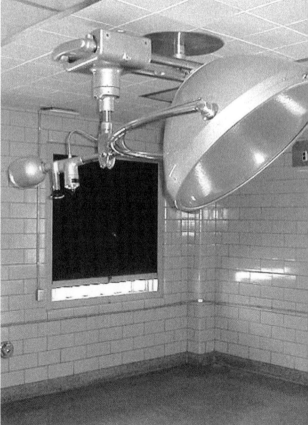

Plunkett Hospital Bleeds

We were six teenagers from Pittsfield with nothing better to do one night, so we decided to roam around the grounds of the abandoned W. B. Plunkett Memorial Hospital, in Adams.

We climbed up what must have been the steepest hill in Adams to a sight straight out of a teen slasher flick.

At the top of the hill sat an eerie, broken-down building seemingly surrounded in darkness and death. As we reached the building, we noticed a broken window and climbed in.

What awaited inside amazed us. A great deal of equipment was still present: wheelchairs, gurneys, cabinets and tools. The walls were in horrible condition and the entire place smelled musty. Ten minutes into our exploration, it became obvious that I was the only one not totally freaked out. So I led everyone into an examining room and began retelling the old tale of the nurse who went on a murderous rampage through the hospital and slashed the throats of three of her patients. While this was going on, her husband had learned of her affair with a doctor there, and he proceeded to find and murder the doctor in his own office. The nurse, upon learning of her lover's fate, committed suicide on the third floor, in the small attic forming the "tower" of the building.

After hearing this tale, everyone else wanted to leave. But being the adventurous type, I practically ran up the stairs to the second floor, and they reluctantly followed. We spent quite a while exploring the dark halls and eventually found the office of the philandering doctor. We froze at the sight before us: an overturned desk, a couch torn to pieces. Pints of blood were splattered on the walls, which had turned dark brown as the blood aged.

Two of the girls screamed and I turned around to see

dust rolling down the immense hallway, directly toward us. We could hear the ominous plodding of slow footsteps following the dust. Remembering the story of the nurse, I ignored the dust and walked directly through it. The footsteps ceased and the dust seemed to wrap around me for just a moment before disappearing.

I began to climb the steps to the attic in hopes of finding a dead body or more blood. I was halfway up when my friends screamed. I bolted down the stairs, and just as I cleared the landing, a gurney shot past me at an amazing speed. The group dove out of its way and the gurney crashed into the wall. No one in our group had pushed it, however. I looked around the corner. No one was there.

Finally coming to my senses, I turned to my friends and said "We're leaving. Now." There was no argument.

We returned two more times, once to the morgue where a friend of mine immediately ran out, screaming that he was attacked by the nurse's ghost. I was never able to get anyone to go in with me after that, and now they're putting condos on the site. –*Chris*

INDEX

Page numbers in **bold** refer to photos and illustrations.

ACKNOWLEDGMENTS

As with all the books in our *Weird* series, the creation of *Weird Massachusetts* was very much a team effort and would not have been possible without contributions by and the collective talents of Joanne Austin, Ryan Doan, Abby Stillman-Grayson, Chris Gethard, Emily Seese, Gina Graham, Leonard Vigliarolo, Marjorie Palmer, Alexandra Koppen, and all those folks who have sent us letters over the years offering stories, photos, or simply cryptic tips leading us off into parts unknown. We thank you all!
—*Mark and Mark*

I'd like to thank Mark and Mark for the opportunity to write *Weird Massachusetts*. I'd also like to thank the many seemingly normal people who helped out with the research, who weren't afraid to crawl into a cave without a flashlight, who didn't mind cracking their car's oil pan on roads so remote it doesn't seem fair to call them "roads," and who offered me insight into this sometimes odd place we call Massachusetts. Thanks to: Chris Balzano, Josh Mantello, Derek Bartlett, Ron Kolek, Maureen Wood, Ben Garvin, Russ Boisvert, Steve Alpert, Brian Poynton, Clif Read, Giles Corey (wherever he may be today), Don and Nancy Featherstone, Bob Wilder, Tom and Arlene D'Agostino, the New England Antiquities Research Association, and the Bellingham Public Library, who helped me procure just about every book ever written on Massachusetts. Thank you also to the many people whom I had the opportunity to interview: Your stories and expertise were a critical part of this book.

I'd also like to thank my wife, Megan, who not only put up with the strange hours and assignments this book required but also lent her editorial eye and thoughts on each of the entries. Thanks for putting up with my weirdness—who would have guessed it would eventually pay off.—*Jeff Belanger*

PICTURE CREDITS

All photos by the author, contributing authors, or public domain
except as listed below:

SHOW US YOUR WEIRD!

Do you know of a weird site found somewhere in the United States, or can you tell us about a strange experience you had? If so, we'd like to hear about it! We believe that every town has at least one great tale to tell, and we're listening. It could be a cursed road, haunted abandoned site, odd local character, or bizarre historic event. In most cases these tales are told only in the towns in which in they originated. But why keep them to yourself when you could share them with all of America? So come on and fill us in on all the weirdness that's lurking in your backyard!

You can email us at: Editor@WeirdUS.com,
or write us at:
Weird U.S., P.O. Box 1346, Bloomfield, NJ 07003.

www.weirdus.com